Selected Works of Zinaida Hippius

"THE PAGE," LEV BAKST (1868–1924).

The Hermitage, Leningrad. 1905. Courtesy of V. A. Mamchenko, Paris.

Selected Works

of

ZINAIDA
HIPPIUS

TRANSLATED AND EDITED BY

Temira Pachmuss

UNIVERSITY OF ILLINOIS PRESS

Urbana   Chicago   London

ISBN 0-252-00260-1

To Volya

Preface

The selection of stories included in this volume has been determined by the following considerations: first, they are helpful to the uninitiated English reader in illuminating various aspects of Hippius's philosophy and in revealing her basic attitudes; second, they are indicative of the intrinsic value and everlasting significance which all her stories had for her; third, her fiction, which stands among the most curious of twentieth-century literary documents, re-creates chronologically the gradual evolution of her thought—her path to God which began with introspection and ended with a concern for sociopolitical issues and preoccupation with matters of universal spiritual significance. A more detailed exposition of Hippius's *Weltanschauung* and manifold activities may be found in my recent study, *Zinaida Hippius: An Intellectual Profile* (Southern Illinois University Press, 1971), which also contains a listing of her voluminous published and unpublished works and a selected bibliography, the latter intended to provide a general guide to readers. The Introduction to this book, therefore, has been limited to a discussion of the essentials of the poet's complex aesthetic, religious, metaphysical, and sociopolitical views.

Responsibility for the English translations of the works by Hippius included in this volume rests with me. The translations merely attempt to convey the meaning of the texts and not their poetic qualities, such as the lyricism and sonority of many passages, their rhythms, and the sound, weight, and accent of words in relation to one another. It is my belief that if anything is to be sacrificed in translation, it should be form rather than meaning. To the usual difficulties one encounters in translating from Russian into English—for example, the emotional and semantic richness of the Russian language due to the abundance of diminutives—may be added the "impalpable quality," as it were, of Hippius's literary style. She often shows a certain reticence in finishing a thought or fully expressing the idea or feeling behind her words and images, especially those of color and fragrance. Hippius's language, like Chekhov's, lends itself easily to reading between the lines, but it has proved extremely difficult to render adequately in English the intangible quality of Hippius's mode of narration. Some passages must be explained; others, unfortunately, have acquired a melodramatic character; still others have become somewhat distorted due to a new emphasis which emerged in translation. Sometimes new words and expressions alien to the original have been added of necessity.

The translation of Soviet slang expressions in Hippius's stories dealing with the Soviet people and Soviet life has also presented certain difficulties. In "Metamorphosis," for example, Hippius—in addition to raising some other issues—points out the deterioration of the sonorous and semantically rich Russian language in the Soviet Union. This is particularly true in the semi-educated strata of the population. Soviet slang expressions, broken sentences, and distorted images and ideas, as Hippius depicts them, can be rendered only with great difficulty, if at all, into adequate foreign equivalents.

Yet another point which may cause some bewilderment should be clarified: many hypotheses, often ludicrous, were proposed concerning Hippius's use of masculine endings of verbs and personal possessive pronouns. Hippius herself explained to her close friend Georgy Adamovich, a Russian émigré writer, that she preferred to write not merely as a woman but as a human being, "kak *chelovek,* a ne tol'ko kak zhenshchina." A woman, the poetess insisted, can be, and must be, a human being above all. She may be a woman only after having established her status as a human being. In order not to stress her femininity, Zinaida Hippius frequently used the masculine forms which are also applicable to "chelovek" ("a human being"). The italics found in the text are in the original sources. "Heavenly Words" was translated by Dr. J. Douglas Clayton and edited by me. His assistance is herewith gratefully acknowledged. I should also like to thank the Library, the Russian and East European Center, and the Department of Slavic Languages and Literatures, all at the University of Illinois, for various grants given for the support of research, for the final preparation of the manuscript, and for the acquisition of the necessary source material. Finally, my heartfelt thanks go to our doctoral candidates Nina Awsienko and William E. Napier for assistance in a variety of ways.

Naturally, I assume full responsibility for all factual information and interpretation of ideas.

TEMIRA PACHMUSS
Urbana, Illinois

Contents

Selected Works of Zinaida Hippius

Introduction

Only a few readers in the West are familiar with the works of Zinaida Hippius (1869–1945) or are aware of her influence upon the spiritual and cultural life of St. Petersburg during the Silver Age of Russian poetry, and later upon Russian émigré circles in Paris. Although one of the most refined and original poets in the history of Russian literature, she was largely underestimated by her contemporaries. However, Hippius's "long and glorious past," to use D. S. Mirsky's description of her artistic career, and especially the period 1900–1917, has accorded her a permanent place in the history of Russian Modernism. A writer of both fiction and poetry, Hippius attained her greatest fame through the latter. Yet her voluminous prose is also remarkable and deserves closer attention by critics and scholars.

After her marriage to D. S. Merezhkovsky, who pioneered Russian Symbolism at the turn of the century, Hippius became, in Renato Poggioli's apt formulation, "the uncrowned queen of the literary life" [1] of St. Petersburg. "Clever and beautiful . . . she acted not only as the

[1] Renato Poggioli, *The Poets of Russia: 1890–1930* (Cambridge, Mass., 1960), p. 111.

Sibyl but also as the Sylphide of the philosophical and religious circle that formed around her husband and herself." [2] Like other Russian Symbolists, the poet regarded literature as part and parcel of the "general areas of culture, that is, of philosophy, religion, ethics, and science." [3] She shared Andrey Bely's view that "art is not only art; art contains the essence of religion." [4] Literature was for Hippius a profound spiritual experience; she conceived of poetry as a struggle to break away from the fetters of a sordid and pessimistic reality and an attempt to fly toward an ideal world. The central theme of her creative work is the portrayal of the spirit and its endeavor to attain the ultimate reconciliation of love and eternity, love and death, and the real and the miraculous. Literature and art serve to reveal the bond existing between the universe and the individual; literature is a means for embodying the merging of the transcendental and the phenomenal for humanity. "We are using art," she stated in 1908, "to promote an evolution of the world toward the ultimate goal of mankind," [5] i.e., the attainment of love, harmony, and unity in the world. Art is more exalted than beauty; it is more encompassing than virtue. Art is that beginning which gives birth to beauty, refinement, morality, and religious thought. Beauty can be conveyed only through the poetic imagery and experience. In Dmitry Merezhkovsky's opinion, "Without faith in the Divine origin of the world, there can be no beauty on earth, no justice, no society, no freedom. . . . One needs to cross the chasm to the *other realm,* to the other *shore*—that is, to the sphere of free and Divine idealism." [6]

Together with Merezhkovsky, Vasily Rozanov, Nikolay Minsky-Vilenkin, Andrey Bely, Alexander Blok, Valery Bryusov,

2 Ibid., p. 112.

3 Andrey Bely, *Simvolizm; kniga statey* (Moscow, 1910), p. 1.

4 Ibid., p. 10.

5 Z. Hippius, "Iz dnevnika zhurnalista," *Russkaya mysl',* no. 2 (1909), p. 157.

6 D. S. Merezhkovsky, "O prichinakh upadka i o novykh techeniyakh sovremennoy russkoy literatury," *Polnoe sobranie sochineny* (St. Petersburg-Moscow, 1912), XV, 302.

and other Symbolist writers and critics, Hippius protested against positivism, social "tendentiousness," and crass materialism in works of art. She rejected the sociological approach of Chernyshevsky, Dobrolyubov, and Pisarev, and the political and ideological interpretation of belles lettres by Mikhaylovsky and Plekhanov. Challenging the appearance of social discourses in creative art in general, she emphasized loyalty and respect for universal culture and claimed that it was the critic's duty to divine the mystery of aesthetic beauty and harmony and convey it to the reader. It is false, she insisted, to separate art from life, for the "artist is able to show a *new* reality; he is able to create *new* objects and new conditions. . . . He is justified in his creative work only when his artistic will can lead the reader to truth, i.e., to the improvement of reality." [7] The ultimate goal of art is the reorganization of life: "The aim of art is to better reality, to move it forward, *to assist* in the transformation of reality. This is the eternal objective of art, but it is also our contemporary objective, since it has been placed before us more or less consciously for the first time." [8] She had in mind spiritual reality; material reality always held little interest for her.

Hippius expected literature to treat God, love, loyalty, and immortality as its main themes. The point of departure for both the poet and the critic, she insisted, should be in mystical content, symbols, and the intensification and deepening of the reader's artistic perception. She asked that more attention be paid to the eternal properties of art—love of God, Christian ethics, poetry of feeling, and elevated thought. In the pages of the Merezhkovskys' journal *Novy put'* (*The New Road;* St. Petersburg, 1903–4), she advocated untiringly a future religious culture which was to be true and universal, and attempted to reveal to her readers the aesthetic nature of the word and artistic

[7] Z. Hippius, "Iskusstvo i lyubov'," *Opyty*, no. 2 (1953), p. 116.

[8] Anton Krayny [Z. Hippius], "Propisi," *Novy dom*, no. 1 (1926), p. 20. For more information about the Symbolists' emphasis on the aesthetic qualities of works of art, see Johannes Holthusen, *Studien zur Aesthetik und Poetik des russischen Symbolismus* (Göttingen, 1957).

form. She always viewed beauty and culture as two indispensable conditions for human life. In accordance with her metaphysics, Hippius called upon other writers to seek out those new external and internal attributes of works of literature and art which are based on refined and strictly individual poetic and religious sensibility. She held that men of belles lettres should develop to the utmost their capacity for religious contemplation and mystical clairvoyance, for she was convinced that the mysteries of, the universe cannot be resolved by technology and science. Furthermore, she stipulated that an artist should uphold his individuality and aristocratic distance from the crude and vociferous crowd. An incessant search for a love which encompasses the heavenly and the earthly was characteristic of Hippius's aesthetics. At the base of her *Weltanschauung* lay the idea of God as a philosophical and religious principle, the concept of restless, inquisitive thought as a creative law, and the notion of the eternal quest for an ideal as the ultimate truth and the foremost purpose of life. These assumptions were fundamental to the metaphysical outlook which she maintained throughout her life.

A typical Symbolist writer, Hippius sharply distinguished between the empirical world and a spiritual world of mysterious purport and immanence. Like Goethe, she maintained that *"Alles Vergängliche ist nur ein Gleichnis,"* and in her works she depicted the world as a chaotic interplay of spirit and matter. Her poetry and prose, including her brilliant critical essays (for which she chose the pen names of Anton Krayny, Comrade Herman, Lev Pushchin, and Roman Arensky) and the keen psychological profiles in *Zhivye litsa* (*Living Portraits;* Prague: Plamya, 1925; 2 vols.), clearly reflect an antipositivistic, dualistic concept of a world divided into the sphere of physical phenomena and a higher reality, indivisible and unobservable. She designated poetry as a path to the knowledge of ultimate mysteries and as an intuitive access to pretersensual reality, whose truth is above intellectual and ethical categories. Poetry should originate in the artist's spiritual and religious upliftings. Following Nietzsche and Schopenhauer, Hippius asserted that the man of the future would be a prophet, endowed with intuitive perception, intellectual acumen, and artistic efficacy. Her own law in art was formulated in an aphorism: "Art should materialize only the spiritual." In an article, "Khleb zhizni" ("The Bread of Life," 1901), she held that art is real only when it strives toward the idea of God and merges with Him. The "bread of the flesh" then becomes the "bread of the spirit," and both of them form an indivisible entity, the "bread of life." The poet viewed each concrete phenomenon in life as if it were imbued with divinity, and in her poetry she aspired to express rhythmically and melodiously the "spirit without the tedious details of life." In a letter (of May 2, 1938) to Victor Mamchenko, an émigré poet and one of Hippius's close friends, she reminded him of "Christ's beautiful words: 'How can you say that the flesh is not useful? All flesh is animated by the Spirit.' " [9] Art reveals the Divine Spirit; in art the Divine Logos assumes the human image. The objective of art is "to transform the Word (the principle) into the Flesh (the content of human activity)." [10] In agreement with Andrey Bely that "Art, embodying the Symbol in the Flesh, subordinates the most metaphysical definitions to theurgical practice" and that "The Word is the Flesh," [11] Hippius strove to embody His spirit in the "flesh" (substance) of her poetry. Longing for the perfection of human beings, she wished to assist them in developing their capacities to feel and think to the utmost and in living in communion and harmony with others.

It is evident that in her philosophy of aesthetics Hippius was indebted to many thinkers, among them to Vladimir Solovyov. His views on the function of art as "theurgy," on love as being beyond the realm of physical time and death, on the existing organic union between the spirit and the flesh, and on sexual

[9] Cf. John 6:63—"It is the spirit that giveth life; the flesh profiteth nothing [without the spirit]; the words I have spoken unto you are the spirit, and are life."

[10] Andrey Bely, *Simvolizm: kniga statey*, p. 94.

[11] Ibid., p. 95.

love as an experience which may raise two persons to one ideal and absolute individuality deeply impressed the young poetess toward the end of the nineteenth century. Hippius never freed herself entirely of these influences. However, she did not simply continue the themes and ideas which she received from the philosophical systems of other thinkers and writers such as Plato, Zoroaster, Mani, Goethe, Solovyov, Bergson, and Dostoevsky, to mention only a few. She transformed and enriched them to fit her own metaphysical and religious system of thought, with its own code of internal laws.

Hippius's characteristically Russian Symbolist verse is rooted in the cultural and philosophical tradition of her country, originating on the one hand from the poems of Boratynsky and Tyutchev, and on the other from the works of Dostoevsky. Tyutchev's concept of God and his glorification of God's creation were akin to Hippius's, as she herself readily admitted.[12] "The tone of her poetry is undoubtedly close to Tyutchev's," wrote D. Svyatopolk-Mirsky, "but its kernel forms a cycle of poems unique in Russian literature. Hippius' poems present her metaphysical and most profound experiences in imagery that is strikingly, uncannily concrete. Her best poems are written on the Svidrigaylov theme—on eternity; that is, on a Russian bathhouse with spiders in one corner, on metaphysical *ennui* and metaphysical vulgarity, on a hopeless lack of passion and love in the human soul. . . . These poems are so original that I do not know anything in any language which resembles them." [13] In Hippius's ethereal poetry, her passionate love of God, which does not exhaust but fortifies the poet's will, is a frequent theme. Her haughty loneliness, the sensual intensity in her early verse, and the restrained yet plastic beauty of the images and sound scheme all set Hippius apart from her contemporaries as an original practitioner of versification. Her poetic universe, es-

12 Z. N. Hippius, *Sobranie stikhov: 1899–1903* (Moscow, 1904), p. v.

13 D. Svyatopolk-Mirsky, "Godovshchiny," *Vyorsty*, no. 3 (1928), pp. 142–43.

pecially the one described in the first volume of her poetry, appears as a horrifying vision, a Manichaean world in which evil often gains the upper hand over good and the devil overpowers God. The thematic features which can be discerned throughout Modernism—the demonic element, a renunciation of life with its joys and spiritual pursuits, the leitmotif of resignation, and the theme of death—all of these impart a peculiar charm, intensity, and pathos to some of her finest poems. Colors, sounds, outlines, and inherent moods blend in the eerie spectre of Hippius's universe, a physical and emotional void which instills mystery and dread. Her "decadent" moods, however, are always counterbalanced by idealistic strivings, and an ardent faith in God and His mercy forms the thematic basis for many of her poems of the period. Hippius's early works reveal her fondness for opposing one mood to another, her inimitable, exquisite sense of artistic control, and her discipline, all of which indicate profound ingenuity and range in the realm of versification. Her poetry is gripping in its seriousness, sincerity, and poetic finish. The nobility of the poet's lonely, nostalgic spirit which aspires for higher values can hardly pass unnoticed.

Hippius's poetic prowess springs partly from her ability both to express abstract ideas as living entities and to present religious, moral, and philosophical views in aphoristic, epigrammatic, yet euphonious and verbally elusive lines. Her poetry is based on music made tangible in a stream of images and ideas. This musicality is achieved through a sophisticated pattern of sound repetition, that is, consonant instrumentation and melodic phonemes with characteristic "dark" (low tonality) and "bright" (high tonality) [14] vowels prevailing in the structure of the poem. On the level of syntax, "poetry as music" means the repetition of words or sentences as an echo or refrain, parallel sentence structure, and parallel rhyme scheme. Music, the initial impetus

[14] Cf. Kiril Taranovsky, "The Sound Texture of Russian Verse in the Light of Phonetic Distinctive Features," *International Journal of Slavic Linguistics and Poetics* IX (1965), 114-24.

in Hippius's creative process,[15] may be heard distinctly in most of her poems. She fulfilled the premise of primary importance in Symbolist aesthetics: "Poetry impregnates music with images; through poetry music assumes tangibility,"[16] or "Poetry is an interior music which is made exterior through rhythmical speech."[17] This special kind of musicality enabled the poet to transmit evanescent emotions and intricate ideas, otherwise inexpressible. She, too, regarded poetry as the "Music which governs the World and our souls."[18] Because the intrinsic musicality of the verse and the ingenious images and concepts used in the poems fuse perfectly with the other artistic effects in Hippius's works, several Russian composers, among them Prokofiev and N. Myaskovsky, set many of her poems to music. The emotional effect of Hippius's poetry is heightened by an intense feeling of love for nature, a spontaneous perception of the universe, and the *persona*'s earnest desire to transcend the vulgarity and prosaic coarseness of daily life.

Interested in moral and intellectual ambiguities, Zinaida Hippius often placed them at the center of her poetic world. They reflect her frequent fluctuation between nihilism and an ardent desire for belief in God, between worship of God and the temptations of the devil, life and death, strength and weakness, spirituality and the sensuousness of life. Like some of Dostoevsky's characters, she often experienced two selves with diametrically opposed thoughts and feelings within her personality. Her religious poetry is a dramatic chronicle of defeats and victories, when, wishing to be right but fearing that she would be wrong, she often was discouraged and downcast by her simultaneous inner strength and weakness. She was especially given to these contradictory feelings toward the end of the nineteenth century while becoming increasingly immersed in religious activ-

[15] Ref. Temira Pachmuss, *Zinaida Hippius: An Intellectual Profile* (Carbondale, Ill., 1971), pp. 21–22.

[16] Andrey Bely, *Simvolizm: kniga statey*, p. 179.

[17] Konstantin Bal'mont, *Poeziya, kak volshebstvo* (Moscow, 1915), p. 19.

[18] Ibid., p. 82.

ities. An artistic expression of these antinomies may be found in her themes and moods: affirmation versus negation, immortality versus mortality, fortitude versus apathy and ineffectiveness, desire to love and inability to love, and freedom of the spirit versus eternal imprisonment in the fetters of the flesh.[19]

Marietta Shaginyan, author of a study on Zinaida Hippius's verse, cautioned her readers that Hippius is a complex poet and that her art should not be discussed in "general terms." [20] Each poem should be analyzed individually and interpreted with great care; otherwise both the real and seeming contradictions in her poetry might confuse the reader. Shaginyan assures us that the poetry of Hippius deserves this effort. It is indeed true that Hippius's religious experiences and states of mind, although intimately connected with one another, are nonetheless distinct. Her lines are so different in content, mood, rhyme, and rhythm that it is necessary to view her religious and metaphysical concepts and their artistic applications individually. The poems of Hippius reflect single moments in her thought. In the introduction to *Sobranie stikhov: 1889–1903* (*Collected Poetry:* 1889–1903), she stated that her poetry, like Boratynsky's, conveys the experience and mood of one particular moment. After this experience has been expressed artistically, a poem is complete. The poet's following sensation corresponds to the next moment, which is entirely different in its nature from the preceding one. Experiences and poems are thus separated from one another in the sequence of time and sensations. Hippius, moreover, likened poems to prayers: "We, modern poets . . . pray in our verses . . . sometimes unsuccessfully, sometimes with success. But we always use the essence of our own beings, our very kernel, the entirety of our 'Ego' at one unique moment—such is the nature of prayers." [21] People who have lost their capacity to associate

[19] Ref. Z. Hippius's poems "Ona," "Syznova," "Imet'," "Ne zdes' li?," "Pobedy," "Uspokoysya," "Dozhdichek," "Soblazn," "Tikhoe plamya," "Svoboda," "Opravdanie," and "Tak li?"

[20] Ref. Marietta Shaginyan, *O blazhenstve imushchego* (Moscow, 1912).

[21] Z. N. Hippius, *Sobranie stikhov: 1889–1903*, pp. ii–iii.

with one another in prayers are no longer able to experience religious ecstasy. Since they have their own individual gods, their prayers have become ineffectual.

As paradoxical as it may appear on the surface, Hippius did not use her poetry exclusively as an outlet for her religious thought, even during this revival of spiritual culture when poets endeavored to reveal Divine truths to the uninitiated. The secret of the poetic and religious exaltation of Zinaida Hippius's verse sprang from an awareness of God within herself: of His will, command, desire, and supreme perception. This attitude explains her never ceasing fear that she might lose both her ability to act and her longing to fathom concepts and phenomena still inaccessible to her. She neither sought peace and tranquillity in her personal feelings toward God, nor did she accept the idea of the Russian Orthodox Church that one should submerge one's personality in a beatific love of God. Hippius rejected the path of Christian resignation and what she referred to as a "lack of will" in Christian asceticism, asserting that man ought to undergo the tribulations of life in order to be able to exclaim, like Dostoevsky's Dmitry Karamazov, "I exist in thousands of agonies— I exist! I am tormented on the rack—but I exist!" Only through suffering can man comprehend the reality of his own being; only suffering can bring about the harmony between his spirit and flesh. These two "half-truths," like two semi-circles, can form one integral, harmonious whole only in God Who represents the perfect and complete circle. Man can synthesize the reality of the spirit and the reality of the flesh only through mental agony, which originates in the fullness of his life experience. "One must drink one's cup to the dregs," Hippius said in one of her poems. As long as man resists the acceptance of suffering, he is not ready for the kingdom of God on earth. To attain God and the man of the better ennobled future, we must travel through mental torment and come to the knowledge and acceptance of life with its joy, pain, and loss.

It was logical that, once she began her pursuit of an unconditional acceptance of life, Hippius assumed great ethical responsibilities. Hence her fear that she lacked strength and was liable to err; hence her regrets that she had not chosen an easier path, a path of resignation; hence her moments of spiritual fatigue and torpor, almost a metaphysical prostration. Fully aware that her salvation depended on the intensity of her desires,[22] she was afraid of losing the determination and will necessary for their execution. Two lines from one of her poems, "My soul, escape temptations, / Learn to desire, learn to acquire!" may serve as the motto of her creative work and life. She advised Mamchenko in a letter dated August 30, 1937, to learn to desire with his whole heart: "It is very sad that all of us desire only 'more or less' . . . Make your desires strong, and you will be able to achieve a great deal. If you are unable to achieve everything, God will help you in achieving the rest. Only remain loyal and keep faith in God." On March 3, 1937, she avowed to Greta Gerell: "I long *to desire* something. I am afraid I no longer desire anything." A human being who did not strive for his ideals was no more than a nonentity.

The early work of Hippius in the 1890's reveals her as a poet of aestheticism and aristocratic individualism, voicing her longing for an ideal vision of the universe, for "that which is not of this world." Only occasionally did she experience rapture in nature and life, having been inspired by the Italian Renaissance and Hellenic pronouncements concerning the sanctity of the flesh. She shared these views with Merezhkovsky, Minsky, and Akim Volynsky (pseudonym of A. L. Flekser, 1863–1926), the latter a critic, art historian, essayist, and editor of *Severny vestnik* (*The Northern Herald;* St. Petersburg, 1885–98). Hippius's predominant moods—melancholy, solitude, alienation from her fellow men, and an intense nostalgia for the miraculous—became particularly poignant at the turn of the century. At this time the tenor of her artistic work underwent a change: conscious of her personal will, fortitude, and calling, she became engrossed in religious matters. Her abstract ideas now assumed

[22] See, for example, Hippius's poems "Zhelanya byli mne vsego dorozhe," "Kak veter ognenny moi zhelanya," "Zemlya," "Opravdanie," and "Sosny."

a more concrete form as she continued to oppose the positivism
and primitive utilitarianism of the nineteenth-century radicals,
and as her former concept of God became fused with a new idea
of freedom and a strong desire to attain true faith in God. Abandoning both the Greek notion of the sanctity of the flesh and the
Christian concept of the sanctity of the spirit, she expressed hope
that these two realms might be synthesized and later merged as
one organic world into a religion of the Holy Trinity. Hers was
an "apocalyptic" Christianity which believed in the second coming of Christ in the same way that historical Christianity believed in His first coming. Neo-Christianity formulated as its
goal the synthesis of the Holy Flesh and the Holy Spirit in their
mutual wholeness and equality, and Hippius supported and amplified this religious renaissance in her poetry.[23] Culture, man's
abiding effort to move forward, and the evolution of his spiritual
and religious awareness were always of great significance to her.
She wished to share her mystical experience with her fellow
seekers. In essence, her early poems may be called a discourse on
abstract ideas in rhyme and verse; they are spirited psalms,
méditations religieuses, reminiscent of pious hymns or chants in
praise of God, such as the "Gloria in Excelsis." They are also
reminiscent of the ecstatic presentiments and expectations of
Ephrem Syrus, the "Harp of the Holy Ghost." The homilies of
Andrew of Crete and especially his great penitential canon,
which is sung on the Thursday before Passion Sunday, appear
likewise to have exercised an influence upon her poems. Moreover, they resemble solemn religious odes rooted in the principal
beliefs of Manichaeism with its concept of duality in the structure of the world, and there is a resemblance to Gnosticism with
its central thesis that an emancipated spirit is the result of knowledge. Hippius's poems are dreams about a kingdom of new
people endowed with new souls and a new religious mentality—

[23] See, for example, Hippius's poems "Molitva," "Neskorbnomu uchitelyu,"
"Khristu," "Za dyavola molyu Tebya, Gospod'," "Gospod' Otets," "Khristianin," "Drugoy khristianin," "Ya," and "Predsmertnaya ispoved' khris-
tianina."

a kingdom which can never be attained, yet which man must always strive for.

Hippius was eager to participate in the creation of a new man, one with his spirit enlightened and exalted and his flesh transfigured. One of the salient traits of her poetic temperament was the decision to serve mankind. She felt a spiritual and religious urging, as it were, and a conviction that in all her actions she was prompted by the will of God. Hence her determination to reveal and put into practice the knowledge she had attained. Her verse, written in the tradition of neoclassicism with clearly romantic and idealistic content, discloses the poet's tragic, almost heroic spirit. The mystical and religious evolution of her views gradually led her to the conclusion that a new "religious consciousness" should replace the "lifeless dogmas" of the historical Church. Opposed to the Russian Church's subservience to the state, she wished to reorganize both the Church and Russian sociopolitical affairs of the time. From 1905 to 1914 her religious, mystical, and philosophical ideas became linked with plans to achieve social and political order.

The characteristic features of Hippius's early poetry also can be seen in her prose. The first two volumes of her short stories, *Novye lyudi* (*New People,* 1894) and *Zerkala: vtoraya kniga rasskazov* (*Mirrors: The Second Book of Short Stories,* 1898), convey a rejection of conventional moral concepts and norms of behavior. Protagonists seeking new world outlooks indulge in lengthy debates concerning harmony, the beauty of the world, God, and love. The feverish atmosphere is reminiscent of Dostoevsky's novels. The descriptive method shows a certain affinity with that of the Belgian poet Georges Rodenbach and his "aristocratic cult of solitude giving rise to an adoration of *lonely canal waters,* of the solitary moon, of everything that is secluded, deserted, and silent." [24] Val'tsev, the hero of Hippius's "Luna" ("The Moon," 1898), roams the deserted streets of Venice at night, thinking about the loneliness of the moon, the canal waters, the hotel, and the isolation of man in general. Like

[24] *Gallereya russkikh pisateley* (Moscow, 1901), p. 515.

Rodenbach's protagonist, he complains of the excruciating pain inflicted upon him by the clamorous crowd. Yan, another lonely man from Hippius's *Mirrors,* is almost paralyzed with his fear of calumny. He expresses the view of the poet that the "pain arising from insults is more agonizing than anything else in the world." [25] In *Contes d'amour* there is an entry of November 17, 1893, in which Hippius likened this pain to a feeling of metaphysical nausea: "The deeper the pain caused by insults, the more repulsive it is. It reminds me of that nausea which sinners must be experiencing in Hell." Her men and women almost proudly parade their loneliness and disgust for the world of finite experience. They admit their way of reasoning is the result of lonely minds and that a better future can become reality only by a miracle. The heroes in *New People* and *Mirrors,* who seek a state of absolute nirvana, dwell on the mystical philosophy of "reflection" to the exclusion of all other thoughts and ideas. They advocate the Nietzschean philosophy of egoism and the pursuit of personal happiness at the expense of social considerations.

Although the poetry of Hippius shows no obvious indebtedness to foreign models, her prose reveals some further influences coming from the West. She inherited from French Symbolism, for example, an aversion to mundane pursuits and a worship of beauty which in her eyes was the underlying principle of the supreme and the lofty. She also shared the hostility of the French Symbolists toward concrete forms, outlines, and a "fetishism of details," an attitude contrary to the artistic method of Acmeism. In several of her early works (in *New People,* for example) she attempted to render an accurate portrayal of the younger Russian generation at the end of the century. However, averse to the accumulation of "tedious details of life," she failed to give a realistic picture: her young people appear as symbols and abstractions rather than as living human beings. These early narratives resemble medieval novelettes in their mysticism, refine-

[25] Z. N. Hippius-Merezhkovskaya, *Zerkala: vtoraya kniga rasskazov* (St. Petersburg, 1898), p. 32.

ment of word, artistic imagination, craftsmanship, and occasional sophistry and pertness. Sergey Makovsky, a Russian émigré writer, maintained that Hippius is impressive as an "author of remarkably elegant short stories, permeated with perspicacity and poignant feeling and which at times are based on complex psychological problems. And what beautiful language, always psychologically true, always striking in its descriptive beauty and in its veracity of colloquial intonations!" [26] It is indeed unfortunate that Hippius's early miniatures of prose, which deserve detailed analysis and evaluation, have escaped the attention of contemporary literary scholars.

Many of Hippius's short stories and novels of the period display the positive aspect of her religious world view. Her protagonists proclaim "enlightened love" in God, a sublimated flesh, and the importance of understanding and harmony among people. "Love must be infinite," says Shadrov to Margaret in *Sumerki dukha* (*The Twilight of the Spirit*, 1902). "It must be an open window, a light into one's consciousness." [27] Some other short stories, in the volume *Aly mech: rasskazy, chetvyortaya kniga* (*A Scarlet Sword: Short Stories, the Fourth Book;* 1906), for instance, are tendentious. Whereas mystical clairvoyance, religious musings, and considerations of beauty and harmony occupy a central position in the earlier narratives, social ideas and a candid preaching of neo-Christianity and ecumenity (*sobornost'*) are emphasized in *A Scarlet Sword*. In "Zhenskoe" ("The Feminine," 1912) and "Net vozvrata" ("There Is No Return," 1912),[28] new characteristics appear in her artistic method. The straight narrative technique of her previous short stories is now subordinated to a figurative mode of narration. Hippius's portrayal of prostitutes, servants, soldiers, and particularly of St. Petersburg housemaids is excellent in its psychological verisimilitude and gentle Goncharovian humor. The

[26] Sergey Makovsky, *Na Parnase Serebrayanogo veka* (Munich, 1961), p. 98.

[27] Z. N. Hippius, *Tretya kniga rasskazov* (St. Petersburg, 1902), p. 190.

[28] Z. Hippius, *Lunnye muravyi: shestaya kniga rasskazov* (Moscow, 1912), pp. 127–54.

educated and sophisticated characters, on the other hand, again
lack veracity, caught as they are in complex situations and engaging in discussions that abound in psychological and metaphysical ideas. They concentrate on their search for a "new religious consciousness," for a new path toward God.

The religious orientation of Hippius's poetry and prose of the
first formative period remained the marked feature of her entire
art. She never abandoned the premise she had formulated at the
turn of the century: art is real when it directs the reader to the
spiritual and stimulates his search for God. A sense of responsibility toward her fellow men in seeking a new religion as a guid-
ing principle in their lives (a search which she later conceived as
her *raison d'être*) also found its artistic portrayal in her works of
the early period. A desire to be of spiritual service to mankind
toned down her cult of aristocratic detachment and individualism and thus brought her closer to the idealistic aspect of
Dostoevsky's metaphysical philosophy. The great Russian novelist and Zinaida Hippius dreamed about a "Golden Age" when
the earth would merge with heaven into one blissful kingdom—
that great miracle when the impossible would materialize, when
human life would be transfigured in its wholeness, and when the
Word would become the embodiment of truth encompassing
and disclosing the All. Like Dostoevsky, Hippius saw the tragedy
of human existence in man's intrinsic loneliness, his inability to
love, his aloofness from the spiritual sphere, and his shallow
faith. Finally, like Dostoevsky she searched untiringly for truth,
determined as she was to alleviate the plight and suffering of her
fellow men. Her indebtedness to Dostoevsky may be seen in "On
—bely" ("He Is White," 1912), for example, a remarkable story
of a later period and of great significance to the author herself.
It first appeared in *Lunnye muravyi: shestaya kniga rasskazov*
(*Moon Ants: The Sixth Book of Short Stories;* Moscow, 1912),
and later she selected it for publication in the Russian newspaper *Poslednie novosti* (*The Latest News,* Paris).[29] Like the
short stories "Ivan Ivanovich i chort" ("Ivan Ivanovich and the

[29] No. 2258 (1927).

Devil," 1908) and "Oni pokhozhi" ("They Are Alike," 1912), "He Is White" utilizes an esoteric myth about the devil as a bewitcher, although here Hippius also exposes his seraphic nature. In her works the devil almost always appears as a symbol of temptation; only in a poem "Grizel'da" (1895) he is portrayed as the "misunderstood Teacher of great beauty." Sometimes she associated the devil with an erotic element and often with *poshlost'* (vulgarity), as in the works of Gogol and Dostoevsky. The poet's devil theme is the expression of her own spiritual surrender to the temptations of withdrawal from other people, of inactivity, and of spiritual exhaustion.

Hippius's preoccupation with the devil is religious in its nature. As Olga Matich pertinently remarks in her "The Religious Poetry of Zinaida Gippius," Hippius's " 'devil poems' provide a very significant insight into the continuous struggle that the poet waged with stagnation, or what she herself calls 'nonlife' or 'antilife,' and with the very attractive escapist state of solitude or isolation from life's movement." [30] In "He Is White" Hippius seems to understand and even partake in the devil's melancholy, from which there is no salvation. The devil appears before Fedya, a student at St. Petersburg University who has been stricken with pneumonia, in order to teach him to accept and love death. Sent by God from heaven as one of the seraphim so that man can exercise freedom of choice between good and evil, the devil is a great sufferer, an angel grieving over human spiritual torment. He took upon himself the heavy burden of suffering for the sake of human freedom. Fedya, whose hatred for the devil and fear of death are erased, dies peacefully in the devil's affectionate embrace. He is convinced that the devil will ascend the throne of God, clad in white garments. "Sharply, as if by a sword, Fedya's soul became illuminated with his new understanding of death. And this understanding became crossed with another sword, a similarly sharp understanding of life."

Among the other short stories of the period Hippius favored

[30] Olga Matich, "The Religious Poetry of Zinaida Gippius" (Ph.D. dissertation, University of California at Los Angeles, 1969), p. 184.

"Vsyo k khudu" ("It's All for the Worse," 1906), "Strannichek" ("The Pilgrim," 1908), and the above-cited "There Is No Return." The first two later reappeared in a collection of her stories, *Nebesnye slova i drugie rasskazy* (*Heavenly Words and Other Short Stories*).[31] The eternal problem of the relationship between God and man is in the foreground of "There Is No Return." As Hippius reminisced many years later, in the spring of 1905 the Merezhkovskys stayed for a few days in Odessa, on their way from Constantinople to St. Petersburg. A ship with wounded Russian soldiers from the Russo-Japanese War arrived there at that time, and a few wounded officers from Port Arthur were given rooms at the same hotel with the Merezhkovskys. "There were both seriously wounded persons and convalescing ones," Hippius recalled in her *Dmitry Merezhkovsky*. "With one of them, who had lost a leg, I became friends, and once, when the nurse stepped out and he developed severe pains, I injected him with morphine. He told me, 'They kept on hacking away at me, but they did not kill me.' I witnessed so many strange things in their rooms! And I was left with the impression that all of these people who had 'returned' from the flames of war had become (or were still) insane." [32]

These observations found their artistic expression in "There Is No Return." Grisha and Nadya, participants in the Russo-Japanese War of 1905, have lost all contact with external realities and life in general after their return from the war. It has forced them "to live in their separate world, on their own planet." The emphasis here is on the human mind which cannot be cured without faith in God. Without God, they are incapable of communicating with people. A similar thought forms the central theme in "It's All for the Worse." Dementyev has murdered his wife. He does not, however, feel any remorse or desire to repent because he believes that there is no real bond among people, or between people and God. He instructs Father

31 Paris, 1921.

32 Z. N. Hippius-Merezhkovskaya, *Dmitry Merezhkovsky* (Paris, 1951), p. 136.

Methodius, a monk, that every man, without exception, performs evil deeds; even monks, although they do not live in the world with its "secular evil," indulge in "monastery evil." Nobody believes in God, nobody thinks of Him. Hippius demonstrates here the relativity of genuine faith—which of these two men, the sinner or the pious monk, is closer to God?

Religious considerations are also the basic issues in "The Pilgrim." Spiridonov, an industrious and kind peasant, and his wife Mavra have lost their only son, whose dying was accompanied by harrowing agony. A pilgrim who spends the night in their hut assures Spiridon and Mavra that God has punished them because of their insufficient love, and that it was because of their sins that their child died so painfully. Mavra indignantly orders the pilgrim out. As in "It's All for the Worse," Hippius again raises the question—who is right and who is wrong; who is closer to God, a devout pilgrim or a loving mother? She also expressed doubts concerning the faith of pious people in a letter to Mamchenko from Italy, dated September 17, 1937. "The present, real actuality of the world—this is the real root of my sadness. . . . Looking at the Pope's palace beyond the lake and at the crowds of monks and nuns who pass by my windows, I think: you understand nothing; there is no help from any one of you, with the exception of my little Thérèse [de Lisieux, of the Carmelite order]." In this letter, moreover, the poet reiterated her former view that heaven, earth, and the human being sustain one another, and the three of them form one inseparable entity. Man, rooted in the earth, must experience all the trials which God sends along his path ("one must drink one's cup to the dregs"). One who emerges from the full life experience, with his personality well preserved, is closer to God than one who withdraws behind the walls of monasteries, cathedrals, or the Vatican.

Several of Hippius's stories are valuable not only as an artistic portrayal of her *Weltanschauung*, but also as works of an autobiographical nature. In a short story entitled "Aly mech" ("A Scarlet Sword," 1906), for instance, she described the beginning of her religious activities, her "Cause," [33] or *"la question principale," "la question essentielle,"* and *"le but de l'Humanité,"* as she referred to the "Cause" in her intense and frank discussions with the Swedish artist Greta Gerell. The characters Belyaev, his sister Lyusya, and their friend Alexey are eager (as was Hippius herself) to create a new church and a new religious mentality. During a conversation with his sister, who here seems to echo D. V. Filosofov's apprehensions, Belyaev says:

Man needs God more than anything else. God is more important, more significant than any deeds, however indispensable they might be. God is the prerequisite for these very deeds. God is eternal, He is ours and everybody's, but we have no unity in our love for Him; we have no prayers, no temple. He who understands this knows that a new temple is needed; he knows what prayers will be required. And we . . . within our capacities and strength . . . will serve this cause with our intellect, abilities, and lives. Our path (specifically "ours," and *only* a path as yet) is through art. And so long as there are three of us, we are strong.

The indecisive Lyusya—like Filosofov, always hesitant and at times even hostile—answers, "But how am I to believe, to the very end, that the walls of our temple will be tangible, made of stone and earth? How am I to believe that the Great Mother, tangible and made of marble, will stand in it? How am I to believe that the birth and resurrection of Christ will be presented on the walls or on the canvases with paints, evident to everybody? Such tangibility is necessary for me, for us, for everybody." These doubts were characteristic of Filosofov, one of the members of Hippius's central religious circle, who frequently caused her much grief and anxiety.

"Nebesnye slova" ("Heavenly Words," 1906), another story of the time, likewise may serve as an artistic record of Hippius's religious activities, but it also reveals several important details from her personal life. Like *Contes d'amour,* the story portrays the poet's own physical attachment to a person "who had

[33] Ref. Temira Pachmuss, *Zinaida Hippius: An Intellectual Profile,* pp. 111–65, 213, 217, 249, 428n–429n.

dragged her down into a pit" after she had deluded herself that they were both on an ascending road. For Hippius, an "ascending path" was the only acceptable way to love. As in her diary, *Contes d'amour*, the protagonist in "Heavenly Words" experiences a feeling of tenderness and compassion for his mistress, but is incapable of loving her. He complains, "All the time I sensed only my body, which was so lonely and oppressive," because his physical attachment had not been accompanied by real love. He expresses Hippius's own views that she recorded in *Contes*: "Cruelty is a weakness. One must not be without mercy to any creature." Like Hippius herself, the hero returns to St. Petersburg after intentionally ending his love affair in order to devote his life to a religious cause. And as Hippius many years later will ponder in another of her diaries, *Korichnevaya tetrad'* (*The Brown Notebook*), the narrator of "Heavenly Words," having grown old, meditates, "Will anybody speak and write about it? About the Cause? Not about me—of what significance am I? Nobody knows me. It is the Cause which is alive. Glory and joy to it!"

"Heavenly Words" is a work which never lost its significance to Hippius. In a letter to Mamchenko dated September 19, 1938, she gave the following evaluation of this story: "I have re-read it with great interest, though also with considerable boredom (it is too long). The book can be viewed as a record of my own 'history,' but there are two levels: an 'outer crust,' devoted to presentations of temporal questions, and another layer, concerned with the eternal aspects of the problems raised." "They will remain forever, these questions," she continued. "God keeps me, though, from saying that I have solved them." In Hippius's opinion, the artistic value of "Heavenly Words" lay in precisely these problems of everlasting significance: "Not a single word about the Eternal, even if only whispered in a corner, should be lost," she admonished her friend in the same letter. "As a sign [from Above], somebody—if only one, or two, or three from all humanity—may come across you and suddenly 'hear' you. We have no right to try to determine on what day and at what hour

all others may hear the voice [of the Eternal], if they are destined
to hear it at all."

One of Hippius's central themes, the mysticism of "sublimated"
love and passion, is reflected in several stories.[34] Temptations
of bisexual attraction are described in "Ty—ty" ("You—Are
You," 1927) and "Perlamutrovaya trost'," ("The Pearl-Handled
Cane," 1933), and polygamous love in "Miss May" (1907). New
forms of beauty, harmony, and love are portrayed in "Smekh"
("Laughter," 1908). Hippius attached special significance to
Memuary Martynova (*The Memoirs of Martynov,* 1927), which
she called a "novel about love," and to "The Pearl-Handled
Cane." The compositional pattern of *The Memoirs of Martynov*
is a series of stories resembling Lermontov's *Geroy nashego
vremeni* (*A Hero of Our Time,* 1840) with one common narrator, Ivan Martynov, who relates various unusual episodes from
his childhood, adolescence, youth, and manhood. Martynov's
love experiences form the plot. In "Sashen'ka," for example,
Ivan appears as a schoolboy who cherishes friendly feelings and
platonic love for Sashen'ka, a young university student. "Skan-
dal" ("Scandal") describes Ivan's erotic entanglement with an
older woman, Magdalina. "Smirenie" ("Humility") portrays
Martynov's first surrender to physical intimacy with a woman, a
prostitute. The action in "Gorny kizil" ("The Mountain Cornel") takes place in one of the fashionable Caucasian resorts.
The work reveals a keen insight into the psychology of both
sexes. "Chto eto takoe?" ("What Is This?") takes the hero back
to St. Petersburg, where he becomes betrothed to Anna, the
daughter of a university professor, but later succumbs to a love
affair with Anna's beautiful, youthful mother. "Falsity in love,"
Martynov says, "is given to man as mercy, as a garment to conceal the excessively cruel and incomprehensible truth of love." [35]
Hippius here poses a question of paramount significance to her:

34 See, for example, "Ne to," "Dvoe—odin," and the volume *Nebesnye
slova i drugie rasskazy* (Paris, 1921).

35 Z. Hippius, "Chto eto takoe?" *Zveno,* no. 1 (1927).

"Can human eyes endure the nakedness of Love?" [36] Perhaps the most interesting of all these narratives is "You—Are You," with its portrayal of Martynov's love, which overwhelms the skeptical and rational hero for the first time during his sojourn in Nice. This is his first passion for a person who at the end of the story proves to be a young and handsome Frenchman. He becomes Martynov's "only 'you' in the entire world."

Another narrative by Hippius, which reveals her deep musings on the essence of human love, places the same hero in yet another unusual situation. In "The Pearl-Handled Cane" Martynov, who is now in Sicily, is surrounded by strange young men and women. Ivan's friend Franz von Hallen is in love with Otto, who lives in Berlin with his young wife. Nino and Giovanni, two handsome Sicilians, are likewise infatuated with von Hallen. Ivan, too, yields to a temptation of homosexual love. Franz instructs Ivan that "genuine love is a great gift given to man. This gift is happiness and sorrow at the same time, but whoever is granted this gift must bear it, whether it be happy or tragic." [37] The narrative is based on Hippius's own observations in Taormina in 1896, where she witnessed a variety of psychological entanglements in the people whom she met and whom she studied with great interest during her stay there.[38]

The artistic presentation of the unity of the heavenly and the earthly as one whole may be found also in Hippius's voluminous works.[39] Her heroes, impelled by their ideas of love and God and their perfect, harmonious interrelationship, spend hours discussing their doubts, fears, hopes, and ideals. Their religious experience suggests to them that they can learn a kind of love which may sublimate their flesh, but in their inherent

[36] Ibid.

[37] Z. Hippius, "Perlamutrovaya trost'," *Chisla*, no. 7–8 (1933), p. 177.

[38] For more detail see Z. Hippius's *Contes d'amour*, with an introduction and annotations by Temira Pachmuss, *Vozrozhdenie (La Renaissance,* 1969), no. 210, pp. 57–76; no. 211, pp. 15–47; no. 212, pp. 39–54.

[39] See, for example, "Ushcherb," "Sud'ba," and "Svyataya krov'."

weakness their efforts are doomed to failure. The voice of Hippius herself, with her hopes and presentiments, clearly resounds in the chorus of her frequently anguished men and women. We can see this agony, for example, in Shadrov, who expresses Hippius's views on the transcendental mystery of sex. Sexual love for Hippius was a manifestation of the Godly Trinity in the human flesh and the only possible physical contact with the spiritual world. Sex, she maintained, is the first flesh-and-blood touch of God, the Three in One. So Shadrov says to Margaret, the woman he loves:

> I love in you . . . the Third Person. I am not allowed to love Him directly; I may love Him only through another person who is akin to me. You are my window to the Third Person. . . . Only through you can I reach and feel Him closely. This is His will. When you fell in love with me, and I saw His reflection in your eyes, I thought that love was your preordained path [toward God]; that through the dark power of your love you will reach His light, if you surrender the whole of your being to an experience of love. . . . Do not be ashamed of your flesh, just as a man should not be ashamed of his words which accurately express his thoughts. For our soul, our consciousness, is the reflection of His thought. Can He express His thought through unfit and unnecessary flesh? [40]

Hippius dealt with love, marriage, sexual fulfillment, and movement toward God in many of her other narratives. Her novella "Sud'ba" ("Fate"; published in 1906 under the title "Vymysel, vecherny rasskaz" ["Fiction, an Evening Story"]), for instance, treats the complex interrelationship of mystical clairvoyance, love, human life, and fate. The work is indicative of her indebtedness to Turgenev's artistic method. It is a story within a story, a group of middle-aged bachelors sitting around a burning fireplace during the late evening and entertaining one another with reminiscences from their earlier years long gone; one tragic story, with strong mystical undercurrents, prevails over all other episodes related; there is an ever increasing dramatic tension as the story develops, and so forth. The deeply rooted

[40] Z. Hippius, *Tretya kniga rasskazov,* pp. 198–200.

interest of Hippius in psychological complexities, married life, true love, and human understanding in general is also manifest in a story "Vechnaya zhenskost'" ("The Eternal Woman," 1908). Child psychology likewise attracted her attention, as the remarkable stories "Sashen'ka" and "Julien ili ne Julien" ("Julien, or Not Julien," 1931), among many others, show.

"It's All for the Worse," "Stranny zakon" ("The Strange Law," 1915), "Serdtse, otdokhni" ("Rest, Heart," 1932), and "So zvezdoy" ("With the Star," 1933) disclose the opposition of the poet to war. According to her, no war can justify human slaughter. She saw the only difference between murder in civil life and murder in war in that wars are "organized" and sanctioned by government. Every murderer, including a state at war, was for her an apostate. "I say to the war today, from the depths of my human heart and my human reason, 'No!'" she stated emphatically in her reminiscences *Sinyaya kniga: Peterburgsky dnevnik 1914–1918* (*The Blue Book: Petersburg Diary 1914–1918*).[41] She amplified her opposition to war thus: "I reject wars because each war, which ends with the victory of one state over another, carries in itself the kernel of a new war, because it engenders the emotion of national embitterment. And indeed each war slows down the attainment of our ideal, i.e., ecumenity." [42] "Under no circumstances shall I ever say 'Yes' to war, just as I shall never say 'Yes' to Bolsheviks," Hippius hazarded resolutely in a letter to Gerell dated October 14, 1938. "Politicians who start wars are often dangerously insane. It is quite natural that there are one or two politicians of that kind, but of course it does not mean that others must not wholeheartedly resist becoming their puppets." A convinced pacifist at the beginning of World War I, she maintained in her speech to the Religious-Philosophical Society in St. Petersburg in November, 1914, that war was a "debasement of the universal human condition." [43]

A rejection of war is expressed in many of her poems, short

41 Belgrade, 1929, p. 12.
42 Z. Hippius, *Sinyaya kniga*, p. 10.
43 Z. N. Hippius-Merezhkovskaya, *Dmitry Merezhkovsky*, p. 216.

stories, public addresses, and essays at the time. In the poem "Bez opravdaniya" ("Without Justification," 1916), she condemns violence and bloodshed, saying that if wars were sanctioned by God she would rise against Him. Later, having realized that it was not in the best interest of her homeland to oppose the war, she began to consider it a "necessary, general madness," [44] accepting it only from a religious viewpoint. She now saw war as ordained by God, as a sacrifice through blood and fire. The Russians, she believed, had to take upon themselves this sacrifice with full realization that it was a step backward, a regression in the "universal pilgrimage of mankind." [45] "We must enter the flames [of war] not as treacherous cowards, but fortified by our spirit as well as by a joyous hope that the redemptive flame of this conflagration will become for us also a purifying fire. Let us hope that this purifying fire will fortify our will and determination to struggle anew in the name of a new Truth." [46] World War I became for Hippius a step through bloodshed and ensuing suffering—"along the path of a Great Movement" [47]—to a new order, religious theocracy, the kingdom of God on earth.

The apocalyptic religion of Hippius was thus inherent in her concept of the war. She maintained that Russia could win World War I only through a reinterpretation of Christianity, with an emphasis on religious sociality (*religioznaya obshchestvennost'*). Whereas before the uprising of 1905 she had cherished hopes that revolution would transform her dreams into reality, in 1915 she expected that it would be the war which would realize her ideals of the apocalypse. The war would bring to an end the old bourgeois, mediocre mentality and way of life; it would signify the advent of a new society, a new order, as yet unknown, but passionately desired. Peace, liberation, and the establishment of religious sociality would come with this beginning. The

---

44 Z. Hippius, *Sinyaya kniga*, p. 13.

45 Z. Hippius, "Veliky put'," *Golos zhizni*, no. 7 (1914), p. 15.

46 Ibid.

47 Z. Hippius, "Priyatie i nepriyatie voyny," *Byulleteni literatury i zhizni*, no. 9 (1915), p. 553.

war, however, deceived her expectations just as the Revolution
of 1905 had disillusioned her before. Although deeply affected,
Hippius—an incorrigible idealist—did not abandon her hopes
for an ultimate victory of freedom even after the catastrophic
consequences of World War I when the Bolshevik *coup d'état*
took place in October, 1917.

First in Poland and later in France, where she and her husband found themselves in 1920, Hippius encountered considerable difficulty in continuing her life's work. She could not find
any co-workers among the Russian émigrés who horrified her
with their apathy and mediocrity. As the stories "With the Star"
and particularly "Prevrashchenie" ("Metamorphosis," 1936) indicate, the poet, like Gogol and Dostoevsky's Ivan Karamazov,
saw the devil's participation in the trivial activities and banal and
shallow attitudes of man. In the disguise of a "poor sponger,"
with the appearance of a typical representative of contemporary
middle-class society, he was everywhere. He was active in all aspects of bourgeois existence. He was in those social, religious,
and cultural pursuits which fostered striving for material well-
being and revealed a placid, unconcerned mentality. Such an
existence, especially with wife and children as the eternal justification of the bourgeois way of thinking, represented for Hippius
and Merezhkovsky a perpetual negation of genuine culture and
true religion. They called it a "kingdom of mediocrity," fearing
that this mediocre kingdom might dominate the world, which
would then be ruled by the Philistines. The Philistines would
create a new society in which freedom, individuality, and the
likeness of human personality to the Divine Image would be
eliminated. It would be the kingdom of the Antichrist, of the
devil himself, whose objective would be the destruction of all
hopes for the establishment of the kingdom of God on earth.
Hippius was shocked by the low cultural level of some of the
Russian exiles, especially those living in Poland, as well as by
the discord and animosity among them, and at all times she endeavored to recall them to their heritage. As the article "Zemlya
i svoboda" ("Soil and Freedom," 1926) illustrates, she entrusted

the Russians in France with the preservation of the Russian cultural tradition. "Culture is an inner value, a string made of many threads which extend from everywhere, from all aspects of *life,*" she reminded them. "A nation (I use this word in the largest possible context) is a living organism; culture is its breath." [48] Freedom is necessary for this breath; freedom is the child of culture. Aware of the chaos arising from the breakdown of cultural tradition and artistic expression as early as 1900, she never could tolerate the ignorance of beginning writers who claimed to be artists, but who had no knowledge of Russian culture: "Almost none [of them] have read Dostoevsky (perhaps in childhood, fleetingly), or the 'outdated' Gogol," she remarked tartly. "They have scorned Turgenev with condescension; they have scorned Nekrasov without condescension, yet they have never seen their works. It goes without saying that they know nothing of earlier, less outstanding writers. . . . Little by little, they have developed their own style, some bizarre mixture of refinement and illiteracy. Their nature . . . has forced them to distort every Russian word when they can." [49] It was particularly the young Russian writers of the second decade, like the Futurists, Imaginists, and "other 'ists,' " who amazed Hippius either with their apathy or their "bold strokes" and "prancing." She was bewildered by their absurd neologisms, devices, images, and their "means toward positive goals," which she could not understand, such as "der . . . bul . . . shchir, the predilection of babies to commit suicide, and the pregnancy of men." [50] She had serious doubts that these futurist "der . . . den' . . . etsy" represented a "blazing star" in the history of Russian culture. In Esenin she saw a typical representative of those Russians who were "untouched by culture." [51] She viewed his ruin as man and artist as springing from his insufficient restraint and his ignorance of the Russian spiritual heritage, a reproach she also made regarding Gorky.

[48] Z. N. Hippius, "Zemlya i svoboda," *Poslednie novosti,* no. 1903 (1926).
[49] Z. Hippius, "Nov'," *Sovremennye zapiski* XXIII (1927), 423.
[50] Anton Krayny, "Moy *post-scriptum,*" *Golos zhizni,* no. 19 (1915), p. 12.
[51] Z. Hippius, "Sud'ba Eseninykh," *Poslednie novosti,* no. 1772 (1926).

Esenin has a purely Russian—Rasputin-like—lack of restraint. . . .
He has lost his wits from a freedom which knows no bounds. If he
wants to express the "new" in poetry in a nastier way, Esenin has
everything at his disposal, including Mayakovsky. If blasphemy is
required, no Komsomol member could offer a better version. But the
main thing is the smashing, smashing, smashing, the pathos of destruction which intoxicates better than wine. . . . The main principle in contemporary Russian poetry, the one of *destruction,* carried
now underground, now above ground, but unremittingly, has finally
touched the very heart of poetry, even the very heart of the Russian
land, that is, of the Russian language. . . . The process (in its
general outline) happened thus: with the Futurists, the smashing of
sound; with the Imaginists and other "ists," the shattering of art,
the banishment of life from art and of music from poetry; finally,
with the aid of the untalented Esenins, the smashing of sentences
and words themselves. . . . [The younger poets] publish their own
poems. One cannot laugh at them as one does at the Futurists; it
is impossible to be exasperated by them. In them all smashing of the
essence of poetry has come to an end: sound, rhythm, sentence, and
word are dead. (I do not talk about thought and meaning. How
could I!) Words—in a very shaky, unstable line—rattle like bones.
All intrinsic laws of language have been completely broken.[52]

Using Esenin's fate as an illustration—for, as she said, "a primitive drawing is always more transparent" [53]—Hippius wrote: "Esenin is interesting as a convincing example. He is a pure chem-
ical product. One can observe in Esenin's case the process of
human disintegration and final ruin." [54] She warned the Russian
émigrés "against the temptation of losing themselves and . . .
against those who have already lost themselves." [55] Esenin-like
"lack of responsibility," "lack of will," "lack of culture," and
"lack of restraint" she regarded as graphic illustrations of human
tragedy. Only true culture, she insisted, can avert the tragedy
of waywardness, hopelessness, and extravagance of feeling.

[52] Anton Krayny, "Poeziya nashikh dney," *Poslednie novosti,* no. 1482
(1925).
[53] Anton Krayny, "Sud'ba Eseninykh."
[54] Anton Krayny, "Lundberg, Antonin, Esenin," *Poslednie novosti,* no. 680
(1922).
[55] Anton Krayny, "Poeziya nashikh dney."

Since culture, freedom, and religion were matters of primary importance to her, Hippius urged the Russians in Paris to consider these as conditions indispensable for human life. These treasures must be preserved by mankind as the highest values in its spiritual heritage. "Freedom is as necessary for life as the air we breathe," [56] she asserted. Culture, art, the creative process, and knowledge cannot exist without freedom; loss of freedom is identical with spiritual and physical death. Empirical knowledge and positivism could only be allowed to gain the upper hand over other attitudes at the expense of universal culture, that is, self-restraint, nobility of thought, and the inner harmonious development of mankind. Real culture can spring only from the mutual relationship of people's inner and outer worlds. If harmony and equilibrium are lacking in this relationship, one of these two worlds would develop excessively and suppress the other, thus disrupting their simultaneous and harmonious evolution.

Germany was for Hippius an example of the discord in which the outer world entirely suppressed the inner world. The shallow thinking of the Germans and their excessive freedom of action in warfare were symptoms of growing disharmony in the German nation; they showed a disrespect for the values of universal culture. The mission of the Russians living in exile was not, therefore, merely an irreconcilable and permanent battle against Stalin and Bolshevism, but also an opposition to Germany in the name of Christianity and religious culture. With their irreconcilability toward Bolshevism and Germany, the Russian émigrés, Hippius argued, could save Europe from barbarism, positivism, belligerency, and automation. To fulfill their historic, religious, and cultural mission, the Russian people must constantly remember their own Russian culture, that is, the harmonious development of their inner and outer worlds. With her story "Metamorphosis," among many others, Hippius wished to prove her case *ad contrarium* by criticizing the Russian émigrés'

[56] Anton Krayny, "Dorogie pokoyniki," *Novaya Rossiya*, no. 25 (1937), p. 15.

placid, unconcerned state of mind in politics and religion, and their disregard for culture and national dignity, two "lofty treasures" which could impart religious meanings to all of their thoughts and actions, and to their very lives.

All of these stories reveal the originality of the personal and metaphysical universe of Hippius and her emphasis on the aesthetic and philosophical content of the literary works which helped set the stage at the beginning of the century for a new literary movement, Russian Symbolism. Her poetry and fiction evidence a particular stress on the importance of the individual and the significance of intuitive and spiritual revelations. Since Hippius also represents the current of religious and sociopolitical thought of the time, her fiction is of importance in the study of the Russian intelligentsia during and after the religious renaissance of the twentieth century. Her works, animated with personal visions of Christ and the Holy Trinity, emanate from and embody the poet's fertile, complex experience and concerns. They are evidence of her firm belief in the exalted and the lofty. Although obsolete in the view of modern existentialism, the philosophy at the basis of her art still has the power to stimulate the reader with the Christian ideals of eternity, absolute reality, and all-embracing love. In her poetry and prose the principal constituents of Russian culture—art, religion, metaphysics, and sociopolitical philosophy—are fused in their harmonious integrity.

HEAVENLY WORDS

UPWARD

People have always talked much nonsense about the heavens. Poets have described their pleasant appearance; astronomers have made calculations on them—they even have a number for every star; ordinary folk look at the sky when they are afraid that it is going to rain, and in general everyone is convinced that there is very little connection between human affairs and the heavens. Religious people, however, do not say this; instead, they regard the sky as a blue curtain which is not important in itself, but only hides from them what is important and is connected with them.

I will not talk about the heavens as a curtain. For me heaven is alive, like the face of a living human being, and it is always with me, participating in the most intimate fashion in all my thoughts and actions. The face of the sky is more comprehensible than the face of the earth —people practically never see the earth in its true, naked form. More often they see it changed by their own hands, and how could it be otherwise? For the heavens are pure and very broad, and therefore expressive as well.

I am going to tell a few old incidents from my life, and it will be clear that the heavens live with us, talk to us, only we seldom listen to their words.

Poets are particularly unbearable. Their heavens are allegorical, but I am not at all interested in allegorical heavens. The poet describes a thunderstorm in lengthy detail simply in order to add, "Such storms often seize my soul . . ." Or they talk about the sun and compare it to the "sun of love." Doctors are inclined to think that storms affect the human organism, the external man, in a very natural manner. But all this is just not it.

We are engrossed in our affairs; we are in hesitancy and doubt —and the sky is with us, smiling, frowning, counseling, explaining, consoling, chuckling. One has only to understand its words.

It isn't difficult to understand them if you are attentive, particularly if you possess certain abilities and the tendency to look upward. I know one old woman who in all perplexing circumstances turned . . . not even to the Bible, and not to the Gospel, but to a breviary. Heaven is much broader than a breviary, and what is more, it is a book which is always open at the right place.

II
THE RAT

I lived for a long, long time without noticing the heavens— probably until I was ten years old. I used to be annoyed when water poured from the roofs, and I skipped like a goat around the garden when blotches of sun lay on the sand, but somehow I never looked up at all. We lived in a village in Little Russia [the Ukraine], and I was brought up freely—more precisely, I wasn't being brought up at all. I was constantly alone and was very spiteful, stubborn, and dull witted.

One Sunday, after breakfast, I went to the old barn to catch a rat I had spotted there. The old barn in the backyard was the one place where I had been forbidden to go, so I constantly hung around it. But today this was especially naughty, because that morning I had been taken to mass and was dressed in a blue silk shirt, which I knew I was certain to ruin around the barn. I must add that I liked the shirt and was a little sorry for it, but there was nothing to be done.

Next to the abandoned barn, which was gray and had a little colonnade, thick grass grew almost as tall as I was, while around it other buildings were huddled. It was very remote, and no one ever came there. I squatted in front of the hole I had noted earlier under the twisted gallery of the barn, took out a piece of squashed cheese which I had pinched at the breakfast table, placed it by the hole, and proceeded to wait. I had no weapon at all and didn't know how I could hope to catch the rat, and in general why I wanted to, but still I waited and hoped.

I waited so long that, when the rat appeared, I went absolutely crazy and hurled myself upon it. With the speed of lightning, it scampered up onto the gallery. As I remember, I shrieked and rushed after it onto the rotten boards and caught hold of the cross-bar of the balustrade. The beam immediately broke in two, and I fell on my back from a considerable height. But the fall did nothing more than stun me, for I had fallen on the back of my neck onto the thick grass. Instead of a rat, I held in my hand a gray piece of the balustrade. The thin green stems waved around me, and right above me, very high up, was a piece of sky, blue like the silk of my shirt. I knew that this was the sky, but I looked at it properly for the first time, thought about it, and took a liking to it. It was perhaps even bluer than my shirt and stood above me as if nothing had happened. However, it had seen me fall, and I was ashamed. Yet it was still pleasant to lie and look up, and I didn't move.

Above all, I liked the fact that the sky was so spacious and uncluttered by anything. If the rat had run about up there, it would have had nowhere to hide, and I would undoubtedly have caught it. But down here barns and holes had been invented . . . It was good, too, that it was uninhabited. And the sky, although it saw my defeat, remained pensive and did not censure me very strictly, so that I ceased to be ashamed and liked it even more. I looked at my shirt. It had a torn sleeve and seemed very lacklustre in comparison with the sky. I lay there a little longer, then got up bravely, straightened myself, and again looked up. So I didn't catch the rat, so I had torn my shirt, but instead I now had the sky. It had seen everything—and didn't mind; it stayed the way it had been. It was good that I now had the sky.

Why I needed it, I didn't know. What I should do with it, I also didn't know. Anyway, I also didn't know what to do with the rat I wanted to catch. Yet I had such a feeling of satisfaction —as if, in addition to all the old playthings, of which I had by no means grown tired, I had unexpectedly been given a new one. I had the barn, the garden, the rat, the grass, myself—in short, everything down here. But now I discovered that up above there was also something good, and that it was also mine. I'd like to see who could take the sky away from me!

Apart from that, it was mysterious as well—no one ever talked about the sky, no one suspected that it was mine, and I didn't want to say anything—indeed, how could I? Even now, as I am talking about it, it's still incomprehensible to others; so at that time I would not have known how to say a single word about it.

That night, reciting the Lord's Prayer, I stopped at the words "which art in heaven." What was this about heaven? I had a nurse, a nasty woman that I didn't like and even secretly despised. Nevertheless, I asked her what they meant by heaven. She coldly explained to me that God is in heaven.

I didn't say anything, but I didn't like her explanation. Has God got so little room that He has to choose heaven to live in? How about in church . . . Yes, I'd heard someone say that God is everywhere. Well then, it's all the same to me—let Him be in heaven as well. Anyway, the sky is mine, just like the barn, the garden, and the rat's hole. No more than that, but by no means less. Let God have everything on earth—the barn, the grass—I know they're mine as well, and let God have everything in the heavens—the sun, the sweeping storm-clouds (now I recalled seeing sweeping storm-clouds)—so long as it's still mine. It doesn't make any difference.

III
THE EXERCISE BOOK

I was being packed off to school in the city. It was a bright, sunless day. The sky was spread above me as evenly as could be, all white, like the pages of a new exercise book. I wasn't in the least sad that I was going away. Why be sad when there are sure to be other houses, other trees, and then there will still be others —it didn't seem to me that I was losing the ones I had. The road along which I was going to travel would join without any interruption this piece of earth with the other; so they would both be mine. In exactly the same way, the sky covered these two and all other parts of the earth without interruption, and it was all mine. I couldn't see everything on the earth at once, because I was small and stood close to the earth, yet I could see all the sky at once, because the perspective is much wider from a distance. Though basically, of course, it's all the same.

But now the sky, although it was welcoming and sympathetic, kept silent, all white and even. I understood this to mean that it did not want to distract me. I had to work and study the things they study in school, and in the meantime it would keep quiet and wait. After all, it was impossible for us to part company anyway. Whenever the need arose, it would always be there. But one has to study, too.

So I set off in great merriment.

IV
FREEDOM

I am writing my heavenly reminiscences every night, little by little, like a diary. I am writing unhurriedly, and I almost have no hope that anyone will read them and understand how close the sky is to us, how intimate, like the earth.

It is worth noting, however, that whenever people recall words which they have said and forgotten long ago, they almost all recall the place where the words were uttered. Sometimes both the thoughts and the feelings which provoked the words have disappeared from memory, but the place is remembered, and whether it was light or dark at that moment. In this way I always recall—the sky. Even if I didn't see it, if I was beneath a ceiling, I knew what it looked like, what it was saying, and I was thinking about it.

Sometimes I hated it and quarreled with it. It was repulsive to me, but I couldn't help thinking about it.

Two friends and I were walking one white night along the Neva embankment. (I was already about to graduate from the university.) Above us was the sky, pure and of a liquid green color. Not a single shadow of a cloud disturbed its cold evenness. We were talking about freedom and quarreling terribly. I in particular was borne aloft. It seemed that there were no limits to my ravings. I cannot even recall everything I said. My companions also talked without listening to me, just as I did not listen to them, and they apparently were saying exactly the same thing as I.

Then suddenly I stopped and fell silent, as if I had been jolted. My dreams of freedom were terribly complicated and knew absolutely no bounds. The sky curved above us evenly, spacious, and everywhere equally bright. Because of the buildings it was impossible to see the line where it joined the earth, but you could guess how the sky, this green cup, firmly and precisely thrust its rim into the earth, and how surely we were locked in this circle. I always loved the gentle and clear line where the sky touched the earth, their kiss, their wedding. What is the freedom that I spoke of? I knew and know, I felt and feel, that within this circle I am free, and that everyone can be free in it, as I am, if he will love both the earth and the sky equally, as I do. Free inside the circle, as far as that bewitched, uncross-able limit. Yet that other freedom—which?—is so unattainable that it is absolutely impossible and unthinkable even to want it.

This was not a thought, not knowledge, and not feeling or sensation—this was what I call conscience, that is, a feeling com-bined with knowledge, and sensation combined with thought. And I fell silent and no longer talked of any freedom, whereas my companions talked for a long time afterward, each listening to himself, neither noticing that I had fallen silent.

V
MY WIFE

Clouds are the thoughts of heaven. In the same way the shadows of thoughts frequently pass across the human face, and the face changes. It seems to me that I can sometimes read the thoughts of people—and can almost always read the thoughts of heaven. As the features of a person change, so do the features of the heavenly face—today's sun is different from yesterday's, and it will never again be as it is today. I have never even seen the same moon. As for the stars, it goes without saying. Rare is he who looks at the sun, but, of course, we rarely look a person straight in the eye.

At the end of my life I don't know whether people will under-stand me, but in my youth I was naïve and thought it natural for all people to look up as much as they look down.

However, before the sky won me irrevocably, here is what happened. When I discovered for the first time that people live in ignorance of heaven, without paying it any attention, and live simply and even quite well, my confidence was deeply shaken. Suppose I am wrong? Suppose I have just invented all this, and the sky is an ordinary ceiling which has nothing to do with us? Why shouldn't I live simply, like everyone else, looking no fur-ther than my feet? I must admit that at that time the constant in-terference of the sky in my affairs was simply confining for me, it wearied and angered me. So I decided to be alone, to do anything I wanted without witnesses, by myself, ignoring precept and morality, and live simply, just like everybody else. I decided to forget about the sky forever, because it would otherwise, of course, be impossible to get away from this witness and teacher.

At that time I had just finished college. I didn't get a position and didn't even know whether I ever would. I had a little money—not a lot, but enough for myself. When my father died (my mother had passed away long ago), he left me that humble little manor in Little Russia where I grew up. I wrote verse, considered myself a poet, and dreamed of devoting my life to literature. I might add that I graduated from the university as a mathematician.

One should keep in mind that at that time I was only twenty-one years old.

Despite my extreme youth, I decided to marry. It wasn't that I had anyone in mind—I simply decided to marry as early as possible and to spend my life as normally as possible, as Tolstoy taught. Such intentions were not easily reconciled with my verse and my thoughts about the "struggle on the battlefield of poetry" —but at twenty-one years of age what can one not reconcile?

In Petersburg the young ladies were all unsuitable in some way. So I went on a trip through Russia to see how people live and, by the way, to look for a bride.

In Kiev (I didn't visit my manor), I had the occasion to make the acquaintance of a whole crowd of young ladies who were completely different from those in Petersburg, and whom I, therefore, liked to the very last one, i.e., considered suitable as wives.

Anyway, I soon fixed my attention on Verochka Bets and Anna Lovina. They were very different, yet each was beautiful in her own way. Verochka was a lively, boisterous, and if not intelligent then an inventive girl, blond but without any gold in her hair, which was sort of dusty yet beautiful. Anna was swarthy, quiet, gentle—perhaps stupid, but pleasant, with a long black braid. Her gaze was slow, gliding. I couldn't choose at all between the two.

So I decided to relate to both, separately, of course, what I had thought in the days of my early youth about how the sky had lived with me, how it had hindered and angered me until I finally decided to abandon all this madness and live like everyone else. Of course, I didn't want to talk about the decision I had arrived at, but only to relate the facts and discover whether either of them was predisposed to the heavenly malaise. This was precisely what I was afraid of and didn't want. I felt vaguely, despite my youthful bravado, that I myself hadn't completely recovered—if this was really a malaise.

On the very first evening, when the whole party was strolling in the park above the Dnepr, I contrived to be left alone with one of them, either Anna or Verochka. I managed it with Anna.

We were sitting on a bench by the river. Above us there was a blue-black summer sky and various patterns of fairly large stars. I myself turned my eyes away, afraid that the sky would begin to speak to me against my will and that I would start to listen to it, and I said to her:

"Look. Do you see the sky?"

"Yes," she replied timidly.

My first question sounded pretty stupid—it even irked me that she did not burst out laughing. Then I decided to continue with poetry.

"What do those stars say to you?"

This was conventional poetry, yet at the same time the question was to the point.

She replied, after a moment's hesitation and quietly.

"I don't know how to say it . . ."

"But they do speak? They do?" I insisted.

Again she was silent for a long time. I was about to lose my patience.

"Yes, lots . . ." she said.

"Well, well, 'Lots,' she said! Listen to what I am going to tell you."

I briefly told her all I had thought about the sky as recently as the previous year. I got carried away and was even going to add that now my thoughts had changed, when suddenly I noticed with astonishment that Anna was crying.

"What is that for?" I asked unsympathetically and thought to myself that things were in a bad way.

"I . . . oh I understand you so well . . ." said Anna excitedly. "That's precisely . . . I don't know how to express it . . . but I understand it fully."

My heart sank. If I had loved her, I would, of course, have understood immediately the brazen folly of my puerile nonsense about the heavens, and the blindness would have passed, as it did of its own accord several months later; but I didn't love Anna.

I inwardly congratulated myself on thinking up such a fine test and got up from the bench.

"Calm yourself, Anna Vasilyevna . . . We will have another talk . . . But now, I'm afraid they're looking for us . . ."

This was extremely crude but, absorbed in my tests, I decided to continue them immediatly. Before Anna's very eyes I began to seek a *tête-à-tête* with Verochka, and with no great skill I deflected her onto the same bench.

"Well, what did you want to say to me?" she began hastily. "Quickly, because everybody saw us come here."

"Let them see."

"All right, but what's this about?"

"I can't say it in just two words," I said, unexpectedly piqued.

She sat next to me and smiled demurely:

"It's all the same—you can take ten."

The astral patterns swirled before my eyes, although I kept looking away. To my surprise, I didn't know how to begin the conversation. Then I decided, without further deliberation, to begin exactly as I had begun with Anna, so I asked:

"What do these stars say to you?"

Verochka burst out laughing.

"So that was your important matter! Oh, you poets!"

"Don't laugh, Vera Sergeevna. Wait. Listen to what I am going to tell you."

And I told her the same things I had told Anna, but even more briefly. Verochka again smiled ironically.

"Well, what do you say?" I asked.

"What do I say? Nothing. I don't like to pretend, Ivan Ivanovich. I'm lazy. Perhaps one could think up some poetic words for this poetic . . . or astronomical story of yours, but I swear I'm too lazy. I don't care about anything. Of course, the stars are the stars . . . It's interesting, of course . . . but I don't care."

If I had loved her, then again I would have divined my blindness to the fact that she was of that breed of creature which does not look upward and, therefore, does not suit me, as I do not suit it. If I had loved her, I would have stood up and left her, but I did not love her. Despite this, I still did not feel like proposing; however, I was so ashamed of myself—hadn't I decided? What is this nonsense?—I quickly forced myself to gasp out:

"Vera Sergeevna, would you like to be my wife?"

She seemed to be surprised.

"That's not poetic license, is it?" she asked.

I was not disposed to mirth and frivolous jokes.

"Would you like to be my wife?" I repeated.

She was silent.

"If you're serious, then . . . then I'll think about it. Or no, it's all the same anyway. I will. It's all the same."

I respectfully kissed her hand, and we returned to the party.

It was true that Verochka did not like to lie. It was with great sincerity that she had said, "It's all the same." She had no parents, and her affairs were run by some trustee. She had to get married in order to gain her independence, and it was all the same whether she married me or another. She liked me less than Kozitsky, for example (all this she explained to me herself with childish simplicity), but probably Kozitsky would lock her up and force her to be faithful—he loved her. Whereas I . . . Verochka saw clearly that I did not love her, and she kept saying with surprise after the wedding, "You know, I don't understand why you married me?" I would be embarrassed and gloomily keep silent—I no longer understood it myself.

Of course, we did not have any family; even the honeymoon almost failed to work out. We set off to spend it at my small manor. At first it was chilly, and Verochka caught a cold—there were drafts everywhere, and we had a terrible dislike for one another. It took the isolation to make this clear. Then the warm days came, thank God, and with them guests blew in to visit us —mostly men, students from Kiev, officers. Verochka gaily came to life.

I think she began to be unfaithful to me after one or two months. Almost everyone, women too, has a vocation: one feels himself to be a born doctor, another—a traveler, a third—a bureaucrat . . . There are mistakes, but they don't come to any good; yet a person's strength is in finding his own place. Verochka was a born courtesan. A real, sincere, naïve, ardent priestess of love. Every way of life is either good or bad, depending on whether it really belongs to the person who follows it or not. If Verochka had become a village schoolteacher or a nun, it would have been a bad thing. But she was a courtesan, unselfish and amiable, because she was born to it, and so it was a good thing.

She, of course, felt—unconsciously, however—that it was good. Nevertheless, it had been driven into her consciousness that that is *always* bad. Therefore, at first she tried, though without any sensation of guilt, to hide from me and others her involuntary deceptions. She hid it badly—she didn't know how to lie—and only became spiteful and vulgar, for she felt her justification without knowing it.

I understood her quickly, more quickly than I would have understood if I loved her, or was in love with her. However, there was none of that to prevent me. I saw her growing embittered, tortured by my presence, beginning to hate me, not free in herself, and I didn't know how to untie the knot without hurting her. She had an ever so tiny mind; such creatures are easily insulted, are insulted at everything, and then suffer aimlessly.

I understood all this on the day when I again accepted the sky as my teacher, as something alive around me, subordinated myself to it again, and this time—forever. Having accepted the heavens, I accepted the earth too, for I had, without knowing it, denied it as well when I denied the sky. I accepted and understood . . . For me they were—and again became—indivisible.

This happened on a hot July day while I was lying in a field on the edge of a wood. The gray earth became lilac toward the horizon and merged with an equally lilac sky, which imperceptibly changed toward the zenith, becoming a translucent blue, and then again, sinking toward the other horizon, where it became hazy, lilac-colored, merging with the earth. Where they were divided, I didn't know, and indeed were they divided? I lay face upward and felt only this earth-sky and life itself. Apart from the earth-sky and life, that is, the movements of my own heart—and the other movements of other hearts, of course—there was nothing. This I both felt *and knew*—and I became almost relieved, although I understood my responsibility, that of my separate life among other lives. I think it was then, at that moment, that I stepped out of my infancy for the first time.

Toward fall some officer on leave from Petersburg fell in love with Verochka, apparently quite seriously. I was waiting for just this. She was attracted by him, and I saw that parting would be unpleasant for her, that she was upset and didn't know what to do.

Before the officer left, I said to her:

"Vera, it's boring here. Would you like us to go to Petersburg?"

She flushed and looked at me strangely, as if she were afraid that I was setting a trap for her and had some evil design. I hastily added:

"I have to, Vera. Business . . ."

Another, more "virtuous," woman would have been glad to have such an accommodating husband and would hold on to him, but her straightforward character was repelled by it. She understood neither me nor herself, and she was tormented—I could see that.

We arrived in Petersburg in October and stopped in a hotel.

I talked about an apartment, but vaguely, for I knew that we should finish everything as quickly as possible.

Vera would disappear for days on end. We met in the evening, and I kept wanting to begin and never knew how, afraid to hurt her. From that day in the field she had become dear to me, like every life, every breathing thing. Everything is right that is alive.

While I was getting up courage, Vera, who was more direct and decisive than I, herself could not hold out.

"Where were you?" I asked her by accident, without any hidden intent, simply to say something.

She flushed.

"What kind of a question is that?"

I didn't answer, and indeed she didn't expect any answer. Suddenly aroused, and apparently at her wit's end, she began to attack me, clumsily, wildly—and naturally.

"I know, I know what you're thinking! You think I have been seeing Anatoly Ilyich!" (That was the name of the officer.) "I can't bear the way you look at me! What a mean way to torture me! We've finally got to have things out, Ivan Ivanovich!"

"Yes, Vera, of course we must," I said gently.

She was on the point of calming herself; then she cried again: "I've wanted to tell you for so long that I can't stand you! I hate lies. I'm not afraid of anyone. Yes, I've been seeing Anatoly Ilyich! Yes, I love him! He's not like you. You think I don't see that you don't love me in the slightest? You're a strange person! You shouldn't have gotten married. You're interested in your astronomy, or poetry, or I don't know what, but not in a wife! I'll be a faithful wife for Anatoly Ilyich, if you give me my freedom. You must give it to me."

The poor thing sincerely clung to her love as a justification, sincerely thought, perhaps, that she would be a faithful wife. How could I tell her that I wanted her well-being and dreamed only of giving her her freedom?

"Vera, don't be angry. I myself wanted to suggest a divorce, although I don't think . . ."

"You don't believe that I'll truly love the other man, forever, you don't believe it?" she cried in desperation, tears in her eyes, and I understood that I had insulted her. Did I have to lie here, too?

I went up to the window. Behind the blackness of the window was the sky, resembling nothing at all, emptiness. I knew that it was there, but couldn't see it or hear it—it was silent.

Well, then—should I lie?

The heavenly emptiness, unseen, unheard, told me, "Be silent."

So I watched and was silent until Vera had said everything she wanted, both for herself and for me, and, calming herself, came to the conclusion she wanted to reach: namely, she decided that I was in agreement with her about everything and agreed to everything.

We parted almost lovingly. I soon gave her a divorce. However, she did not marry the officer or anyone else. She stays in Paris all the time and seems to be happy. It is even certain that she is happy—she has found her vocation. Everything will be forgiven her—if she has any sins.

VI
LAUGHTER

I am not writing a chronological history of my life. These are only those fragmentary events which are most memorable to me and most related to the heavens.

I was still very young when I went abroad for the first time, to Italy. I had already emerged from my infancy—the incident with my wife made me more thoughtful, yet at times quite childish; irrational daring still seized me. At times I seemed to myself a disenchanted seeker of new beauties, almost a demoniac, which did not prevent me from being at heart a young romantic with more than a tinge of sentimentalism.

And so I set off for Italy. I decided to be original and begin from the end. To go straight through Germany, Austria, and the whole of Italy, without stopping anywhere, even in Naples, to get on the steamer at Reggio and open my eyes only in Sicily.

So that was what I did. I hardly even glanced through the windows of the railway carriages. In Naples, where I arrived in the evening, I immediately got on another train, and by morning I was already rocking on the waves of the Ionian Sea.

I didn't stop in Messina either, but traveled on to a little town; I had a letter of recommendation to a family that lived there all the time.

It was spring. The family, Germans, greeted me joyfully, gave me a room in the lower story with a long balcony above the steep terraces. On the terraces were orange trees in blossom, and behind them—the broad, icy slopes of Etna; to the left, in a semicircle, the expanse of the sea filled the horizon and was brighter than the sky.

I began to live here and soon felt a little at home. At first I walked around gaping, like an imbecile, at all these wonders, unusual and astonishing in a coarse but powerful way. I was not overwhelmed, only amazed, and for some reason very proud that I was here, seeing such unnatural things.

The pride and intoxication did not pass completely, even after I began to feel at home. The intoxication even increased gradually, because each new day gave birth to new flowers, new clinging fragrances, and also new sights.

My unsophisticated but generous hosts introduced me to the local colony of foreigners, as well as to some Sicilian families, and I began to penetrate the life of the little town.

And what a town it was! All white and blue. The little white houses, looking as if they were braided out of flowers, and below and above—nothing but blue, blue—the sky like a sea, the sea like a sky. Then I understood what the sea was. It was the earth, masquerading as the sky, imitating the sky; only the features of the sky—the sun, the moon, the stars, and likewise the thoughts of the sky, or rather the clouds—were not always reflected accurately, but distorted. I don't like the sea, yet at that time I understood nothing, and it seemed to me that I was reaching the heights of beauty, bliss, and the most refined wisdom.

The people who lived there more and more often seemed to be sages who were discovering the cherished secrets of pleasure, deep, great, and bold. Of the foreign home-owners, who had settled permanently in this town, practically none had families. At the approach to the town, along the terraces, clung the white villas of the lonely, rich Americans and Englishmen. There were a couple of German barons, and there was the villa of some count—a Pole or Russian. My host, a nice old man, had, by the way, a wife, a quiet, young, thrifty, and ecstatic German woman who had already begun to look like a Sicilian. She was almost the only woman in the whole circle.

One Englishman, the wealthiest, a young man of enormous build, Mr. Middle, led a rather withdrawn life. He talked little and at times did not come at all to where we held our gatherings. I had not been to his villa, yet they used to relate marvels about it. Externally, it was nothing special—white walls, behind which the roof of a little white house, overgrown with pale wisteria, was barely visible. This house stood to the side, almost immediately at the foot of the gray, rocky mountain called Monte Venere. Whenever I encountered the towering figure of Mr. Middle, intense, politely taciturn, and almost mysterious, on the narrow main street of the town, I would bow to him respectfully, with a strange sinking of the heart, resembling both doubt and jealousy. I recalled my recent, unsuccessful love affairs: as a result, all women seemed to me so flat and vulgar, and all love for them—vulgar, gray, and ugly. Could there be in such a love something corresponding to the beauty of these flowers and this whole fairy-tale, blue-and-white town? No, here everything had to be special, unusual, finely beautiful, insolently bold. I felt myself becoming purified, forgetting everything in the world, and simply adoring beauty and hating my old vulgar ways.

Then one day Mr. Middle invited us all to his house for dinner.

Our hostess grew excited and told me for the hundredth time

how beautiful Mr. Middle's villa was. I, too, seemed excited all day. From the morning on, we sorted the flowers which some acquaintances in the town had brought my hostess the previous evening. They were friends native to the surrounding villages, and they had brought the flowers on the occasion of her birthday (she was rather popular). One could say that I gorged myself on the flowers, but not only did I not develop a revulsion toward them—on the contrary, I received a sort of animal pleasure, sorting the flimsy, silken petals, as tender as the neck of a child. We had not finished sorting them when night fell and it was time for us to go.

Mr. Middle did not like to entertain late. It was for this reason that he had invited us to dinner at seven. It was barely getting dark when we left. My hostess regretted that there was a new moon, because Mr. Middle's villa was even more beautiful in the moonlight.

The villa turned out to be not at all luxurious or big. The garden and balcony were so wreathed and drenched in flowers, and they, the flowers, were so strong here, so enormous and overpowering, that I was reminded of Paradise after the Fall. Deserted after the Fall, it probably grew even more luxuriantly, for Adam and Eve were no longer there to crush the flowers. In any case, here the foolish and irritating chatter of one of Eve's granddaughters would be out of place—it would deprive all this beauty of its mysterious seductiveness. I even looked with distaste at my hostess, but she acted modestly and had no pretensions to anything.

We ate on a terrace that projected into the garden. The illumination was somehow strange, shifting, slowly and evenly changing from red to green and then back to red. Mr. Middle's young servants waited on the table in multicolored Sicilian costumes which fell in long folds. What I ate and drank—I don't recall. I drank little, although I frequently saw at my side a pair of dark, velvety eyes and a swarthy hand filling my glass. It seemed as if both the food and drink smelled of flowers. Because of this I could neither eat nor drink, and yet I liked it.

After dinner we descended from the terrace onto a little space, illuminated by the same spinning light above. Mr. Middle came to life and became almost amiable.

"Now . . . our tarantella . . ." he said and clapped his hands.

From the black obscurity of the garden a chord rang out. Some unseen musicians began to play the tarantella. An uncomplicated, fast, heavy rather than melancholy tune—as passion can be heavy.

The same youths in their long costumes danced on the court in front of us. I remember the dark, lustreless, unthinking eyes with their intense gaze, the pitch-black curls under the crimson ribbon, and the narrow strip of forehead, smooth, swarthy, with its tiny beads of sweat. And their fast, gracefully light—yet at the same time heavy—movements to the heavy, monotonous, and shocking tune.

Mr. Middle also danced—and apparently with great skill. Even my hostess joined the circle with another boy. The latter, dark-eyed, dressed in crimson, kept choosing Mr. Middle. The count also danced, tall, supple, and tender, like the stem of an iris. If I didn't dance, it was only because I had absolutely no idea how.

The musicians, as they departed, still unseen, played some tinkling serenade, an old Sicilian one.

It was already after nine. We departed.

At home I bade my hostess good night, without replying to her lengthy effusions, and immediately went down to my room.

I did not light the lamp and did not remain in the room, but went out onto the balcony. Resting my elbows on the grillwork, I looked down into the dark abyss from which the heavy fragrance of the orange flowers, as heavy as the fragrance of incense, rose up and tenderly smothered me. The sea murmured in the depths; to the right the gray mountain of the goddess of Love rose sharply.

I was in love. In love as never before with everything that surrounded me, with myself, and with the fact that I was in love.

My body ached, sweetly and weakly, and I felt it growing weaker, soft, with neither will nor strength. It seemed to me that I was reaching for and touching the heights of beauty, from which vulgarity is as remote as I was from those base, vulgar people with their coarse, "normal" love on their coarse, ugly earth. New paths, new forms of beauty, of love, of life . . . I was approaching them, I would sense them, I could feel them!

I raised my eyes—and saw the sky.

At first, I remember, I didn't think anything, I didn't yet understand, but a minute shiver ran down my spine.

I couldn't turn my eyes away. I kept looking and looking . . .

The sky was laughing.

The very next minute I saw and understood that it was laughing. It was black and pure, seemingly resonant and cold, despite the huge stars which squinted, blinked, and quivered with laughter. The young moon was about to move behind Etna; it almost lay on the blunt summit, indeed it did lie, for its sharp ends, both of them, were turned upward, like the corners of a smiling pair of lips. Again the sky spoke to me, and again I understood and listened to it—and accepted its judgment of me. For this was its judgment—its laughter, so unexpected, almost cruel.

I looked—and from my body, from my soul, something warm, sticky, enfeebling, and pitiful was gradually sloughed off. The new beauty, the new love! Heavens, what had happened to me! It was as if the light had gone out of me. No, all this, despite its coarseness, was not even frightening, but simply laughable, so laughable that I too smiled in the darkness. Above me the sky laughed, and I deserved it.

The bulky Englishman, his dinner in the light of the spinning lanterns, the sinuous, gentle count, the champagne that smelled of flowers, the lustreless eyes of the boy in the crimson band, the sweat on his forehead, the dubious music of the hidden musicians, the solitude of the distinguished foreigners, the solemn pensiveness—this life, this crumbling Etna, and the squirming sea, which it was impossible to look at without exclaiming, "*Comme c'est beau!*" and the ill-fated mountain of Venus, where they sometimes sent young citizens caught in the act—yes, all of this—the beauty of Mr. Middle, that huge man, as he skipped about with a serious mien in the tarantella, and his heavy golden chain pounded against his stomach.

And it was like this to the death, the mindlessness, the dilapidation, the sickness . . . these ways and forms were neither new nor human, but old and simian. A pitiful retrogression—pitiful and comic. I recalled myself in the pose of a proud, blissful, enamored sage, and it was no longer a chuckle, but a roar of laughter which constricted my throat.

The stars blinked and squinted, the moon touched the blunt summit of Etna, and no sooner had it touched it than it immediately slipped down, so that one could scarcely see its crimson extremities. The smile had disappeared. The sky had forgiven me.

Two days later I left for Florence.

VII
PITY. THE DEATHLY SHADOW

This heavenly diary of mine is somehow terribly sad, or more accurately—tiresome. It's mostly "psychology," though today's youth pronounces this word—if you only heard them—with such contempt! But what can be done?—In my day people weren't afraid of "psychology." Of course, it is possible to keep silent about it, as they do nowadays, yet it still lives in the soul, has its value and significance, occupies its place, and, if it is not externalized, sometimes crushes someone. Besides, in my mind the sky is so linked with psychology and psychology with life that I cannot separate them.

Psychology—and love . . . True, you might think that it's a woman who wrote these notes, or even an inveterate Don Juan . . . There are such types. In my time they could be met particularly among poets. However, I'm not in the least a Don Juan. In all my life I loved only one woman—and that love left such a bitter furrow in my heart that I was happy to forget love, and thereafter I kept my distance from women I might like.

This solitary love affair of mine began and ended with heavenly words. I will tell it very briefly, because it is painful and boring to listen to love stories of others, although no one has ever confessed that fact to anyone.

At the time I was twenty-five or twenty-six years old. I had business and other matters in Petersburg, and I didn't have a bad living. Yet I abandoned all this and there I was, in the middle of November, going to Rome. There a woman was waiting for me whom I had seen in all about ten times previously; I met her by chance that summer at a spa. I knew almost nothing about her, and I could not even remember her face clearly—but I loved her.

We corresponded. She said that she was going to spend the winter in Rome and invited me there. She loved me terribly, but it seemed to me sometimes that my feelings for her resembled tenderness rather than love. I don't know what it really was— isn't it all the same now? If it were tenderness—then it was enormous, almost passionate, and enfeebling.

I was approaching Rome early, at dawn. A gray, gloomy, autumnal dawn. An hour before Rome I had already arisen, was ready and gazing intently through the window of the car at the pallid Campagna landscape, from which I was unable to tear myself away.

I had never seen it in the late autumn. O terrible! O majestic Campagna! Along the ground live, sluggish mists were passing, creeping like the dead, heavily, their white garments trailing after them. There swayed—and probably rustled drily—right by the very windows of the car, yellowish-brown rushes, walls of rushes, tall and thick, with stems like trees. Sometimes the semicircles of distant aqueducts quivered, as if made of the gray vapors; a fearful fen, damp, limitless, plunging the soul into an incomprehensible, happy languor, into a quiet, joyful horror. This is a place where it seems as if everything that was and everything that will be—*is*, where you cannot feel time. But at this moment I could not completely emerge from time; some little piece of myself stayed inside me—and this was even more fearful.

It was growing lighter and lighter; the white garments of the dead were still there, and the dead rose ponderously from the marshes, up toward the sky, across which steely shadows, growing darker all the time, were already on the move. Yet in the dawn sky there was no merriment. Its vault was quiet, mournful, and the more I looked at it, the tighter was the sadness that gripped my heart. As if I were traveling not toward love, but toward a parting.

I told myself that she loved me, and that if she loved me then everything was all right; whatever kind of woman she was, she would be good—real love would give her everything necessary. And I would give her everything her love should desire of me. I did not pity myself, but . . . suddenly I saw clearly, understood, felt—that the sky pitied me. The train was moving slower and slower; the breeze through the lowered window had a quiet, moist freshness; on the edge of the heavens I saw the pure white, quiet, transparent light of the immense morning star. Oh, how gentle and tender it was! Huge, low, like a rolling tear. The sky was silent; it could not help, because what had to be—had to be, but I understood its grief for me, its love, and tenderness. My sorrow did not go away because the sky had taken pity on me; yet it became easier for me to bear, for I was not alone.

When I got off in Rome, trembling with the morning cold and inward tears, I could still see the star in the gap between the railroad cars. It was slipping quietly lower. But passing along the dead, sleeping streets, I could no longer see it in the sky. Probably it had already set.

The whole winter passed.

In the spring we moved to Florence.

I love those towns, as one might love living souls, though at the same time I am glad that life did not bring me there again, and will never bring me there again, for there is practically no life left—I am an old man. I left too much there, all my youthful romanticism, all the personal joy peculiar to me. Although, perhaps, these are all empty matters, like all *naïveté;* however, one loves them. One loves the follies of one's childhood.

It was not in vain that the sky took pity on me. All these months had been one blind torture, from the lie which at times seemed true, at times a lie—like the rotating lantern at the villa of Mr. Middle—from the unnecessary yieldings of my heart, from the consciousness of my powerlessness.

My Cause, my thoughts—everything I let go to hell. I almost didn't understand what a sin I was committing. She, the woman that I loved, was simply a cunning little animal, incapable of further inner development, yet I kept fussing around her and believing—because I wanted to—that we could hear each other, and that words had the same meaning for her as for me. She was dragging me into a pit, but I was convinced that we were both climbing upward. Ugh, it is unpleasant even to write about. I am glad that it finished like this. I couldn't harm her even involuntarily.

It ended—strangely—one hot, cloudlessly clear day in May.

We had gone together on a jaunt on the electric train to a rather distant hamlet outside Florence. Earlier I had been there alone and knew that a path led from it up a hill into a pine wood.

It was sunny and hot. The narrow road into which the rails were set rose continually between the low white walls, behind which endless, continuous gardens were spread out, green and glistening.

The car was empty. I went out onto the rear platform and looked at the pure sky, without the slightest trace of a cloud, and at the green. Soon the road ended. The car kept climbing; from this height we could see far around. I looked without thinking about what I could see—and suddenly I somehow felt vaguely queasy.

It wasn't even queasiness. I simply thought, "I don't know what's the matter, but I must be ill."

I went into the car, sat for a little while—and went out again. It was the same again—nausea or sicknesss. All the pure, bright blue dome seemed to me—and then again it didn't seem—to be covered with the finest web of soot. Wherever I directly looked—

there was nothing, but next to it, where one could see out of the corner of one's eye, there was a black film. I transferred my gaze to the green of the gardens, and there it was the same—the green had darkened, although it stayed green, and the sky, though it had darkened, still remained blue.

I became ill. I don't know whether it was fear or pain, but something forced me to close my eyes, to go into the car, and sit there in silence.

My companion asked:

"What's the matter?"

"Nothing. It's hot. Why don't you go out onto the platform?"

She went out, stood for a while, then returned. I looked at her eagerly, but she didn't say anything. So there was nothing wrong. So this earth, this soot was covering my eyes, and not the sky.

I went out again. The sky seemed to me terribly close, with the sheen of cast iron. The motionless leaves looked as if they had been covered with a film of ash. Yet again it was as if there were nothing wrong.

Then we arrived. I expected to be unable to walk, that I would fall flat on my back, and the sky over me would immediately turn into earth. I didn't fall, however; my head didn't even turn, and the sky kept darkening slowly, imperceptibly, so that for an instant I hoped it had all passed. But when we reached the broad square of the village, I saw that it had not passed.

Immediately it struck me—I was bowled over by the thought:

"There's something wrong with the sun!"

I stopped and raised my eyes.

"Don't you notice anything? Doesn't it seem to you that the sun . . ."

"Yes," she said hesitatingly. "Perhaps you're right."

The sun, however, stood pure in the cloudless blue. Only it seemed as if there were fewer rays; they had become shorter and paler.

In the open doors of a shop I saw a fat Italian woman. She was looking up, too. Two lads came toward us. I asked them

about the sun, and they explained to me that an eclipse was expected, not a full one, yet almost full, and that it had already begun. I was surprised that I didn't know this. On the other hand, though, I lived in seclusion and didn't read any newspapers; I had no occasion to hear about it.

We stood around for some time and then went along the narrow street and up the path to the wood.

A silence, not a full one, but a semi-silence, a hush, surrounded us. The gray, deathly blue trees, assuming a continually more death-like appearance, did not once move a single leaf. The ashen leaves seemed to have suddenly curled up and withered. Only the pines stood as straight as ever, petrified, and all a thick green color. Occasionally, a bird would emit a ragged cry, like a sob—and again everything fell silent in the darkening, as it were, slowly cooling air which was too motionless.

I was silent. I was seeing something I had never seen—a dying sky. It was really dying, moving away, retreating, slowly revealing the emptiness, the black space which we know exists but have not seen, because we are covered with the blue of the sky. The emptiness, like a dark jaw, bared itself above me. The sky was dying, and with it the earth was dying, too; inseparable from it, the earth was becoming covered with cadaveral shadows and blotches. With them, with the sky and the earth, my life—and the tremor of my heart—was being extinguished as well. Life is linked to them, just as they are linked to it.

Of course, I knew that this was not death, but only the foreshadowing, the ghost, the threat of death, for the eclipse would pass. However, I was not thinking about this—was it not all the same, *such* an insight into death and *such* a death itself? We were dying—the earth, the sky, and I—together. In order that I should be, it was necessary that the earth and the sky should be. And in order that they should be—it was necessary that I should be.

The tranquil horror of this moment, this dying of the whole creature—for both the earth and the sky are a creature—was not a new feeling for me. This I immediately understood. It was as if the former dull ache that had earlier lived only outside consciousness suddenly emerged, gathered itself into a sharp point, penetrated the barrier between heart and thought, and found form, manifestation, word. My blind sufferings, the torture of spirit and body—this dying of my soul, the murder through me of earth and sky—that was precisely the eclipse, the eclipse, the eclipse itself!

The sky was telling me, "You're sick—just look at our sickness. You're dying, perishing—just look how I shall share your death. Whoever is blind—has no sin. But whoever sees and does not accept—for him there is no forgiveness."

And all my life, now ending, that I had squandered in the aimless torture of unnecessary love, became precious to me, as every single life of every single creature is precious. The deathly shadows, the blue rays wandered about me, yet the measure of the powers of life had not been fulfilled. It was not yet the end, and hence such a shiver, such a tremor seized the creature. No, it was necessary to live, to live—to see, if one had eyes; this was not yet the angel—this was the demon of death; not an assumption—but a murder; this was an eclipse.

For two hours the deathly gray gloom squeezed the air. The resurrection was slow, barely perceptible—it only became easier to breathe, the heart beat more loudly, and the birds, timidly, began here and there to call to one another with joyful bewilderment. The sky was coming out of the emptiness, returning to me.

My companion fell silent, like a bird, but she was not a bird that could be resurrected instinctively only with the general resurrection. And she was not I who understood life, the sky, and the earth as a gift, and who was also resurrected only with the general resurrection. She was between us, at a halfway stage. With the semi-instinctive nature of the animal and the semi-rational nature of the human being, she quickly oriented herself, knowing that this "is a normal astronomical phenomenon, and it will go away; at first it's unpleasant, but then it's very interesting."

She began to talk, and I fell silent. She was angered—with

us every insignificant matter led to a quarrel—and became moody, as I recall. We went up the hill a little way and sat down. It was already starting to get light then, and my heart had come to life a little. There was no time to be lost. In only one case could I tell her directly everything that I thought and felt—only if the eclipse of my spirit still continued. For she would not hear anything. I said:

"Why are you angry with me? I'm silent because I am thinking that we will have to part."

She looked at me in astonishment, but I already understood her looks. So I continued:

"For you said that you wanted, for several reasons, to remain for a short while in Florence, whereas I have to leave now."

We really had talked about this. She had been confused in her "reasons"; I had not wanted to pry; I was afraid, yet I had demanded that she go with me. She had screamed that she "had to be free," but I no longer understood anything, because I saw everything from the point of view of "love" where no "freedom" was necessary.

"So now you agree! You understand that I have to feel free?"

We talked for a long time. Let her have her way! Heaven forbid that the child be hurt! My tenderness remained, lonely, enormous, unnecessary. There was no love. She, this woman, had been my eclipse.

For some reason she cried a great deal, piteously, but with childlike, somehow bitter tears. She herself did not understand what she was crying about. "After all, it's only a few weeks' separation."

Mixed feelings of tenderness and pity gnawed away at my heart like salt. If I had cried, perhaps it would not have been so painful. But the tears did not come. The whole time I could feel only my body, and it was so oppressive.

We returned to the hotel long before dinner. Having wearied and cried herself out, she lay down on the high bed opposite the window, next to which stood a little divan. She lay down, turned to the wall, and immediately fell into a sleep, a deep and sudden sleep, as if she were a hurt child. Not knowing why or for what reason, I instinctively took a sheet of grayish paper and a pencil, sat on the divan by the window, and began to draw the cushions, the golden knot of her hair, all her helpless, thin, small body, the folds of her dress of white piqué that hung down a little, and the tip of her foot on the blanket.

I draw badly. I didn't know why I was doing it, but I painstakingly drew every fold and every shadow on the pillow, as if it were vital, as if I wanted to put my hand on the deathly shade of love that had crossed my life.

I finished the drawing, which was clumsy, yet charming and fearful at the same time. She and I most often talked in French, and I instinctively wrote underneath it in French:

"Voici mon enfant morte."

Our fortnight's separation became a permanent one—simply, easily, almost without words, of its own accord. She probably did not even notice it happening. I did all I could so that my child would not notice it. Cruelty is weakness. One must show mercy to every living creature. I returned to Russia in a strange condition, as if after a long illness. Looking back, I now understood many facts more clearly, more truthfully, differently. The tenderness had finally turned into a pity which was as unnecessary to her as the tenderness had been.

My eclipse had passed. I had to live. I had to live.

VIII
MACKEREL SKY

Before evening the clouds, high and almost motionless, broke up and covered, as if with tresses, even and soft, the deepening green of the sky. It was May. I was traveling in a rickety cab along the Vozdvizhenka [Holy Cross Street] in Moscow.

Everything was bad. Nothing was going successfully. There were various minor matters, but they had wound themselves around me, little by little, and now it seemed that I couldn't tear myself out of this web. I felt a vague weariness with life, as if my feet had become numb from wearing uncomfortable shoes.

Perhaps it seemed so bad because I was with my friend Volodya, whom I had seen little of since college but whom I loved. He and I were returning after seeing Father Geronty, where I had again heard Volodya's ideas. Volodya had been talking with him and now was talking nonstop to me, looking not at me but down at the quivering fenders of the cab. Volodya had a pale, rather long nose and hollow cheeks, covered with an uneven black beard. His lips moved and, although I could not catch all his words because of the noise and rattle of the cabs, ours and others', I guessed that he was still talking about the same thing.

I had already understood him, I already felt bad enough; around me was the web, in the pit of my stomach I was nauseous, I was tired of living—yet he kept on talking and talking . . . Why? He had found an escape for himself—he was going into the monastery, but then I couldn't go into the monastery, so why was he poisoning me? One can never forget such minutes for the simple reason that I loved Volodya in my heart, always believed in him, and even after losing him could still not tear him out of my soul.

During this time together—I had been staying with him in Moscow for more than a week—he had completely drained me. We had been to see priests and elders, had talked with them, had talked to each other. Volodya had read me some frightening books, and I had constantly seen before me his thin, white face with the moving lips and the downcast eyes. He had invited me in order to "seek my advice" precisely about this step of his— entering the monastery—yet from his first words he had acted as if he had already decided irrevocably and was only explaining to me the whole time why it could not be otherwise. I already believed that it could not be otherwise. My heart became heavy inside me, and my weariness with life grew. My love for Volodya was somehow being extinguished, replaced at certain moments by a vague hostility.

"Oh, to escape . . ." Volodya repeated over the clatter and rumble of the wheels. "Life is just filth and abomination . . .

These are not people that surround us, but animals . . . Oh, what abomination!"

Why did he keep repeating this? Didn't he see that he had convinced me? Why this increasing persistence, this strangely growing ardor?

"It's impossible, impossible to do otherwise," Volodya continued. "There's darkness everywhere. I'll choke in this filth. Yes, darkness everywhere. Do you understand that it's impossible for me to do otherwise?"

I didn't reply. Along the narrow, bright street people were walking, hurrying, flashing by. The signs on the buildings gleamed golden. A boy shot under the nose of the horse and chuckled, giving a little skip. Volodya was talking again, but I wasn't listening to him any more. I was absorbed by a single thought: "What if Volodya is trying with such persistence and such growing ardor to convince me that he is correct precisely because he does not fully believe it himself? What if he wants not my encouragement, but support for this niggling doubt? What if he doesn't know whether in fact everything is only gloom and desperation?"

"Are you listening to me, Vanya?" he said. "Do you understand?"

"Volodya . . ." I began—and stopped.

Lord, how fortunate it would be if he had some doubts. I believed in joy—and I believed in Volodya. I had to lose one faith or the other. But what if he had doubts . . .

"Volodya . . ." I said again.

He became angry.

"Well, what? What are you trying to say? Were you listening to me? Do you believe in God? Or do you at least understand my belief in God? For it's because of God that I can't live here. I have to go away, escape, lock myself up, weep in the darkness for my soul, curse every kind of joy, because joy was created by the devil, and not by God . . ."

"Volodya, Volodya, but that . . . ," I pointed upward, and I remembered the tears suddenly starting to burn in my heart and sear through the web that bound me. "That up there . . . was that also created by the devil?"

Never did I see such a triumph of gladness in the heavens as that evening, over the dirty, narrow street. A silvery fleece had spread over the greenish-blue field, as transparent as quiet, earthly water, as rock crystal. There was not even a smile in the heavens, but only a shining, joyful caress for the earth; not a solemn dispassionateness, but love from the intimate maternal countenance.

"Everything I give to you, everything is yours," said the sky, "as you too are mine."

Volodya, after me, raised his eyes for the first time to the heavens.

That, against which his soul had struggled and which it had already fractured, was crushed by the gaze of the heavens, by the strength of their joyful love.

I remember we just arrived at the hotel in silence and then spent the whole evening weeping together. What we wept about —I don't know. It was just—from joy.

IX
LIKE A TIGER AT PLAY

I had just found out that because of Ostap everything was going awry.

He was the most destructive peasant I had ever met. Stubborn, wicked, cowardly, and stupid, and on top of that he was the village elder as well and had influence.

Having conceived of a very serious undertaking, which was thereafter to become the main purpose of my life, I decided, before giving myself up to it completely, to take a trip down to my estate and set my affairs in order there with regard to the land and the peasants.

I did not want to spoil them, but to settle accounts with them fairly and squarely, not losing my own and not acquiring the due of others, as an equal with equals. Yet I ran across insurmountable difficulties and was reminded of Nekhlyudov in *Resurrection,* the novel Tolstoy wrote in the last century. My situation was very similar, although, I repeat, there was none of his suspect seigneural magnanimity about me; moreover, the people in Little Russia, as I thought, were more businesslike, freer and more sensible, and after all, times had changed.

However, the business dragged on, and I rather frequently flew off the handle, especially when I saw that Ostap was causing the trouble—I would explain until I became exhausted; they would agree; it would seem they had understood; then I'd look —and Ostap had twisted it all his way again, and again I would have to start from the beginning. I still do not understand what he was after—he must have sincerely thought I was somehow pulling the wool over his eyes.

I was enraged by the fact that he was a coward and bowed and scraped in a stupid fashion before me, and yet at the same time it was absolutely necessary to intimidate him. I fell into voluntary exaggeration and at times acted without restraint toward him, although it seemed repulsive to me.

October had come, but the weather still held.

I was walking across the yard to see the old odd-job man Matvey, who was cutting wood by the barn. The night before it had appeared that everything had been completely settled between me and the peasants, but I had just found out that they had again gone back on their word.

There was no doubt that it was Ostap's work.

The yard was wide and empty; the grass had yellowed and was trampled down. I went up to Matvey, who stopped chopping. The short day was coming to a close.

"Matvey," I said, not recognizing my own voice, for my anger so quieted and restrained it. "Go down, please . . . to the village . . . tell Ostap to come and see me. Tell him to come immediately, you hear?"

Matvey looked at me sympathetically.

"Oh these Ukies!" (He himself was a Russian.) "More stubborn than the devil, God forgive me, and more stupid than a pig. This Ostap—what's he causing trouble for? Doesn't he understand? He should be taught a thing or two—then he'd understand, no mistake about it. He's a swine. One look at that ugly mug of his, and you know how much brains he's got."

"Go down and get him, please," I repeated quietly, through my teeth.

Matvey again looked at me.

"I'm going, I'm going," he said, and we both moved together —I toward the house, he toward the servants' quarters, presumably for his jacket.

Opposite us were the trees of the orchard and the west. I was looking down and kept my teeth clenched from the pain of my anger, but looking by chance at Matvey's face I saw that it was sort of red and purple. Involuntarily I lifted my gaze, to the western sky behind the orchard, and stopped.

Matvey stopped too.

After a moment's silence he murmured, "Look at that, what a sky! It went like a tiger! Looks just like a tiger at play!"

But it was not even a tiger—it was the spotted skin of a panther or some vicious snake. The spots, half flame and half blood, stained the sky. They spread, moved over into the clear areas, burned, forced themselves into one's eyes, repulsive, thick, ponderous, malicious, animal-like.

I looked away; along the ground hopped "bloodstained boys," [1] and a shamed, fearful, and repulsive feeling crept over my spirit. It was as if I had seen the color, the face of my own soul.

"Look, Matvey," I murmured, "perhaps you don't have to go for Ostap now. Go down tomorrow morning. Then I'll have a chat with him in the morning. Let's forget him."

Matvey did not seem to approve my decision, but he didn't go for Ostap.

The spots in the west soon began to fade and disappear, the

[1] In Pushkin's historical drama *Boris Godunov* (1831), Boris, the sixteenth-century Russian tsar, sees "bloodstained boys" which remind him of the infant Dmitry, heir to the throne.

panther's skin turned gray and rubbed away, the snake slithered away, and the sky became tranquil. I became tranquil too.

X
SHAME

Here is another apparently unimportant and very "psychological" event from my life which is not very pleasant for me to recall, although I did not actually commit any transgression or sin. However, the greatest transgressions are not as painful to recall as the occasional inane, petty awkwardness, the misunderstanding, the most innocent mistake, neither noticed nor even unnoticed, but of the sort that it is impossible to explain because of its insignificance. So it is compressed into a little lump in the soul, and at times, when you begin to stir about in there, it presses, not painfully yet nauseatingly.

Everybody, even the most respected, most serious person, believe me, has such lumps; though they by no means prevent him from being both serious and respected.

I cannot say, in all fairness, that in thirty-odd years I ever lacked seriousness, or was foolish or idle. But there was one point inside me where I had sort of lost touch with myself, and when an actual event came in contact with it—I both reasoned and felt differently; that is to say, I felt rather strange and reasoned very little.

As I have already said, I only loved one woman, seriously indulged in love only once, and from that time onward steered clear of love with all my being, whether it concerned me or others, keeping my strength for other things. But as I was handsome (although my face often seemed unpleasant to me personally), and as I never courted women, I appealed to them. They themselves courted me, and I had to keep my distance from them skillfully, with persistent attention. I swear that this did not flatter me every time—I know that I am not an exception, I am like everybody; it was only in the way I avoided them that I did not act like everybody else. Yet I was spoiled, pampered.

Every woman became suspect for me—what if she suddenly fell in love with me? So I became fastidious, self-confident, and irascible.

After a five-year separation I met Vladimir, the same one who had wanted to enter a monastery. Having sat down and hardly spoken, we understood that we were closer to each other than we ourselves had thought. Our thoughts went in the same direction, and our dreams were almost the same; our concern was almost the same and soon became completely the same. And it was so wonderful and joyful that I saw why heaven had once warmed us with its embrace—for the salvation not of us alone, but of God's Cause, which had become the Cause of our lives.

Vladimir had a wife. He told me simply that she was a poor girl whom he had met by chance, that she helped him when he needed help, and that they had married. I didn't question him. I saw that a firm, tender friendship and trust bound them; through Vladimir even I seemed to relate to Natalya Sergeevna well.

She was slight, not particularly pretty—a pale face with a rather pointed chin, dark tresses which she wore plaited and wound around her head, and a firm, penetrating look. This firmness seemed unpleasant to me. Her look seemed to be searching for something illicit in the other's soul, and when she found it, she revealed and then judged it.

However, I felt this only the first time, and then, when she began to treat me with kindness, affection, and friendship, I no longer felt any coldness. But then I began to fear that Vladimir and I were gradually losing our independence because—who knows?—suppose she suddenly turned out to be more energetic, imperious, and firm than we?

This was petty of me. But soon this phase too passed, and I simply slipped into my usual idea—that Natalya Sergeevna was "in love with me," and here I stayed.

Our Cause progressed gradually, sometimes unsuccessfully, sometimes picking up again; it demanded attentiveness, strength, and love. Volodya and I became closer and closer and so, in appearance, did Natalya Sergeevna, who did not diminish her affection for me and in no way hid it. Yet, after I had convinced myself that she was in love with me, I began to look on her as any other woman in love—the forced proximity with her irritated me, her kind words did not move me, and the familiar half-contemptuous, half-flattered feeling came over me more and more in her presence. I could not leave, for that would mean leaving Vladimir, and he was my alter ego, just as I was his.

However, I did not fear for myself. Natalya Sergeevna's human power was not dangerous for me after she turned out to be a weak, enamored woman; her feminine power did not threaten me because this woman did not appeal to me at all.

So I led a double existence, partly involved in our Cause, rejoicing, grieving, contemplating, working, and getting tired, and partly—remembering that this intelligent woman was in love with me—getting angry, regretting, half-flattered, thinking only about how to avoid saying one word more than necessary to her, so as not to give her false hopes.

Once, in May, when the long white nights had already begun, I came to see them in the evening and stayed late. Vladimir was not well. Shortly after midnight he said that he was going to lie down.

"Vanya, you finish this conversation with Natasha. She'll show you the letters I was telling you about."

I stayed. In the room where we were sitting the curtains were tied back because it had not become dark, and against the pale blue light I could see the face of Natalya Sergeevna seeming even paler. Moving without haste (all her movements were quiet), she went to the table, took out and gave me some business letters which I read by the window.

We started to talk about the Cause, then about Vladimir. She talked softly, but quickly, with vivacity. All the time I kept in mind that she was in love with me, and therefore I could not talk with sincere enthusiasm either about our Cause or about Vladimir. As I listened to her, I again found that she was intelligent and businesslike, and in my soul was born a complex feeling of excitement, conceit, and spite, with a slight admixture of contempt.

I don't rightly remember what we were talking about. Apparently, it ended up being about me. She recalled how right at the beginning of our acquaintance she had predicted that we would come together and that I would become involved in the Cause.

I paced the room.

"Yes, because you wanted to be close to me . . ."

"Of course I did," she said.

Such frankness even surprised me. I was afraid that I had said something I shouldn't. Again I led the conversation onto other things, though in fact my mind was not in the least on them. All my words and their tone, all came from the one thought: "There! You're in love with me, and I am not in love with you, but as I cannot break off relations with you, I shall be very, very diplomatic, and you had better understand this, for you're an intelligent woman."

Here I was even ready, in my magnanimity, to flatter her.

So we talked for a long time, because this meeting did not seem to me to be at all unpleasant.

It had already grown completely light; it was time to depart. The high window and door of the balcony looked out onto the square and the eastern side of the sky. There was a great deal of sky, for behind the square some kind of vacant ground began.

Natalya Sergeevna got up and went ahead of me to the door. I was walking behind her, stepping quietly. Although we couldn't disturb Vladimir—his bedroom was not close—but because of the silence of the dawn, because of the silence around we kept talking with our voices lowered, and this gave a mysterious significance to our basically simple conversation. After all, I had known earlier that she was in love with me, though my words had never breathed such a frank recognition of her love.

Half-saddened, half-satisfied, I followed her. I remember her slim figure, the bright worsted dress, the black tresses, smooth, draped around her temples, and her head, inclined forward a little.

Right at the door she stopped, turned to the windows, and said very simply:

"There's no sun."

"Why not? There has to be. It's already late."

"No. When there is, it's here. It's not here today."

She looked directly at the sky, turning her face toward it.

I looked, too.

The heavens were pure, green, shadowy. But low in the east there lay a strip of clouds, white, silent, heavy, hard, as if made of stone, and they were cut as evenly as could be. There was not the slightest sun, and indeed there couldn't be. Above these strips, the sky burned with a tender, roseate fire.

How could I not know my native sky? How could I not understand what its features were saying? I had lived with them and grown accustomed to them.

The face of the sky was burning with shame.

The fire was transmitted to my own face. Perhaps it was only the reflection. But no—Natalya Sergeevna was as pale as before. And her look was quiet and firm.

Although it was directed at the sky, and not at me, I understood that it was penetrating me, judging me, and perhaps forgiving me, but that was the worst part. I understood with the clarity of the damned that I had behaved shamefully, had talked like a fool (I was no longer sparing with my words), smugly, like a boy, like a schoolboy, like an officer . . . like who else? Because she was not the tiniest bit in love with me. Yet she had clearly seen that I was convinced of it. So where did I get this conviction? It was only because others had fallen in love with me. She had been kind, had related to me with warmth . . . And so I . . .

But why, if she saw that I was acting like an idiot, oh why did she not say that it was not so?

Common sense whispered to me that at that time I would not

have believed her words anyway, and finally, perhaps she had had pity on me. Or perhaps she had her own motives. She had a right to keep silent.

I could not bear this any further. I decided to tell her everything, to explain immediately, to punish myself, to ask for forgiveness. In the unlit hall I held out my hand to her . . .

She did not notice my hand in the darkness, however, and I didn't say a word, couldn't find any. How could I have found something to say when no words existed for such explanations? Each word would only have increased the horror of shame between us. Everything that happened was the sort of thing that seems to exist, and it even overwhelms a man, and yet at the same time it doesn't seem to exist at all. There is no form to it; there are no means for expressing it between two people. So I went away, completely helpless, into the yellow light.

It was impossible to reach an understanding. To live through it in silence also seemed to be impossible, yet that was precisely what had to be done. However, shame had eaten into me too deeply. I almost hated Natalya Sergeevna, and I thought that there was only one hope for me to achieve tranquillity—this was if she still said to me at last:

"I'm not in love with you at all!"

I thought if I could bring her to say these words, I would somehow abase her, and I myself would feel a little better. Otherwise, I would suffocate.

That's how complicated psychology was in my day. Perhaps it was aimless in itself; we were taught by it, nevertheless.

And I became almost rude to Natalya Sergeevna. The more gentle and restful she was, the ruder I was. She tried to calm me down—I became even more enraged. In an almost improbable fashion I kept showing her that I knew she was in love with me, that there was no love in me and no desire for closeness. I even pushed it so far that I—may God forgive me!—said that I had no faith in the success of our common Cause, thanks to my distrust of her.

This seemed to sadden her.

"Yet you love Volodya and believe in him."

"But he doesn't love me!"

I just didn't know myself what I was saying.

"Come now, we both love you," she said, as if comforting me. "This will pass."

So I didn't get my way. She didn't change her attitude toward me one iota; not once did she put me in my place or even lower her gaze. She was sort of invulnerable. I think that she understood a great deal. But without precisely understanding the state I was in, she decided that I was unshakable in my conviction. Why did she permit me to think that she was in love? Did she have pity on me? Or did she have her own motives?

I was walking along after visiting them one evening. There were such long, calm clouds in the sky, and they stretched quietly to the south, probably to the distant sea. I too wanted to calm down, to rest, to outlive this nonsense, though in such a way that I would never come back to such things.

I went away for three months. In the fall I met Vladimir joyfully and Natalya Sergeevna gratefully. That suspicious, contemptuous, and irritated feeling that I had toward women has almost disappeared since then.

With Vladimir and his wife I lived almost one life, doing one work. They were my only helpers; it seemed that one could not be closer. Yet throughout the whole of my life something unsettled could be felt between me and Natalya Sergeevna, something buried by the years and events, insignificant in itself, but worrisome because one could not approach it with words, and because one just couldn't do anything about it.

XI

ON THE WANE

I'm old. I don't even remember rightly how old I am—whether it's ninety-two or -three, or maybe it's less.

I'm lonely. Volodya and Natalya Sergeevna have died. My Cause and some of our helpers and disciples are alive, but when

I had given everything I had and when my strength had faded, I myself left it and them. The Cause is alive, growing without me; I have fulfilled the measure of my strength and have finished my share.

I don't want to write about this work of my life here and now, although like everything it was born from heaven. However, it was not born in a single moment, nor by a momentarily changing expression on the face of heaven, but by my whole life on earth beneath the heavens, by the heavens that incomprehensibly blend into the earth, by the earth that equally imperceptibly and incomprehensibly blends into the heavens again, and by the feeling of my life in them, between them, by them—the strange feeling which is inseparable from knowledge. And in order to talk about what I was doing and have done in these thirty or forty best years of my life—the fragmentary words of heaven are not enough. To them must be added the words of the earth, as well as the words of life.

I will not find them—I'm already too old. Someone will find them, say them, and write them down. Not about me, for who am I—no one knows me—but about the Cause. It is alive, glory and joy to it.

The joy is in me, constant and unmoving, like a sunless, shadowless light. I am quite alone—but I mistakenly said that I was lonely. I am never lonely. I have great big windows, which I do not hang with any drapes, looking onto a square. On the square there is a church, and behind the church—the sunrise. I sit long and late in the armchair by the fireplace; the fire barely breathes. I keep my legs under a thick plaid blanket, for I have become sensitive to cold, and I don't even need to go to bed—I have insomnia anyway. I sit like this, and before morning, just as the sky starts to brighten, the moon rises from behind my church, it hangs right above the cross, and I look at it and love it. It is so weak and thin, and just isn't enough to give the necessary light; it has become all emaciated and bent. It sinks low and hangs there, doesn't have the courage to climb. Both of us are approaching our death, and since it shows its old face so late at night, I alone see it, while the young ones sleep, for they need their strength.

The sky loves its little old moon; the sky understands what kind of death the moon dies. The sky loves me, too; it understands my death, too. The moon and I are both identical children of the sky and the earth.

And it is even strange to think that there are somewhere people who to this day believe they have lived with the earth under their feet and the sky over their heads, and that afterward everything will change, that both below them and above them there will be only earth, and there will be no sky. They, I think, have simply never thought deeply about the immutability of the laws of life. If they consider it, however, they will understand that the laws will not change for them, either.

The earth will not take away life and will not take man away from the sky. Indeed, how could it take man away when all three of them—sky, earth, and all living things—are alive only in each other, and all *three form—one?*

What is—will be. This same thing will be—yet perhaps in a different form, because of the movement that changes everything.

And when I have a different, new life, there will be a new earth, and there will be a new sky.

Glory to them!

FATE

I

Late one evening, about midnight, five old friends were sitting around a dying fire and exchanging stories.

Many suppose that nowadays such things no longer take place. They did take place occasionally at the beginning of the last century, then more often toward the middle of the century, and in the time of Turgenev it seemed that old friends were constantly gathering somewhere around a fireplace and telling each other stories. Nowadays, however, one hears nothing more about it, neither at home nor abroad—not even, for example, in France. At any rate, storytellers never tell us anything about it. Whether they are afraid to prolong their narrative and thus fatigue the busy reader, or whether they prefer to pass off indubitably as their own a story which a friend has told them—who knows? Or perhaps there really are no longer such people, pleasing to one another, who would sit around a fireplace together and listen to one another's stories? No, the fact is that, although it indeed occurs only rarely, such gatherings do take place even in our times. At least, one took place on the evening I am about to describe.

Not only were they old friends, but they were old people as well. That is, not very old—between forty and fifty at the most—and all of them bachelors. This last circumstance could have been the reason for their sitting together by the fire listening to each other—some smoking cigarettes, others taking quiet puffs on scented cigars, slowly sipping a marvelous, thick wine from their glasses. There is some sort of gentle, marked dignity about an old, peaceful bachelor. He is never absent-minded, always has his wits about him, is always ready for friendship, and when he listens, he does so with pleasure and attentiveness. He is interested both in the world around him and—almost equally so—in his own and other people's relation to the world. On the other hand, the man who is not a bachelor is primarily interested in his relation to his own little world, and if it does not interest him, it worries him, and if it does not worry him, it annoys him, but in any case this little world of his, if only in part, shields the larger one from him.

They gathered in the apartment of Lyadsky, a stately, youthful-looking man of about forty-five with wavy gray hair and an affable smile. His eyes, however, were not without a trace of severity. He was the director of some department where he was well liked. Nearly all the rest were not colleagues of his, but old friends from school and the university who had embarked upon different paths. Despite this, however, they were able to preserve their former intimacy.

Dark wallpaper. Dark curtains. Dark carpeting. Dark, heavy furniture. A solitary electric light was on, shining gently under its low shade, and in the hearth there were gentle crimson coals with their flickering blue flames. They were speaking about the future—in a word, about the obscurity of every man's future fate, about every man's longing to penetrate this darkness, about various predictions, presentiments, prophecies. Why should these people who were no longer young, who had lived their lives almost to the end, why should they be interested in the future? They were speaking, however, not only about themselves, but about all men, young and old, about their aspirations, and the laws of fate.

"In ancient times," Lyadsky said, "although people believed in the invincibility of Fate, they still made use of horoscopes, invoked the oracles, the prophets; why was this? Aware of his fate, Oedipus did not try to escape it. Now we believe in free will—just at the time when we need prophets, horoscopes, and faith in such things. Nowadays the knowledge of the future might change life and make some sense out of it."

"Do you think so?" asked one of his friends, a tall, lanky man, very handsomely dressed, with a graying moustache. Sitting in an armchair right beside the fireplace, he had been silent most of the time. From his singular manner of conducting himself, in a modest and sober way, one might have detected in him the qualities of a diplomat, a man who frequently listens but who also knows when to speak. His name was Politov.

Lyadsky answered him dispassionately:

"Yes, that is how it seems to me. While you . . ."

"I am of a different opinion. You have reminded me of one strange occurrence . . . One particular meeting . . . I have never forgotten it. It is a long story, but if you wish I will tell it to you. I have never told anyone about it—I don't know why. Perhaps there was simply no occasion for it. However, today's conversation has touched upon my own recollections. So many years have gone by . . ."

This is what Politov told them.

II

When I was young and had just begun to serve, I was attached to the embassy in Paris. I lived there a year or two, made myself at home, became close with some of the people and, oddly enough, became closest of all with a circle of artists and men of letters. Some of them were the most unbearably trite people, yet there were also some lively, intelligent people to whom I could speak without feeling bored. Despite my youth—I was a mere twenty-five years old—I wasn't captivated by that idle-sounding French merriment, which seemed rather primitive and tedious to me. But I didn't shun society and never avoided social events whenever they presented themselves.

One time, through a friend of mine, the artist Lebrun, I happened to find myself at an elaborate banquet given by another most distinguished artist, whom everyone knew as Eldon. The banquet was given in his own residence. The affair was held for some occasion . . . I cannot recall which. *Fermeture . . . ouverture* . . . I don't know, but it was a feast and a celebration and, as they said, the whole artistic and theatrical world was present. There were ladies in attendance as well. I remember a long table and how it sparkled. I also recall flowers with a breathtaking fragrance on the tables, and the hostess, charming Mme Eldon, a heavyset, magnificent, ruddy-complexioned woman, who likewise sparkled all over. I even remember her saying something and expressing thanks, as she smiled and clinked glasses with a calm, pleasant gesture.

Since my friend was engaged in lively discussion with his neighbor on the left, and since my neighbor on the right was not speaking with me either, I found myself alone among a noisy assembly that laughed and enjoyed itself without me. I was grateful for the chance to be silent—I could play the observer. I gazed at the row of faces directly opposite me, beginning at the right. One face, another, a third . . . When you shift your eyes rapidly from one person to another, it seems that one and the same face is transforming itself so strangely because, although the faces are different, there always exists an unpleasant and indisputable likeness in each of them . . .

A fourth, a fifth, a sixth . . . Suddenly my eyes stopped. I had nearly reached the left end of the table where a woman, whose face my eyes had unexpectedly rested upon, was sitting across from me to the left, almost next to the hostess. A bouquet of pale, withering roses practically concealed her from me, but when I inclined my head a little I could see all of her. Don't be surprised at me for remembering such details. But on the other hand, if I were to meet that same Lebrun tomorrow, even if he hadn't aged one bit, I wouldn't even recognize him. As for the woman, I think that even you would recognize her if you saw her after I have finished my story.

It is easy to describe her features, for there was nothing remarkable about them. She was beautiful, pale, and serene. It seems she was young, perhaps not even yet thirty. Her eyebrows were smooth and thin, and angular, as in all antique portraits. Her dark hair, softly enveloping her face, had not the slightest lustre, nor was it very luxuriant. That was all. She wore a black gown with a distinctive, narrow, décolleté neckline, revealing a thin line of white skin leading down into her dress. I had not yet seen her eyes, for she kept them lowered. She was silent, just as I was.

Then she started to speak. She smiled. Her mouth was very small and scarlet, her teeth were set close together. She was young and beautiful, yet ordinarily beautiful, not even very attractive to me. In my heart she aroused neither praise nor dissatisfaction, nor repulsion, but terror. A terror which nothing can explain, a dark, evil fear, which all of us have experienced . . . in childhood, perhaps, at night, alone in the dark. This fear is distinct from all others because it only forms one half of the feeling, while the other half is delight, yet a kind of dark, malicious delight, as incomparable to any other delight as this terror is to any other terror. Since I wasn't a child, I unwittingly began to reason to myself, "What, in fact, was there about her which could inspire terror? She was ordinary, beautiful, young . . ."

Young! That's what it was. That was it. Undeniably young. Not even thirty. Twenty-seven or twenty-eight.

Not at all! Twenty-seven—and fifty, eighty, one hundred and twenty; no, two hundred, three hundred—I don't know—she could be even one thousand years old! Yet all the same it was beyond any doubt that she was no older than twenty-eight.

I turned to my companion:

"Listen to me a moment—who is that lady sitting next to Eldon, on his left?"

Lebrun, interrupting his conversation, looked at me absently and with impatience:

"Which one? In the pink dress?"

"No, no, a little further over to the left, in the black gown. What's her name?"

"Oh, that one. Her name is Countess Yvonne de Suzor."

"And is her husband here, the Count? Which one is he?"

My friend, who had by now turned away from me again, said with surprise:

"Her husband? She isn't married. She is the daughter of the late Count de Suzor, the very same Count who . . ."

He then abandoned me entirely, convinced of having satisfied my curiosity.

I didn't question him further. I looked once again at the Countess, and at that moment she raised her eyes. Such strikingly unpleasant eyes they were! So large and pale, perhaps bluish or grayish—I don't know. Only they were very pale, transparent, as though made of colored crystal, and old-looking. The eyes of a dead person. But at the same time they were young, bright eyes.

I realized that I had been mistaken because of her eyes, and I had involuntarily lapsed into an almost poetical exaggeration when I had persuaded myself that she was "three hundred, five hundred, one thousand years old"!

No! A thousand years—that is almost an eternity for us. Eternal things never grow old. Yet the Countess, with all her youth and beauty, was indeed old, of that old age, of that human decrepitude around which, very close by, lurks man's death.

I noticed that her pale eyes were resting on me. The gaze was completely tranquil, not indifferent, nor even accidental. She looked at me as though she had known me from long ago but was neither glad nor astonished at our encounter, as if it were necessary that I should look—almost to the point of impoliteness —at her unquestionably beautiful young face with my persistent, unbroken stare. This time Lebrun himself addressed me, and I was finally compelled to lower my eyes.

"You asked me about the Countess? It's true she has a very interesting face, don't you think? Although wouldn't you say there is something . . . even alienating about it?"

I thought that he didn't understand anything and never would, so I just said to him, noncommittally:

"Perhaps . . ."

"Yes, a charming girl and a dear friend, although I must admit that I'm not an avid admirer of her creations. There is a certain style, a trend, a very singular quality about them, if you will, yet . . ."

"Pardon me, but what type of creations?"

"Well, I mean her paintings, *parbleu!* Didn't I tell you that she was an artist? At the last exhibition her painting and several *études* of hers were displayed. She is very famous. You have, no doubt, noticed that. Ré. Ré!"

Ré! So this is how she signs her canvases, with those two indiscreet letters! So this is Ré! I couldn't say that anything was made clearer for me as a result of this information. On the contrary, it became more baffling and confused. How could I not know Ré? They had spoken about Ré, had said that her paintings "create a ponderous impression"—everyone understood it; that is, everyone understood it in this way. I, however, understood nothing. I remember walking away bewildered, not so much in my mind but in every part of my being. I recalled immediately her "Campfire," which I had seen during the past year. It is impossible to describe paintings, and it is not really necessary. The thing which upset me about this "Campfire" cannot be reduced to words. Anything expressed in words would be too commonplace. The picture was apparently well painted. It depicted the darkness, with a large campfire situated in the middle. On the left there was a half-naked old woman; there was also one on the right. A shadow was somehow visible from one of them, and therefore it appeared that there were three old women, one of whom was enormous. That was all. About the old women there was a rigid immobility, an earthly heaviness. The third one, the shadow, was immense but light. That was all. There was no sense to it; God alone could make some sense out of all these pictures! But they were really memorable and stirred the soul.

The dinner lingered on endlessly . . . Lebrun began chattering with me. Seeing that I was looking at her again, he once more focused the conversation upon Ré and said:

"When that funny old man died, the Countess's father . . ."

I interrupted him:

"I never heard about the Count."

"Really? I thought you had heard about him. The Countess's fate is remarkable. Suzor, a millionaire and recluse, refused to recognize her as his daughter for sixteen years. She had been living almost in poverty with her half-crazed mother, studying intermittently, running off to the Louvre and art school . . . Suddenly everything changed. The father took her back along with her mother—who, by the way, died soon after—and he surrounded them with royal luxury, hiring the best teachers, sending them on trips, allowing them freedom, showing his love. People surmised that he loved his daughter because he died in her arms and because toward the end he allowed no one by his side except her."

"And now?"

"Now she lives all alone, in her . . . well, it is almost a palace. Of course she is no recluse, but she comes close to being one."

"She never married?"

"*Que voulez-vous? Une artiste!*" my friend replied with the pronounced levity of an impartial judge, and we spoke no more about the Countess.

But no sooner had this lengthy repast drawn to an end, when, without thinking about it beforehand, I began to make my way among the guests in the direction of this woman. It did not even occur to me to ask Lebrun to introduce me.

III

From close by she appeared to be the same as from a distance. I perceived only that she was of average height, rather slender, and that her gown was very long. She stood at the piano with her back toward me (we had passed into the drawing room) and conversed with some elderly gentleman. Hardly had I approached when she turned and, to my surprise, extended her hand to me, again as to an old acquaintance, and said:

"*Bonjour.*"

The old man immediately withdrew. I couldn't understand one thing—could it be that I alone saw something in her which no one else could see? Or, perhaps, they had already grown accustomed to her, took her for granted? Yet even the lighthearted Lebrun, referring to her, said, "*Etrange figure.* She seems to have no life in her." A stupid, vulgar statement, but maybe from his point of view it was so.

I noticed that from close up her complexion appeared very fresh, with that gentle freshness common to light-skinned women. She was younger than I had imagined. Probably around twenty-five . . .

What was I to say to her? She stared at me unrelentingly with her pale, transparent, seemingly vacant, sunken eyes, like those of an eighty-year-old woman; they were also charming. She was smiling faintly.

What was I to say? I wanted to think up some possible topic, to discuss her paintings or something of the kind—and suddenly I said almost the impossible:

"You seem very strange to me."

She looked at me serenely, as before:

"Of course you can account for my appearing strange to you."

Her voice was soft, even muffled somewhat, and young-sounding. She spoke slowly, not uttering her words in an inquisitive tone. In her voice there was something calmly assertive, as though she could not possibly raise it any higher in order to pose a question.

"I can account for it only in part," I declared, involuntarily attempting to be precise, "but not completely. My soul is unable to comprehend everything."

"Yes, it is impossible to understand me entirely. However, in what you do understand, you are correct. I like you very much. You are deep."

"But I don't like you!" I exclaimed against my will, as it were. "That is, I like you an awful lot, yet I don't like you. There is delight in my heart, yet there is also terror. It's inexplicable . . ."

"And it torments you," she completed my sentence. "Tell me everything you can express in words."

And I told her . . . everything, with absolute precision, all I had thought about her while sitting at the table. Yes, I told her everything, not modifying my words at all. My friends, you know me very well. Believe me that in this woman there was something unusual, unequaled, for certainly it is impossible to visualize me, to picture me—a man of good education, reserved by nature, and a diplomat by profession—conversing in such a way with a strange French lady, moreover an artist, etc., etc. However, I assure you that it was impossible not only to lie to her, but even to say something inaccurate. At least it was impossible for me. I don't know how it was with others. It appeared that, in general, they spoke with her very little.

She listened to me with perfect calm, as though I were acting out a part before her for the tenth time. I cannot think of a better comparison. When I had concluded, she said to me:

"You are on the right track. These are merely your first guesses, but they are correct. Thinking along these lines cannot be considered incorrect. I am actually twenty-six years old—and eighty-one. For that is the way it is!"

"What kind of riddle is this!" I exclaimed almost angrily. "Do you wish to take advantage of my inexplicable fantasy, to deepen it, even without letting me know for what purpose?"

She didn't even smile.

"You don't need to become angry, my dear. For the time being it's better that we be friends. Come to see me. I am home during the evenings. Now let us talk about something else. There will always be time to return to this."

With an amazing and casual imperiousness she shifted the conversation to something else, to something simple, yet of apparent importance, because not only did I sense nothing false about this transition, I hardly noticed it at all. We spoke for a long while—about everything, it seems, even about her paintings. In her voice, in her words, there was always present some kind of calm, unwavering conviction, an almost fathomless, melancholy depth —and a young, fresh . . . decrepitude showing through her eyes. In both cases she equally terrified and delighted me. That which could not be united—was being united; furthermore, that which should not have been united—was forming one integral whole.

Though I could have spoken with her about anything whatever, I spoke all the time about one thing—her.

IV

To tell you that I fell in love with this woman would be untrue. That I began to love her—no, this is also not true. The more often I saw her, however (and I began visiting her every week, then twice a week), the more I spoke with her and gazed at her, the more that captivating terror, that fear-instilling delight increased within me. I was no longer able nor did I wish to resist its sway over me.

She lived alone, seldom paying calls, and worked a great deal. Occasionally she would have guests, but they visited her somewhat reluctantly, and she would receive them in the same reluctant manner. I noticed that there was something about her which actually alienated others. Most likely it was the same thing which kept me near her in this unusual, unloving captivity. The others would leave her, not giving any thought to what was really unpleasant about her, and that would be all.

It seemed to me at times that, were she devoid of this perplexing terror which robbed me of my will, I could then love her simply, as I would a lovely woman, with a deep and serious affection. At first I didn't like her; rather, at first I was startled by the incomprehensibility of her face and could think of nothing else; but afterwards, with the greatest effort of my will, I would try sometimes for a moment to picture to myself that colorless face *only* as that of a young person filled with the joy of life. And just as I had succeeded, there again appeared that former sensation of terror, intensified even more by the pain of an overpowering and bewildering loss, as if you were standing beside the coffin of a loved one.

Then I would forget completely about my possible-impossible love and would stand before this terrifying woman, chained only by her unwomanly and superhuman fetters.

We sat most often in a small parlor next to her studio, more exactly, in her study. There the furniture was almost as dark and heavy as it is here, and there too the coals would begin to flicker from time to time in the fireplace. Her residence did, in fact, resemble a gloomy palace. Whenever I visited her, I would pass through several silent reception rooms in order to reach the stairway leading upstairs to her study and the studio.

The Countess always welcomed me cordially. She was always calm, always looking attractive, and always wearing her long black gown, as though she were always in mourning.

Always calm . . . yet I noticed—and she did not conceal it—that her affection and cordiality were steadily developing and deepening toward me. I was always frank with her—I could not be otherwise—and she knew all that I knew about my own attitude toward her. She knew how I was tormented by terror and delight, both of which were increasing all the while, and it appeared that not only did she understand them—she could resolve them for me; however, she had not done so. Sometimes, when I spoke, she would listen and keep silent, or would utter in her quiet voice a few quietly assuring words, with some quiet, mournful, always distant tenderness. As for myself, I did not insist, did not ask or inquire, did not pressure her—I could not do so. It was as if some journey were taking a long time and could not be shortened at will.

Left to myself, I was experiencing an ever growing and intensifying pain, yet she maintained a severe and resigned silence to which, in her presence, I succumbed.

Thus the winter passed. We became almost intimate friends, but I continued to lack an understanding of her and of myself, just as it had been on our first meeting.

It seemed that I could no longer live without her, although with her I wasn't living either. The incomprehensible, disturbing oppression which I had been experiencing grew even more intense. I tried not to see the Countess for a whole week. It was almost spring. Finally, after a week went by, I decided to go once more, although not immediately but after waiting three more days. This did not come to pass. In the morning I received a note from her—the first one—in which she wrote:

"My friend, please come to my house this evening. Yvonne de Suzor."

The thought of disobeying her never even occurred to me. The hour arrived, and I was at her place.

V

The Countess greeted me downstairs. Together we passed through the row of deserted reception rooms and went upstairs.

In the fireplace coals were glowing. The light reached the ceiling, although the walls remained dim. She sat by the fire in a high armchair with a straight back. A scarlet reflection passed over her face, which was proud, young, and frightening. Her transparent, aged eyes did not reflect the burning rays; they were the same pale, lifeless, yet beautiful eyes.

Before looking into them I told her the previous thoughts which had been preying on my mind:

"You were surprised, Countess, that I haven't come to see you for such a long time . . ."

She replied:

"No. I was not surprised."

I immediately understood that she wasn't surprised, and could not have been.

She continued.

"You see, I must tell you, I must reveal something to you about myself. I was unable to tell you before. It wasn't necessary then. Now it is necessary. Because . . . probably, we will soon part."

Before the word "probably" she paused, and she uttered it with a strange effort. I remembered instinctively that it was the first time I had ever heard this word coming from her. She had never before said "probably," "I hope," "I suppose," "perhaps" . . . But the minute I heard it, all my thoughts were turned to the words, "We will part."

"Are you leaving?" I nearly shouted. "Will we part?"

"Yes. I am not leaving. But probably . . . you . . ."

Again "probably," and again with an effort.

"I am not going anywhere. I am not thinking about it, and I don't intend to leave! Why part?"

She fell silent.

"Well, it doesn't matter," she finally said. "It doesn't matter whether or not you are thinking about it. Today I must tell you something which you don't know. I will tell you about it because I love you."

She spoke these words with such a simple, commanding, yet resigned calmness that they echoed within me with the same calmness. I could not even think about telling her whether or not I loved her. Whatever I felt for her was greater and more incomprehensible than any love.

"Tell me, if you must," I said.

"Yes, I feel that now I must."

Her strange calmness, almost rigidity, took possession over me for a time. I, therefore, listened to her lengthy and quiet account, which was simultaneously understandable and frightening.

Here is what she told me.

VI

"You know that for certain reasons Count de Suzor did not recognize me as his daughter, and for seventeen years my mother and I had been living away from him. I hadn't seen him until I was seventeen, until that very day when everything changed. We were living here in Paris, almost impoverished; my mother's illness had even aggravated the situation. Against my will, I grew accustomed to independence and enjoyed a freedom which young ladies of my age . . . of my age then, rarely enjoyed. I had many girl friends and school companions; I succeeded in enrolling in art school, for I had an irresistible passion for painting. I was unusually energetic for my years, extremely vivacious, headstrong, and passionate. The injustice with which the Count had treated my mother endlessly tormented me. It made me indignant, forced me almost to clench my fist at the slightest thought of it; I hated my father. I blamed him for my fate. I could have studied—not as I do now . . . I could have become great . . . for I was very self-confident, and I believed in myself. But if life dealt me a crushing blow, I used to think, I could also perish.

"I was tortured by reflections about my fate. Sometimes I would begin fearing the unknown and inevitable horrors and misfortunes of the future. I thought about how I would struggle with them, about what would become of me and my mother—I felt lost, not knowing what to do, and I would weep at night. Sometimes, on the other hand, my soul would be overcome by a life-giving hope for genuine, all-pervading happiness. I wanted to do something, to get to meet my future—but how was I to act? Where was I to go? Don't forget that I was sixteen years old and all alone with a half-deranged mother.

"Once a school friend of mine, a girl from an aristocratic family, told me that all Paris had gone insane, carried away by some kind of newly arrived fortune-teller who could predict one's future. They said that he was a noted Frenchman who had spent many years in Egypt, India, or somewhere else, studying the ancient occult sciences in their almost unfathomable wisdom, that he shied away from all the most recent charlatans, hypnotists, and conjurers, and was simply more like an ancient seer. He was wealthy and accepted no money—this last factor forced even the greatest skeptics to doubt that he was a fraud—and he would receive anyone. They vied with each other in inviting him to all the fashionable drawing rooms. However, he avoided gatherings of any kind.

"Somewhat later I read approximately the same thing about him in the newspapers. I deliberated over it for several more days, and then I was resolved. Therefore, one evening (for I was busy during the day) I went to see him.

"It seemed to me that I was performing some sort of desperate action. Going alone, just before nightfall, to a fortune-teller . . . What nonsense all this was! What ridiculous superstition! He must be a charlatan . . . Well, what if he were? Why shouldn't I go, just out of curiosity? I tried to visualize the sort of furnishings he must have, what he must have brought back with him from India, Tibet . . .

"Even the staircase which I had to climb was a disappointment to me, and it heightened within me the belief that he was a charlatan. They had spoken about his wealth, but here there was nothing of the kind. It was an ordinary, even drab little flat in one of the cheapest sections of town. I rang at the door, my heart throbbing, expecting to find a crowd of people at his place. This thought, at least, encouraged me somewhat.

"Instead of a red- or black-skinned servant from India, a rather slovenly *femme de ménage* opened the door for me and instantly led me to a tiny waiting room with terribly shabby furniture. There wasn't a soul in the room. I was about to sit down, but at that moment, from the neighboring room, an ordinary old man in a gray dressing gown appeared. He was small in stature, partially bald, and had a small gray beard. This was the seer.

"I did not care for his tiny, wrinkled face, smiling affectionately, yet shyly. There was even something ludicrous about him.

"He asked neither my name nor why I had come—it was not

difficult to guess why I had. He sat across from me at his long, narrow wooden table by the lamp. Affectionately, almost ingratiatingly, he asked to see my hand, which I offered to him unabashedly. What nonsense all this was! He stared for a long time at my palm and then asked the day and year of my birth. After this he looked straight into my eyes several times.

"He was silent for a while, and then he began to speak.

"The longer he talked, the more I was overcome with chagrin, nearly malice, and laughter. Finally, I pulled my hand away from him and laughed—not without contempt—right in his face.

" 'So this is all you can tell me, right?'

" 'Yes, my child . . . I see it in your hand, in your eyes. A most enviable fate awaits you. You will be rich, famous . . . Now you are having troubles, but they will pass. You shall have a long life, brilliant and prosperous, and a happy love—only one . . . You shall fall ill a few times, but you will recover and live a long life . . .'

"In a word, he repeated what he had said in the beginning, adding a bit, yet everything expressed in those same phrases. His hateful, monotonous phrases, which don't say anything or promise anything, nearly infuriated me. Some kind of demon was taking possession over me more and more and, when it finally did take possession over me, I cried out:

" 'Leave me alone with your vulgar deceptions! None of you have any imagination. All the fortune-tellers in the world will make the same promises to simpletons, all those platitudes which apply to everyone equally! A long life . . . Love . . . Sickness . . . Troubles . . . which will pass . . . Any female cook can tell you the same thing from reading the cards; any female cook can make such predictions. What good are all these wisdoms, ancient sciences, India—they are no good at all! How boring!'

" 'My child . . .' the old man began.

"But I interrupted him—I was too disturbed and highly indignant. I sprung up from my chair and, standing before him, continued with sudden ardor:

" 'No, I would believe you only if you told me what my future, do you hear, my future, would be! Just as no two people are alike, there are no two fates alike, and I must know my own fate, my happiness, my unhappiness, my own heart with my future feelings—all this I must know! If you can, tell me about everything, even describe to me the color of the wallpaper in the room where my joy will await me! Show me the eyes of the man whom I will love! Only then will I believe in wisdom, knowledge, and foresight! But you cannot do this. So be silent! Comfort others with your "ancient sciences"!'

" 'My child,' the old man said again.

"I looked at him. He was no longer smiling. He appeared to me suddenly afraid . . . and frightening. I fell silent. He was also silent. Then he uttered—and so mysteriously:

" 'So it is you?'

"And he smiled ironically, but not at all like before. Both evil joy and pity were visible in this smile.

"I didn't know what to say.

" 'So it is you?' he repeated.

"And he went on, not waiting for an answer:

" 'You wish to know your own fate, right up to the end, to the color of your loved one's eyes? To the very last beat which your heart will ever make? Right up to . . .'

" 'You are making fun of me! Repeating my own words for no good reason! Yes, I want that; of course I want to know it! I know that it is impossible, and I despise you with your sciences, because I accept no substitutes. Good-bye.'

"I was about to move toward the door. He did not prevent me—I must be fair—but I myself paused after having looked at him.

"He then said:

" 'So it is you. I was told that one time, just once, a woman would come to me and demand from me what you have demanded. For this single time—just once!—I would be permitted to comply with this request. I am just permitted—I am not commanded to do so. I can refuse to comply with it if you swerve from your desire.'

"He said this in such a way that I suddenly believed him.

" 'I will never go back on it! Never! Oh, if only you can, I beg you! As soon as possible, right now, if only you can!'

" 'You don't have to beg,' he uttered almost severely. 'I will do it if you don't change your mind. I won't do it right now or any time today. You must think about your request. Go home and think it over. After you have thought it over, if you haven't changed your mind—return tomorrow at this same time. If you don't come back tomorrow . . .'

"I understood that it was impossible to argue with him, so I said:

" 'Very well then, I'll come tomorrow. Of course I will come! There is nothing to ponder over, nothing to think about.'

" 'No, there is something,' he said insistently, getting up and showing me to the door. 'Think it over, think it over, my child. And . . .' he suddenly added in a lower voice, locking the door, 'when you have thought about it, pray . . . to someone . . . anyone you wish.' "

VII

"Almost the whole night I could not sleep from expectation, excitement, and happiness. For some reason it was impossible not to believe the old man when he spoke his final words; I believed irrevocably and was annoyed only that out of stubbornness he had postponed the affair for twenty-four hours. What was there to think about? What was there to doubt? Such extraordinary happiness is to be given to me, such power—of knowing! The innermost mysteries of the future would be revealed to me! People pledge their entire souls trying to predict just a part of it—and I would know it all! One would have to be a madman to refuse! I sneered at the old man's advice—'to think it over'— and thought only about how I would find it all out. Would he tell me? But words cannot present a complete picture. Would he show it to me? But eyes cannot see one's feelings and thoughts. He promised, however, that I would know everything, everything! I would see my father, I would find out how I would take revenge on him. For I had no doubt that I would have my revenge on him.

"Night had passed, and the day dragged on. I stayed home the entire day. I had 'thought about it' enough! As for the other advice of the old man, to pray to someone, I had forgotten all about it. I never had been especially religious. Besides, why should I pray, request, or ask when I would know everything!

"The demon of mirth and laughter took hold of me. I roared with laughter the whole day for no reason at all, responding with a laugh to any questions posed by anyone in the household. It was barely dusk when I put on my hat and went strolling along the streets. Outside there was a pre-autumn drizzle. I could hardly refrain from laughter as I looked at the poor, gray people, splashing along in the mud, trembling with every step, with every step entering the unknown, the uncertain, the dark. They did not know what might await them at the first turn in the road. Poor, pitiful creatures!

"The time passed. The appointed hour was approaching, and at the appointed time I was at the old man's door.

"He opened it himself immediately. I saw no one, not even the female servant. The old man held a burning candle in his hand, although lamps were on in the entrance and in the waiting room.

"'It is you, my child,' the old man said. 'You have come. I expected you would come.'

"He wore the same gray dressing gown. He was completely the same as he had been the previous evening, yet at the same time he was totally different—shaking, as though from a gripping, mysterious joy mixed with a wicked fright, almost terror. He resembled an apprehensive and nasty old gray bird, with his bald head buried like a bird's in the wide collar of his dressing gown. He was a cowardly bird, yet a large and powerful one. I sensed the power in him right from the beginning, and again I understood that he would not deceive me.

"In the waiting room, not letting the candle out of his hand, the old man stopped, as if he had become still more apprehensive, and said:

" 'You have thought it over, my child, you have decided for yourself . . . I advised you to think it over. And after freely giving it some thought, you have come to me, have you not, with that same demand that I . . .'

" 'Yes, yes!' I cried out impatiently. 'You don't have to repeat the same words to me. It has already been settled!'

"His trembling had infected me. I was no longer laughing, nor was I joyful. A disagreeable and indistinct anxiety oppressed me. I was frightened that fear would seize me. It was somewhere very close . . . although it seemed that there was no reason for it to appear.

" 'How long are you going to hesitate?' I shouted, almost rudely.

"The old man immediately turned, and with surprising calmness and severity he said, 'Follow me,' and stepped over toward a door in the corner which I had not noticed before. He opened it and passed through.

"I lingered for a moment on the threshold, but only for a moment—it was as though someone's quiet, gentle hand were trying to restrain me. Then it withdrew, and a sudden trepidation crept over me and disappeared, as if a cold mouse had scurried along my body, and I entered after the old man.

"I found myself in a very large, even immense room with a low ceiling, which was totally empty. There was nothing except a ceiling, a floor, and four very smooth, stark, white walls. I did not even notice any windows. However, on one wall a fireplace had been built, gaping huge and black like the open mouth of some old person. My guide set the candle on the mantelpiece. I saw that beyond the fireplace, almost in the middle of the room, there stood a very simple wooden chair—just one.

"It then seemed that I again had expected something extraordinary—soft lights, mysterious carpets, suffocating incense, something magical, frightening—and for that reason the room's unusual emptiness and whiteness deceived me, and the fear which was enveloping me was not the one perhaps which I would have liked, but it was very unpleasant, dull, imperceptible, and drearily stifling, like the dim candlelight in the enormous room.

" 'Be seated, my child, sit down on the chair,' said the old man, fidgeting around, still with the same maliciously affectionate cowardice. 'Sit down, right now . . . Right now . . .'

"I sat down obediently the way that the chair was standing, that is, with my back to the fireplace, facing the massive, unending white wall which blended with the ceiling and the other white walls. I had already gained control of myself a little and was even thinking of what had preoccupied me before. 'Obviously, he isn't going to tell me in words, but maybe I will see myself and everything else on this white wall,' I thought.

"The whiteness of the wall was unruffled, death-like.

"The old man stopped fidgeting.

" 'My child,' he said coldly and resolutely. 'I will be made responsible if . . . For the last time—are you sure you want . . . ?'

" 'Yes, yes,' I replied. But I said it without thinking what I was saying; my tongue seemed to be speaking of its own accord.

"The old man pulled out a white silk kerchief from the pocket of his dressing gown.

" 'All right. All right. Let it take place,' he began to speak rapidly. 'Sit here quietly. Don't worry. I am just putting my hands on your head. However, I shouldn't see it myself. I cannot. I must not. Here, I will cover my eyes.'

"With trembling fingers he tied the kerchief in a knot around his bald head. It was a large kerchief, and its ends dropped down ridiculously. Then the old man slipped behind the chair, and I heard only his mumbling:

" 'Right away. Right away. Are you here? I will lower my hands onto your head. I will lower them, and then I will lift them up. Nothing else . . . Nothing.'

"His babbling ceased. I felt him slowly lower his hands, probably folded, onto my head, still without touching it. Then he

touched it . . . Oh, what heavy hands they were! He touched
my head, he lowered his hands, and . . .

"And then he raised them again. Between the movement of his
hands down and up not a fraction of time had elapsed. No matter how far we reduce time—whether to a thousandth or a mil-
lionth of a second—it is still some portion of time, but here
there was none. Yet it would be most incorrect to say that there
was absolutely nothing. Oh, nothing! No, there was everything—
the only thing missing was time.

"I got up. I turned my face toward the old man. He tore off
the kerchief and looked closely into my new face, the one which
you see now, and I still remember his eyes—pitiful, sorrowful,
hostile, and filled with the fear of death. With such eyes a
murderer or violator looks at the work of his hands.

"He glanced at me and turned away. Without looking back,
I departed. He stayed."

VIII

"It is still not clear for you what happened to me then, in
that . . . interval between the two movements of his hands,
when there was no time. It is hard for a happy, ordinary, living
person to fathom it. I will try to explain it to you, but if there
is something which you do not understand, replace what is
obscure with faith—you have the capacity to believe.

"I had wished to know my future fate, all my earthly life which
lay before me, how I would live this life, how I would feel it.
My entire life, till the moment of my death, every future moment. To attain this, it was necessary to experience every
moment of my life. And I experienced it. You must believe me
when I tell you that in that . . . snatch of timelessness or
eternity between the two motions of the old man's hands I myself—whom I did not see but felt from within (just as I do not
see myself now but feel myself from within)—lived through
every moment, every hour, every year, all of which would be
destined for me; I resolved every thought which I already had

and still would have; I cried all the tears which I would have to shed; I became fatigued from my future work; I suffered every sickness in my life; I heard every word, many of which I would have yet to hear; I found out everything which I would find out, and I saw everything and everyone whom I would yet see. For me everything had already been accomplished—right up to the last tremor of my body in its final moment, its last agony . . ."

Countess Yvonne paused. She was correct—I still had not understood, still had not been able to accept it.

"Believe me," she said after a minute, "with the help of faith in this matter, it will be possible to understand, to imagine what all this is, and what I am now. All human beings know their past. I know my own future, just as all people know their past—I *remember* my future."

"But Countess. . . ," I muttered. "We do forget our past . . . Can one really remember everything? . . . And you can forget . . ."

"We forget . . . yes; of course it is impossible to remember everything with identical, equal vividness. This, however, does not change a thing. You hardly turn your thoughts to something from the past, when it suddenly appears before you with that accuracy which has already been experienced. This is how it is for me, because no matter what I may think about in life—it is already here; it has already taken place. I even know when and which thoughts I shall have. Every thought, every movement of my soul and body comes to me for the *second* time, and I know when they are to come. I have lived through two *second* lives, because my first experience then, in that chasm of timelessness, was precisely a clear and true reflection, an image of my future, my *second* life. That is, this image was exactly the same, the same as the second life itself—life *with knowledge!* My friend, you, a man whom I love, whom I had already loved, whom I will lose, and whom I had already lost—if not with your mind, then with your heart, with the entire freedom and happiness of your heart, please do understand my boundless, unparalleled grief: I never loved you a first time; I again love you—but again it is for a second time! And again I will lose you, merely because I never had a first love . . ."

I did not know whether I understood her. Amid a dull, stifling, petrifying terror some scattered thoughts were spinning around in my head, some questions. I said with an effort:

"Countess . . . Countess . . . Surely we have been given free will, haven't we? You are talking about the Fate of the ancients . . . *Fatum* . . . But I cannot believe that we have no power to change our fate."

"Yes, we do have free will. And I took it and used it up all at once . . . that night at the old man's. I changed my fate by freely desiring *to know*. My fate was changed because of my desire and its fulfillment, according to my own will. I came to know my fate which had already been changed (because of knowledge); but my fate which would have been fulfilled if I hadn't wished to know it, I don't know. Indeed, it is not that one, the unknown fate, which awaits me. The old man foretold it to me on that first night. In outward appearance it resembles my real fate. The part about my only love . . . he had said, however, that it would be a happy love, whereas I have experienced, and will experience, an unhappy one. It is an unhappy one precisely because I wanted to know it; I came to know it—and by knowing I have changed everything."

"But if you had wished, Countess," I went on again. "If you wished to change something anyway . . . to die before it would be time for you? To change something, to change it . . ."

"Earlier than I want? But I know what I will want and, therefore, I will do it. I know how many more times I will have to endure this torturous longing to go against what is inevitable, to interrupt this inevitability, to finish before it is the end . . . I also know which thoughts and feelings will prevent me from doing so. I will tell you about them."

She rose and, supporting herself on the mantelpiece with her hand, she appeared—all in black, frightful—like fate itself. I no longer regarded her as a human being.

"Because of my willful infringement upon the blessed law of

ignorance I have become separated from everything human; I am alone. People live; that is, they desire, believe, doubt, strive, rejoice, hope, suffer disappointment, fear, pray . . . In my life there is neither fear nor hope. There is nothing for me to look forward to, nothing to doubt, nothing for me to ask for. There is no time for me which lasts. There exists absolutely nothing for me. However . . . this is only in time! Only in life! And then? When, for my second and last time, I will again experience the torment of agony and close my eyes—what will become of me? You see, I am asking this because now I still have the joy of ignorance, faith, hope, and expectation! At this point I become close to other people, on a level with them. At this point, while hoping, I fear—and, therefore, I do not wish and cannot wilfully desire to interrupt the extent of my punishment; I want to endure it in its entirety. And perhaps . . . yes, *perhaps,* there I will find repose and my human strength, and a new, everlasting freedom . . ."

She stood before me, her face turned toward the glow from the fire and toward me. Her face was instantly transformed—for one second only—and I no longer recognized it. Illuminated with scarlet rays, young—and only young, even eternal—it was so beautiful that, trembling, I cast down my eyes, not daring to look. When I raised them, it was all over. The formerly terrifying woman gazed at me with the former ancient, vacant stare.

I must have understood her, because an inexpressible terror overcame my soul. In this terror, however, there was no longer that captivating, magnetic delight which deprives us of our will, a delight which is mixed with fear whenever we do not know or understand the reason for our being afraid. The incomprehensible, the unknown, was replaced by knowledge—my fear increased tenfold, was intensified by pain, compassion, and all-embracing pity—but my delight had vanished. My delight remained only for the eternally incomprehensible essence of superhuman laws, but not for her, not for this woman, because her terrible fate itself—if not its meaning—became clear to me.

There can be no delight in the terror of despair. There can

be only dull silence. My soul was filled with the terror of despair
—and with this silence.

Several moments passed.

Yvonne again sat down in the armchair. The coals had died
out.

"I will say a few more words to you," she uttered in her
weary, muffled voice. "It was difficult for me to tell you, but it
is better that I did, and of course it couldn't have been otherwise.
In all my life I have had to tell it to only two people. Only two
people have been ordained to enter my life, to grasp the frightening and mysterious nature of my face, and to be tortured by it.
I have told it . . . to one person because I loved him, and to
another—because I hated him. It would have been worse for you
if you hadn't found out. Whereas if he had not found out . . .
But why talk about it?—Could I have acted differently than I
did? As you see, this second . . . the first . . . it doesn't matter
. . . it was my father, Count de Suzor. As you know, he had made
his peace with my mother and had taken us in. He loved me
insanely, as only he could love, and the object of his love was I,
his daughter, before whom he felt guilty. All his life, until he
reached old age, only two feelings remained alive in him—attachment to me and fear of death."

The Countess paused for a moment, gazed intently at me, and
continued:

"You know what will come next. This is so. For it is all too
clear—indeed, I know my own future and the future of those
people whose lives come into contact with mine; I know precisely how I will come into contact with them. I know the words
which I will hear from them which they have not even said yet!
For example, I know that someone in the future will inform
me of a misfortune which has just befallen him. I already know
of this misfortune from his future words—which he himself
does not yet know. But I do not tell, have not told, and will
never tell anyone about anything I already know. Never! I will
not destroy the happiness of being ignorant, I must not, I cannot. So I go my own way, avoiding contact with people. It is

good that I pursue a lonely path. It is good that only two people have stopped at the sight of my face. As for you, I have been allowed to protect you by revealing the truth. I love you. As to my father—the truth killed him. I hate him . . . rather, I hated him. His love and his insight perpetually tormented him in my presence. I told him that the truth would kill him. He did not believe me. So I revealed everything to him. And . . . I told him the hour of his death. I told him, him alone! How could I have acted otherwise? Of course, his death came at the hour I had said it would. I knew all about his death, and he died in my arms. Love and pity for me, together with despair, and the fear of inevitable death killed him."

Death! Death!

This word, the only thing which still had a ring of hope for her, sent its last cold shiver across me. What am I doing here, wretched, crushed, ignorant being, yet lucky because I am alive? Why am I with this woman? She loves me . . . No, it is not good for a person who is alive to have a dead one loving him. But I also loved her . . . or would have loved her . . . Oh, I don't know, I just don't know! Do we dare to love a loved one when behind that person the doors of the vault are closed?

I got up with difficulty, like someone who was terribly sick.

"Countess," I said, "I cannot tell you . . . now. I do not know whether it is better or worse that you have told me everything. But I have never lied to you. And as soon as I am capable of understanding my own soul, I will tell you everything . . ."

"You will write to me," she answered simply, while rising.

I wanted to ask her, "Why would I write?" but I remembered that she knew everything; she knew better than I—probably I would write . . .

My legs could barely move; they felt heavy, as if numb. She stopped at the door, held my head in both hands, and kissed me on the lips.

In this kiss I felt all the coldness, all the solemnity, all the undiscovered grandeur, and an eternal, menacing fascination— Death united with Love.

With unspoken reverential awe, like an unworthy pilgrim kneeling before the body of a dead yet saintly being, I knelt down at the feet of this woman and kissed the edge of her garment.

. . . .

XI

Now only a few more words remain to be said.

The next day I received a telegram saying that my father was seriously ill; I was summoned to Russia. I decided to leave during the night. Before my departure I had time to write to the Countess . . . approximately the same thing which I have told you—about myself, about my soul. I could not lie to her. I wrote to her that I was leaving and told her why. She had known this the day before! She had said (and I recalled), "You will leave . . ." The day before she had read my soul, because I wrote her everything the following day. Indeed, she had already read my unwritten letter!

I was half-asleep, half-delirious. My unhappiness—the telegram from Russia—was my happiness as well. I had to leave.

My father died. I did not return to Paris again. I did not receive an answer from the Countess, nor did I expect one. I have never seen her again . . . But I have never loved any other woman. Furthermore, not only my love, but everything within me—my thoughts about death, my most fearful, sacred hopes, everything which is beyond human existence, which doesn't enter one's life—all these are still bound within me to my recurring thoughts of her.

My friends, forgive me! I changed her name. I began my story too flippantly and insincerely, a story which I unconsciously hoped you would consider invented. I see, however, that you have felt all the terror of its truthfulness and have understood how this memory has formed one whole, one entity with my soul. Perhaps my entire soul has derived its existence from this pain and terror. I would like you to understand it . . . and if

there is anything which you do not understand, then believe it
—we have the capacity to believe.

The Countess is still alive; many of you have actually heard
her real name. It is quite well known. The Countess is still alive
—she will endure the full measure of her suffering for infringing
upon the inviolable law of ignorance. Nevertheless, there is a
benevolent limitation to her knowledge—and that is death.

The Countess is still living—she is in my every thought. But
I shall not see her. If I do see her, it will not be here, but there,
where there is kindness and forgiveness.

Politov fell silent. His friends were also silent. The coals
were silently burning out in the fireplace. Dark walls. Dark
curtains. A dark, warm, and dense silence in the room. It
seemed that time had stopped—for the dark waves of the dark
Future were surging voicelessly over the immovable border of
the Present, in order to be transformed into the already-known,
already-seen Past.

It appeared as though everyone were afraid to move, afraid to
separate—through the manifestation of the Present—the known
from the unknown.

IT'S ALL FOR
THE WORSE

Dementyev killed his wife.

They held an investigation for one year, after which he was brought to trail and sentenced— due to extenuating circumstances and his eleven-months' pre-trial imprisonment—simply to do church penance at a distant monastery.

His term of penance was drawing to an end, but Dementyev hardly gave any thought to leaving the monastery, since there was really no place for him to go. In the monastery he had conducted himself silently and peaceably, and only toward the end did he occasionally hold a conversation with the keeper of the treasury, the kindhearted, stately, dark-haired Father Methodius. In spring, before twilight, they would meet together at the monastery graveyard and talk with one another. They would sit on a small bench beneath the lilac trees, by the grave of the merchant's wife Bronzova. It was a solid, high monument, on top of which there was an urn, and below the urn—some verses. Although the monastery was far from the capital, it was nevertheless not in some out-of-the-way place, nor was it very poor. It was located near the district center.

One time Dementyev and Father Methodius met at twilight on a spring evening and struck up a conversation. For a long time Father Methodius had wished to ask the penitent about how his sin had taken place, but up to now Dementyev had remained silent on the issue; instead, they would engage in more abstract discussions.

"It is so heavenly, Nikolay Pavlych! Spring is rapidly coming upon us," the monk began chattering, breathing deeply and looking above at the yellow-green sky, fresh and clean, as though it had just been washed. "How big the leaves are already. Oh, it's so nice and warm! Most likely your St. Petersburg still has snow on the ground, or else it must be a cold mudbath. You really shouldn't go anywhere, Nikolay Pavlych, but stay here with us. Why not? It's peaceful here, yet your heart seems to be troubled . . ."

"I probably won't be going anywhere," Dementyev said, smiling ironically.

It was impossible to guess how old he was—he was neither too young, nor too old. He had a grayish, haggard face, grayish-white hair, a sparse, shaggy beard, pale gray sunken eyes, and when he smiled long wrinkles ran along his cheeks.

The answer filled Father Methodius with joy.

"You aren't leaving? Well, that's fine! You could take the vows, with the help of God, and you would live out your life in peace."

"No, I am not going to take the vows, Father Methodius," Dementyev said. "I can do without it . . . these long drawn-out affairs have become a burden to me. There is no point in my leaving . . . yet there is also no point in my staying here. Perhaps I will tell you, Father Methodius—and why shouldn't I tell you, since it's all the same to me—I plan to hang myself."

Trembling all over from this unexpected statement, Father Methodius opened his mouth and began waving his arms.

"What are you saying, Nikolay Pavlych? Christ be with you! Now that you have done all your penance—what new sinful designs are you bent upon? In the monastery, yet planning to hang yourself! Just think about it! And what for?"

"Well, all right then. I'll go away from the monastery, into the grove by the river. Please don't shout. You are a good man, and when a good man hears of this he ought not to shout. Besides, if he is a wise man—then he ought to sympathize and show understanding."

"Can it be that your sin has been torturing you?" Father Methodius asked in a quieter tone.

"What sin? I never repented killing Marya. After all, it just happened that way, and that is all there is to it."

Father Methodius, just about horrified, was on the verge of indicating to his companion the error of his ways when curiosity won out over everything, and he asked him:

"Well, then, how did it happen? Were you jealous of her, or what? Oh, my Lord Jesus Christ!"

"I would tell you, Father Methodius, but I'm certain that you wouldn't understand. First of all, you talk all the time about sin and repentance . . ."

Father Methodius became slightly offended.

"Nikolay Pavlych, you don't know what is in my soul. Do you think that I have never been upset by doubt? It has happened to me, too. Only I keep silent about it, of course. Nowadays, it happens more seldom, but in my youth certain thoughts really preyed on my mind . . . Even now I can't turn away from many of them."

"No, it's not because of that . . . Of course, that happens no matter who you are, even if you're a Solomon . . . But all this is getting away from the point. The point is that there is no communication among people."

"That's true, there isn't," Father Methodius exclaimed animatedly. "I thought the same thing myself while I was still in the world, when my father still had his little shop in town. There is indeed no communication. You explain something to one person, yet you don't know what is on his mind. And even though you realize this, you still make every effort to explain it to him. That's why it's good here in the monastery. What kind of communication do we have here? The smallest possible. You chat with your brothers about the simplest things, you report your business affairs to the Father Superior, you show him the records—that is our communication. However, we communicate with God through prayer. Each man in his own way speaks to the Lord about himself, and He, the Almighty One, will for sure look into everything. Since olden times there hasn't been communication among people. It seemed to me that the devil managed to cast his net in every direction."

"Well, now you see," Dementyev said. "You yourself say that there is no communication. Why, then, are you asking me to tell you about my wife and all the rest? You're asking me merely out of curiosity. Well, it doesn't matter, it's all the same to me."

"Some limited communication exists," Father Methodius asserted, looking somewhat embarrassed. "For example, I became fond of you, but you have said to me, 'I will hang myself.' I must try to grasp why you said this."

"And that is exactly what you will not grasp. Because something like this everyone decides according to his own conscience. But I'll tell you what happened to me, and it won't take very long. Understand it as you want to. My wife Marya was a big, slovenly, nagging woman. We lived together for eight years, and I got so fed up with her, so fed up . . . that it's impossible to describe. I married her while I was a student—I had been a lodger at her mother's place. I was very young and just like a monk—a kind you don't even have here in this cloister. This 'dear Mashechka' would come to my room in the night and kiss me. She was much older than I was, but that didn't matter—she didn't seem bad-looking. Besides, what did I know? As our relationship grew, we became more and more involved. She spoke with absolute conviction about our getting married; my head was filled with all sorts of noble sentiments; so we got married soon after that. Are you listening, Father Methodius?"

Silently and with a meaningful look, Father Methodius nodded his head.

"My mother had been living in the province where she soon died. Marya's mother also passed away soon after that. We had no money. And every year Marya would have a child, and they were such nasty ones, sickly; they all died, and she was very glad of that. I withdrew from the university at once, set out for the railroads, got forty rubles and an apartment—two rooms and a kitchen. It was like that from day to day: I would go out early in the morning, the work was dull—real convict labor—then I'd come home, and she would swear at me and yell; there would be a stench everywhere. She would throw anything that came into her hands at me, for she was just a frenzied woman, so malicious. Even her face looked oily from malice. Little by little I began swearing at her. She opened up a laundry in the apartment and taunted me, 'Just look how you intellectuals treat your wives! You'll have to pay for my tears, you brainless student!' And then she'd start in with her dirty words."

Father Methodius shook his head.

"My, my, that was really an evil woman. That's why it's so good here in the monastery! We don't have any of these terrible women here!"

Dementyev continued:

"Why go into detail? Some kind of dullness began weighing me down, little by little at first, and then still more. I was so sick of her!"

Although Marya was no longer among the living, even now Dementyev's anguished voice resounded sharply.

"I came home one evening and headed for my room through the kitchen. She walked behind me, carrying an iron and a wet towel. She banged the iron on the table and rushed up to me, screaming and asking for some money. I couldn't make it out. I shouted, 'Get out of here!' She hit me in the face with her wet towel and threw the iron at me. I picked up the hot iron and hurled it back at her. It hit her so precisely, right there on the temple, that she fell, without suffering one bit."

"My goodness! Good Lord! Look, Nikolay Pavlych! What was wrong with you? You should have thrown the witch out (God forgive me!) a long time ago, and everything would have been over and done with!"

"Throw her out? She wouldn't go. She followed me everywhere I went—according to the law, she insisted. She wouldn't go anywhere."

"Indeed! What could you do?"

"Anyway, the servant saw that I didn't do it deliberately and that Marya had thrown the iron at me first. I was acquitted because of that. But I didn't try to justify myself. I even said at the trial that I had killed her accidentally and without thinking, but that I wasn't sorry for it. Simply because I was so sick of her."

"Oh, you are an unlucky one, Nikolay Pavlych," Father Methodius muttered hesitatingly. "That evil woman destroyed you. If you only had a good wife, you would have been living a good life now, you would have had enough money, you would have been working, or even . . ."

Dementyev smiled wryly.

"But I, on the other hand, have thought that things would have been just the same. That's the crux of the problem—that it would be the same. If I had happened to get a better wife, I would have been living with her not eight but eighteen years. Do you think that with another wife there would have been no arguing? Or that she wouldn't have become sloppy? Or that she wouldn't have wanted money from me? Or that the children wouldn't have died? If my financial situation had been better, if we had had more money, it still would not have been enough. Everything would have been the same, only longer and even more tedious, and everything would have gone from bad to worse, because we would have run out of strength, and there still would have been sickness, with death following close behind—all in its proper order. Now, as it stands, they will bury me beneath a small bush at the place where I will hang myself, but if I had a good wife, she would have a monument like Bronzova's erected. Thus isn't it really all the same?"

Father Methodius was silent.

"You don't know this, Father Methodius, but I will tell you. I have taken a close look at the lives of different people, and everything seems the same. Every single life is heading for the worse. There may be joys along the road, but they all have one direction—the worse. It's the direction common to them all. At first, in your youth, you think this and that, not understanding that it is for the worse, but when it begins, you understand, alas, that you cannot escape it. You say I'm 'unlucky.' Well, what about Napoleon—have you heard about him? He seemed lucky, but for him, too, everything, including the good part, was headed for the worse; then the worse came, and so it went on to the final misfortune."

"But, of course, life is long," Father Methodius said uncertainly. "And now, Nikolay Pavlych, you are rid of this woman, now you can live with God. You can start all over again, if you are not oppressed by your sin."

"How should I begin? Should I go and look for work? Search for a new wife? So that everything can go along and turn out the same way again? No, thank you, Father Methodius. I've been wearing myself out day after day, never knowing why, and I can't take it any more. I lived out the whole of my life in those eight years, the kind of life which others live out in fifty. But although it is that very same life, theirs is less concentrated while mine is more intense, so that even for this length of time it has been long enough. I have understood this old life we live. Excuse me, Father Methodius, but worldly life is beyond your reach, so you can't pass judgment."

"What do you mean, 'beyond my reach'? It is for the worse, you are right—everyone's life is for the worse. If one thinks about it properly, how could it be for the better? That is why here in the monastery we are truly blessed, for we don't have to dream about accepting life but actually prepare ourselves immediately to do so. So do tell me this, Nikolay Pavlych. You yourself may not know it, but maybe you are so oppressed simply because you have killed another human being? Can it really be that you have never repented?"

"What they have ordered me to do, I have fulfilled. But in my soul I have not repented. I just don't feel that I've killed her. It's as if I hadn't killed her."

Father Methodius gazed thoughtfully at the blackening sky and coughed.

"So then there has been no spiritual repentance?" he asked. sternly.

"I am telling you, it was just as if I had never killed her."

Father Methodius leaned over to his companion and declared mysteriously, "This means, my dear friend, that you haven't killed anyone."

Dementyev was surprised.

"What about Marya?"

"Well, Marya never existed at all. No, listen to the thoughts which occurred to me at one time. I never told a soul about them, but I am telling you. There is a parable in the Gospel in which the sower sowed good seed, but the enemy came at night and sowed weeds among them. Both the good seed and the others came up; however, the sower did not order the weeds to be removed but allowed them to grow together. The weeds, therefore, are the creation of the devil, do you understand? But the wheat was made by God. Just grasp the meaning of it. We all grow together. God has created man with a soul—could the enemy also create a soul? He did it only for appearance's sake, for the purpose of temptation. They walk along the earth as real people, but—oh no!—they are weeds, the enemy's creation, just a mirage, vapor, a temptation for God's children. They have no feelings, it is all the same to them; they just want to tempt and then be destroyed themselves. That's what your Marya was. She was not created by God. She tempted you and was destroyed."

Dementyev listened fixedly and with attention, then grinned.

"Look what you've thought up. According to that . . ."

"According to that, you will say, we can make anything out of anyone!" Father Methodius interrupted him excitedly. "Oh no, that isn't it at all! No, we don't dare know it! It is not granted to us—and we don't dare! I understand, brother, that there is a temptation here in this thought of mine! I have even kept it concealed and have told you alone about it, and I myself don't even know why. It is a great temptation! Now I seldom recall it, but before I used to look at the people, in church or wherever, and think, 'Who of you is really from God, and who is a mirage of the devil?' I was greatly tempted."

"Yes," Dementyev said thoughtfully. "However, it's better not even to talk about it . . . It's oppressive enough without these conversations."

"But it's less oppressive that way! Don't think I'm some backwoods monk, for I can figure a lot out. For example, there was quite an event in town a long time ago—some wench had a baby and threw it alive to the pigs. It is said that she herself confessed to hearing its little bones crack. What do you think—was this a real child? The wench was the guilty one, but what about him, the innocent one, why did he have to be crunched by the pigs' teeth? What was the purpose of his suffering? People will ask, 'How does God permit this?' However, there was nothing to permit, for there was no suffering, and I believe that this child was an insensitive mirage, sent for the wench's temptation—would she throw him off or not? She threw him off, and the enemy was glad that he had strangled God's wheat with his weeds. The wench shall have to answer for it, as if for a real human being. And you shall have to answer for Marya!" Methodius added all at once, with unexpected ardor. "Maybe she was not a real person, but it is not for you to know. You have no remorse, and thus you are tormented by a dull and oppressive feeling. Your heart is lifeless. It has reached the worse before its time."

"You really are amazing, Father Methodius!" Dementyev exclaimed. "You are a monk, yet what ideas you have. But it's all the same to me. You yourself have come to understand that there is no longer any life for me. Why were you frightened, then, a little while ago when I said . . ."

"That you want to kill yourself? That was another temptation for you . . ."

"A temptation for me? It might be a temptation for you. You have figured out my position, so don't bother me any more, leave me alone. Maybe I myself am not real, eh? Maybe I'm a mirage of the devil? What do you say to that?"

Dementyev smiled ironically.

Father Methodius seemed to wither and looked at him strangely. It became completely dark, and Dementyev's face flashed imperceptibly white beneath the lilacs. Both fell silent and remained so for a long time. Father Methodius felt inwardly disturbed.

After being silent a while he feigned a yawn and suggested:

"Well, isn't it about time for us to be going home? It's beginning to get chilly."

Dementyev did not budge from the spot and kept still. Then he said in a low voice:

"You see, Father, we have been talking together, but there has been no actual communication between us. Each of us has been interested in his own affairs."

"No, wait . . . Indeed, it's that one, the devil himself, who is a lot to blame."

"Yes . . . the devil . . ." Dementyev was again silent. "Let me ask you, Father—do you believe in God?"

"What is this supposed to mean? My Lord! Asking a monk such questions! What else should he believe in? I believe and I profess my faith firmly."

"You believe. Well, and what about it?"

"There is nothing more to say."

"There, you see! 'Nothing more to say.' That's where the trouble lies, that's why there is no communication between us. You believe—and there is 'nothing more to say,' while life drags on by itself, headed for the worse. You have only escaped it, and by escaping it you have ended up for the worse. If we believed, that is, let's say, if I believed—then for me there wouldn't be this 'nothing more to say!' Then I would not let it all be heading for the worse! That's something I would change!"

"What would you change? You've said yourself, haven't you, that death would come all the same?"

"Death? You are very perceptive, Father! Doesn't this mean that you don't believe what is said in your books: 'By dying He destroyed our death!'? You don't believe it! For you have just said, 'I believe, and there is nothing more to say!' "

Father Methodius became confused; he coughed.

"Oh, you are carrying it too far . . . These are your words . . . We do believe. Of course, we are unworthy . . . For that reason there is some kind of confusion in our minds, and fear as well . . . We do believe. How could we not believe?"

Again both were silent.

"Look, Father Methodius. I ask you . . . If it should happen . . . If I should end my life some day . . . Well, we have talked about it enough . . . But if I . . . Will you pray for me, as you know how to do? Will you promise to pray for me?"

Father Methodius looked at his companion in a panic and timidly uttered:

"Well, all right . . . Although, of course, it is not proper . . ."

"Not proper? It can't be! Ask for the Superior's permission, seek his indulgence! Insist that it be allowed! How can you not pray for me? Why not?"

"Many will not be able to justify it. Pray for whom? I will seek the indulgence of the Father Superior. There were cases . . . What do you really mean, Nikolay Pavlych? Think about your sin! You shall have to answer for it!"

"Oh, just leave me alone," Dementyev said wearily. "We have talked about it enough. It's late already. Let's go before it gets too dark."

They passed through the dark graveyard together. The air was mild and fragrant; it had the smell of the spring earth, the budding poplar trees, and some other sad and languorous sweetness so often found in graveyards. Large pale stars flickered high above. Dementyev walked with his head lowered. Perhaps he was thinking that even spring was heading for the worse, since its beauty would come to an end with the arrival of autumn.

When the friends parted, Dementyev said once again to Father Methodius:

"Please forgive me if I've frightened you. Don't forget what I've asked you. Do not think that perhaps I am a mirage of the devil, for maybe I am a real person . . ."

They met several more times beneath the lilac trees, but their conversations did not proceed very well. In a week Dementyev actually did hang himself in the grove some distance off by the river. They explained it by saying that he had no way to make his living and that he had been a chronic hypochondriac. Father Methodius begged the Father Superior with tears in his eyes to allow him to pray for the suicide victim. Father Superior found himself in a quandary and promised to have a conference with the bishop of the diocese. It is not known how the matter was settled.

THE PILGRIM

Outside it was a gloomy September evening. The autumn mud along the country road and the sky overhead merged into one blackness, and if everything were turned upside down one's eyes would not be aware of the change. It was warm and immeasurably still; storm clouds lay low. There was no rain.

Out of this steady darkness there emerged that evening a small pilgrim wearing a skullcap, with a sack over his back; he knocked at the door to Spiridon's hut. Shutters covered the windows, but light shone through between the cracks.

The pilgrim knocked, asking for shelter, and Spiridon came out and let him in.

Spiridon's hut was spacious, white-washed, not very new, but warm—the stove had been reset just a little while before. Spiridon was a very upright peasant who seldom drank. As for his family, there were only he and his wife, who was from a far-off village.

Upon entering the hut the pilgrim prayed in the corner before the icon, then bowed on all four sides.

"Well, good evening, master and mistress. May the Lord bless you and keep you who have taken me, a stranger, under your own roof for this night."

"Right then, why don't you just put down your things and set yourself down at the table," Spiridon said. "Supper's ready. And the wife'll set the table. Then it's time for bed. Why waste good firewood? And there's still all that work to do on the threshin' floor. We better hurry up before that mean weather comes. Where'ya from, Father?"

"I'm from the monastery, my good man. Not far, it's the Holy of Holies. But I'm going much farther. My abbot gave me his blessing to go and make a pilgrimage."

"Yeah, well, let's have something to eat, Mavra. Don't you hear me?"

Until then Mavra had been sitting quietly and motionlessly by the table, at the side, beneath a tiny kerosene lamp. A cotton kerchief which was pushed forward over her head had kept her face hidden, but when she arose, in the light her entire face seemed to be in a dark shadow, almost rust-like in color.

She went up to the stove and began getting things ready, but very quietly; she appeared to be in a dream—even at the stove.

Spiridon, the pleasant-looking, red-bearded young peasant, sat at the table, crossed himself, and sighed.

It was warm and rather bright in the hut, yet a certain melancholic grief and emptiness pervaded the corners of the room. Even the white clock with the rosebud ticked in a melancholy way. Only the little pilgrim was busily occupied with his sack on the bench, while whispering something in prayerful words and sighing noisily and officiously.

"Go ahead, pilgrim, have a drop of kvass," Spiridon said. "I don't know what name you go by."

"Pamphily, I am humble Pamphily. Christ preserve you. I don't really need the kvass, for I curb my flesh by abstinence. But maybe since I'm so tired from the road . . . On a journey food is allowed . . . "

"Well, go ahead, have some, Father," Spiridon said with indifference.

Mavra brought in bread, a cup, and spoons, then went away and sat down again in her former place in the corner.

"Ain't you gonna eat?" Spiridon asked.

Mavra answered quietly, as if sighing:

"Nah . . ."

After taking two helpings Spiridon looked at the pilgrim, at his small head and small beard which seemed shredded or motheaten, and at his young but already wrinkled, graying face, and said, without addressing anyone:

"Yes, we're feeling such a grief . . . The wife's awful upset. She mopes around here like a cast-iron pot."

"Is there something wrong at your house?" the little pilgrim inquired. "Your wife's eyes are gloomy, very gloomy, I can see that. What has happened? With what has the Lord visited you?"

"You see, our kids never made it, none of 'em," Spiridon explained. "Friday we took the little boy to the priest. He was already the fourth one. God bless 'em, they lived no more than about ten days. Yes, they're born, then they die, nothin' more to pine over. But little Vasyuta, why, he was already four years old. Such a nice little kid. Don't know why all of a sudden he begins twistin' and turnin' in pain, sufferin' so bad . . . then she takes him to the hospital . . . then he dies."

"If he wouldn't have suffered, it wouldn't have been so bad . . ." Mavra suddenly uttered from her corner in an unexpectedly loud and almost cracking voice. "But he suffered so bad . . . for so many days he didn't have no peace. I takes him in my arms, and that little head just hangs there, oh, how it hangs there! Not even cryin', just keeps a'lookin' me in the eye. 'What is it, Vasyuta? What's it you want, tell me, my precious?' He just keeps on lookin'. Then he says ever so quiet, 'Please, can I have some milk, Mommy, no, I don' wan' it . . . ' He'd want some milk, then say, 'No, I don' wan' it . . .' "

Mavra than broke off and turned aside.

It was probably not the first time that she was relating the story about Vasyuta, and most likely she had concluded with these same words before.

The pilgrim gave a deep sigh, appeared saddened and, making the sign of the cross, he pronounced his blessing:

"Oh Lord, grant peace to the soul of Thy servant, the newly departed child Vasily. It is Thy holy will. Inscrutable are the ways of the Lord. And you, servant of God, Mavra, don't be hardened of heart. Accept this trial with obedience and humility. Great are our sins and transgressions of which no punishment is worthy. Yet God will still be merciful to us for our sins."

"That one was a real nice kid," Spiridon murmured reflectively. "Here we're stuck, as always, on our own. They tell us she can't have kids no more. Somethin' wrong with her insides. So we'll have to live out our life this way. It's hard for us peasants with no kids. That one was such a nice little feller."

The small pilgrim practically leaped up from his bench and his face became a mass of wrinkles.

"You are to bear your cross to atone for your sins," he announced joyfully. "What are you? It is said, 'Love not the world, nor the things of this world, nor the desires of the flesh . . .' It has also been said, 'See the birds of the air, they do not sow, neither do they reap, they have no storehouse or barn . . .' And what about you? You have become attached to the ways of this world, and the Lord will chastise you for your deeds."

"Oh, yeah . . ." Spiridon replied indifferently. "Sure, we're sinners . . . But why's our sins so special? Besides, we ain't stupid; we heard how they said, 'Earn your daily bread by the sweat of your brow . . .' "

"Yes, but where was that said?" Pamphily pounced on him. "When was that said? It was a long time before our Lord Jesus Christ came here upon this earth. Then He came, and it was said, 'See the birds of the air . . .' And further on, 'But whoever of you does not leave his father and his mother, his wife, and his children . . .' There, you see? Didn't He say 'children,' too?"

"Well, maybe He did . . ." Spiridon muttered in dissatisfaction and yawned wearily. "Well, ain't you the passionate one, Father, I can see that. You better spread yourself out over there and lie down, it's late already. Why are you jumpin' on me? I'm just sayin', 'It sure's a shame.' There ain't no more to say, it sure's a shame. The wife's awful upset."

He got up yawning and, heaving a sigh, began to say his prayers. He then took off his belt and climbed up on top of the stove.

Pamphily refused to leave it at that.

"Sure, she's upset. Still the Lord is all merciful and ever patient with us sinners. Why do you love the world so much and all that is in the world? Just look at me—I stand here in front of you, a most sinful man. I don't sow any wheat, nor do I gather it into my barn, but I spend all my days praying or wandering. I don't have a wife, children, or any other such worldly attachments, but all people are like brothers to me; each one is good, each one takes me in and feeds me well. Whoever may die—it's God's will; it's my task to pray for the repose of that soul, and all is well. So it's easy for me. I'm walking in the way of the Lord. But you have grown toward the flesh in the way of the flesh."

"Oh, shut up," Spiridon muttered sleepily from on top of the stove. "Mavra, why ain't you putting those dishes away? It's time to put out the fire."

Pamphily went up to his bench and began stuffing his sack, getting ready for bed. He was talking to himself unintelligibly, sighing, and in the same reproachful tone.

When Mavra went over to the table to collect the dishes, he turned to her and said:

"That's just the way it is, my young woman. Pray and do penance, so that maybe the Lord won't punish you."

Mavra stopped and looked at him from under her kerchief. It was the second time that she had looked at him in such a way.

"Why's He, that's God, I mean, still out to punish me?" she asked. "What've I done? My suffering don't count, but what for did Vasyutka have to suffer?"

"For the sins which you have committed," the pilgrim replied. She wasn't listening.

"But why couldn't he have died right then and there?" she

went on in the same whining, cracking voice. "He didn't die right then and there. But his head was just hangin' there, just hangin'. 'Mommy,' he says, 'please can I have some milk?' He'd want some milk, and then, 'No, I don' wan' it . . .' "

She sat down on the bench by the disorderly table and fell silent.

"That was on account of your sins, I'm telling you," the pilgrim repeated with assurance. "He suffered because of your sins. If you don't pray, then the little one won't have any peace in the next world. He'll be suffering in that same way."

Mavra came to her senses and gazed once again at the pilgrim. "It's for my sins?"

"For yours. And now you are sinning even more by this grieving over it. For it is said, 'Love not the world, nor the things . . .' "

The pilgrim was saying this, having almost arranged his sack in the corner and preparing to say his prayer and finally lie down. However, he had not completed his "Love not the world, nor the things of this world," when Mavra literally tore herself from her place and rushed straight at him.

"Get out of here, go on!" she ordered him. "Out of this hut, you troublemaker!"

The pilgrim was dumbfounded.

"What is the matter, woman, have you gone mad?"

"Get out of here, I'm tellin' you," Mavra repeated. "Oh, it's bad enough already without you. You're like the plague on me, tellin' me all about my sins. Get out of here this minute."

She was a tall, powerful woman, and her face was so terrifying, dark, and almost rusty-looking that the skinny pilgrim got frightened.

"What's the matter with you? Lord, Jesus Christ, Mother of God, Protectress! What's the matter with you? Get a hold of yourself, woman! Let me say a prayer . . ."

"Get out of here, I'm tellin' you," Mavra screamed. "All of your prayin' is about sufferin', we don't need your prayers! Get out of here this instant, before I tear you limb from limb with my bare hands . . ."

By this time she had pushed him over to the door and was lugging his sack behind him in order to throw him out. In bewilderment, the pilgrim cried out plaintively:

"What does this mean? Master, what do you say to this? Are you hearing it? Your woman's gone insane, throwing a stranger out of her house at night . . . Master!"

Spiridon woke up and roused himself on top of the stove.

"Throwin' you out? Ah, don't you worry about it none. She ain't herself today. Don't you pay her no mind, I tell you. Lie down in the hall, it's warm enough there, nothin' to fret about."

"What's this all about? What for? Woman, curse you . . ."

She shoved him into the hallway, threw down his sack with a bang, slammed and bolted the door.

Spiridon stirred again.

"What's the matter, you big fool? What's gone and possessed you? Why'd you go and throw out that stranger? Eh, woman, there's no fear in you . . . Just you wait!"

Mavra stood in the middle of the hut and breathed heavily. Finally she spoke:

"I couldn't take it . . . That one's cursed, Spiridon Timofeich . . . He says, 'My Vasyuta . . . !' He says, 'Because of my sins, in the next world . . .' He says, 'Love not . . .' What is this? D'ya think the little one just suffered only a tiny bit here? Why couldn't he have died right then and there? His little head was hangin' down . . . 'Mommy,' he says, 'please can I have some milk . . . No, I don' wan' it . . .' "

As though she had been struck, Mavra lapsed onto the bench and, not exactly sobbing, not exactly wailing, tearlessly muttered something while pressing her dry face against the table.

Spiridon stirred himself again on the stove, sighed, but remained silent.

HE IS WHITE

". . . He is not evil, but good,
for he was made by the Creator
as a bright and ever-sparkling
Angel, and free—as a wise man."
St. John of Damascus

The student Fenya Smurov fell ill with pneumonia.

At first he tried for a long time to overcome it himself, and when he finally did go to the doctor, his sickness was already at its peak.

He was very opposed to the idea of admitting himself to the hospital. Therefore, he stayed in bed in his own room on the Petersburg Side [a district in St. Petersburg], which he rented from a petty official, a bachelor. The pock-marked Lukerya would bring him something to drink, and he himself would take the medicine whenever he regained consciousness.

Fortunately, he happened to get a good doctor, young and very kind, who would come to visit him every day.

The doctor would frown and advise Fedya to go to the hospital. Besides the fact that he had always been rather sickly, Fedya had a serious illness—he never coughed, but after climbing a flight of stairs he could not breathe for a long time.

However, he showed signs of improvement. His temperature fell, and, listening to his chest, the doctor said that the fever was passing altogether.

"Maybe I can get up now?" Fedya asked in a quiet voice.

"Get up? Oh, no! You have a long way to go before you can get up! God forbid! You have a weak heart. Lie there as still as you can. Have a little more to eat. I'll be back in about two days. Remain as still as possible!"

So Fedya continued lying there.

No one came to visit him; the pock-marked Lukerya did not bother him, and within his soul there was such tranquillity that it could not have been more peaceful. It was just as well that he did not go into the hospital. It was just as well that he had not written anything to his aging mother in Elets. Then she certainly would have come; she would have scraped up the money somehow and come. She would have only worn herself out. Besides, how much money could a deacon's widow have?

At the same time it turned out that Fedya did have some money—he was paid for the work he had done, and it was just enough to cover the cost of his illness. It was too bad that he had so little money, yet he still had to pay the doctor's fees.

Actually, he hardly even thought about all that. Nor did he think about anything else. It was strange, however, that he did not experience the sweet, animal-like feeling of recuperation which occurs after a severe illness. He just lay there quietly.

It was not very crowded in his narrow room—Fedya had practically no possessions. There were books on the stand and on the floor, shoved into a corner. A lamp stood on the worktable behind the bed; shading the lamp was a volume of Dostoevsky. Near the end of Fedya's bed there was a chair on which his cotton dressing gown had been thrown, the one which his mother in Elets had sewn for him; it came in very handy.

Fedya lay very still in the quiet dusk produced by the Dostoevsky volume. Whenever he would happen to fall asleep, he would sleep for a long time. The dreams which he had were quiet ones. They reflected his life, the way he had lived before his sickness. They were the same thoughts which he always had had before his illness, persistent ones, which seemed to weigh him down so that he even began to stoop when walking. In general, Fedya led a very timid life.

However, now in his dream his thoughts did not torment him —they appeared gentle, quiet, and dreamy.

He would now wake up in a very strange manner. He would open his eyes—and there would be those same yellow walls, that same quiet dusk; it always appeared that many, many hours had elapsed, even if he had slept only one minute, and without fail there would come this totally new thought . . . And what a thought it was! What was this thought about? He did not exactly know.

And it concerned death.

Before and during the time of his illness Fedya had always been thinking a great deal, intently, about death. This was one of those tormentingly persistent and fruitless thoughts of his . . . But now, like all the rest, it had abandoned him . . . But what bothered him now was something else.

In one short instant, when after a dream he would cast his eyes upon the shaded yellow walls, all at once in this brief moment he would understand death "from within," through and through. "From within"—here was contained all of its ineffable, unique nature. Before this—there had been the thought, the knowledge of death. At this time—there was no thought of it, but it was there itself, so real and yet so extraordinary, just like his own hand. It lay on the blanket, and if he wanted he could have moved it from within himself. Death seemed unlike his thought about it, just as his concept of the human hand did not resemble his own hand, the one he had known so well before.

Then everything would suddenly disappear, and again there were the walls, the silence, and his quiet submission to the ticking of the clock on the table which faced a medicine jar with a white label.

The most amazing thing of all was that Fedya was not afraid

of these awakenings and never tried in any way to explain them to himself.

"Oh, yes, so that's how it is," he would say in a low voice, opening his eyes. "Oh, yes."

That this understanding came "from within"—he defined in precisely that way and did not think of this experience again, although he remembered it all.

Since it was autumn, Lukerya would carry in the lamp much earlier, and to Fedya it always appeared to be night, just as if there were one deep, lingering night. He seldom looked at the clock. It seemed that the doctor had been there an awfully long time ago, yet perhaps it was only yesterday.

Anyway, what further need did he have of the doctor? His sickness had passed. Fedya was lying quietly.

One time Fedya woke up—and "death from within," as always, swept past him, and then this feeling slowly subsided. It was like the tingling sensation you get when your leg starts losing its numbness.

He could see the yellow wallpaper, the cotton dressing gown, and the clock, in no great hurry, ticking by itself. Fedya did not feel like sleeping. He just lay there.

It seemed to him that on the faded chair seat, beneath the dressing gown, something black was fumbling around.

What fumbled there was something resembling a small kitten. Although Fedya had excellent eyes and was accustomed to the semidarkness, he could not distinguish it right away. He fell to musing about the kitten. Where could it have come from? His interest had been aroused.

All at once he saw it clearly.

A furry black little devil was perched on the edge of his chair, dangling his little feet, with his tail all coiled up. His little feet were most ordinary, only they had small hooves. Generally speaking, the little devil was very ordinary—with his tiny horns and small pig-like snout.

Fedya burst out laughing.

"So that's what you are like!" he exclaimed. "The most commonplace. Was it really worth fearing and hating you all my life, as I have hated you? You are such a little beast! And I knew all along that you existed, even though there was nothing to prove it to me."

The little devil wagged his small head and also laughed in his squeaky voice.

"Suppose I am not even yours now."

"What do you mean, not mine?" Fedya was surprised. "There is only one of you, so please don't lie about it."

"One of me, that's true. But what kind?"

"How should I know? I can see right here what kind you are, and I am totally indifferent to you."

"Yes, yes," the little devil remarked, almost apologetically. "That's how I was in the beginning. Later on I grew up. I became big and strong."

Before Fedya's eyes the devil began to grow, and by this time he was sitting on the chair, big and strong, black as before, but with iron claws. Only his eyes remained like the small devil's: they were quite blue, and somehow out of place on a devil.

Fedya stared and stared and twisted his lips in contempt. "Look how he frightened me! That worthless old piece of trash."

"No, don't think that. That's just how I do it," the devil hissed with his bass voice. "Just take a good look at me: I am handsome, very handsome indeed . . ."

Fedya was a little taken aback; he did not notice anything, but in the meantime, instead of the burly, grown-up demon, a somber yet beautiful creature appeared before him, dressed almost theatrically in a scarlet cape. The cape was also handsome-looking.

"So that's what this is," Fedya said. "We know all about it:

'And the proud demon was so handsome,
So mighty and resplendent . . .'"

"I am very intelligent, moreover," the demon went on hurriedly. "But for this I will have to give up some of my beauty . . ."

All at once there was no demon before him. In his place was someone whose familiar lips were bent in an evil grin, and his frowning, diabolical eyebrows were pointed upward.

"I have had enough of your transformations," Fedya said wearily. "Besides, I have known all of this for a long time . . ."

Mephistopheles leered at him with stern disdain.

"Indeed, that's your human version," he said. "You don't know the real story as well as I do. Indeed, my own skin was at stake."

Fedya reflected a moment:

"Well, okay, continue. I just wanted to say that all this doesn't frighten me. It also seems that you have forgotten one more thing . . ."

He wanted to draw attention to something with his eyes, but the lamp, shaded by the volume of Dostoevsky, was behind the head of his bed. However, the devil understood him.

"Don't be in a hurry, I haven't forgotten anything. Is this it?"

With a smile Fedya looked at the gray, mangy, but strong and fidgety devil with the traditional "Danish dog's tail." The devil sneezed.

"Of course, even with this I cannot get through to you," he said, wiping his nose with his ear. "I am here only for a minute, so I won't leave anything out. After all, I am very conscientious. You ought to be more curious. Indeed, you people are all so different."

And, laughing, he began to turn into a human being, tall, slender, rather pleasant, with his blond hair thrown back. His face displayed a self-assured satiety and a self-assured imperiousness.

"What's next?" Fedya asked in bewilderment, and at that very moment he noticed that the man had wings. His wings somehow did not grow by his shoulders, but extended from beneath his arms, angular and so enormous that they cast shadows upon the ceiling. His right wing stretched above Fedya's bed and, reaching the wall, it struck against it with a dull, empty sound. The color of the wings was yellow, and they appeared to have been formed out of a rubberized material.

But on the whole everything seemed quite all right—both the man and his wings.

Fedya watched pensively. He understood that his self-assured and powerful man—or superman—*could* be more fascinating than any demon, or any little devil with a runny nose; but Fedya himself was a stranger to him. Fedya was neither captivated by him nor afraid of him, and for that reason he did not hate the devil. Besides, these were all some devilish pranks, these transformations and apparitions. This creature was the devil in every disguise—could this mean that there was really no devil at all?

Suddenly, with inexplicable languor, Fedya raised himself slightly upon his pillows. As before, the man was seated next to him. However, there were no longer any wings but instead—simply an elderly gentleman with glasses, wearing a threadbare frock coat. He was so weak—such weak, lanky, apish arms hung down from his torso, his back was stooped over from weakness, and his head dangled from his weak neck in such a way that it appeared he would not even last a minute on the chair. Certainly he would not be able to move a finger or open his mouth. However, he did open it and mumbled:

"I am doing this for your sake. I am yours. Only I wish everyone would leave me alone."

Fedya looked in horror at the devil's face. In that face there flashed oddly familiar traits, and the more Fedya looked the more clearly they showed through—they were his own, Fedya's traits. It was Fedya himself sitting before him—only an old, terrifying, boundlessly weak-willed Fedya, his head hanging down.

"Why do you torture me? For what?" Fedya groaned. "All my life I have been thinking about you, never knowing what you were, and even now I still don't know, because you have done nothing but repeat all my thoughts in front of me. Now you are sitting before me like a weak monkey, in the disguise in which I hated and feared you most of all, wanting to fight with you, yet not having the strength to fight with you . . ."

"You had no strength?" the monkey inquired listlessly.

"If the strength of hatred engenders the strength of battle, then I had! I had!" Fedya practically screamed. "And, therefore, you are lying now as you sit by, wearing my own face! You are a liar! You are a vision, a shadow! Oh, all my life to think and to be tortured—yet to know nothing about you, only to hate you! A curse upon you!"

The devil nodded his head and, babbling on, he echoed . . . "A shadow . . . a shadow . . . all your life . . . to know nothing . . . all . . ."

"Tell me," Fedya suddenly entreated him, "is it really you, or isn't it? If it is, then what are you? Who are you? Why are you here? Why do I hate you? What have you come to me for?"

Fedya now saw the devil indistinctly. The long hands and the head were no longer hanging; a flickering spot continued to glow, not vanishing. There was a head and there was a body, but exactly into what this body had been changed, Fedya could not make out. He saw only the strange blue eyes fixed on him.

"Don't be in such a hurry," the devil said softly.

All of a sudden he leaned toward the small table (his movement resembled someone's long hair being let down) and gazed at Fedya's clock.

"What are you doing?" Fedya shouted.

"I have come to tell you."

The nebulous figure was becoming brighter. It brightened slowly but uninterruptedly. Darkness fell from it in patches and dropped to the floor, revealing a bright nucleus.

"Will they forgive you? Do you want to be sure that they'll forgive you?" Fedya whispered agitatedly, sitting up on his bed.

"No. They won't forgive me. Besides, if I were to be forgiven . . . all of you people, you yourself, all of you, could you really . . . forgive me?"

"No."

"There you have it. Thus there shall be no forgiveness. And there is no need for forgiveness."

"Who are you? Why have you assumed such a form now? Is it you?"

"Yes, it is I. Listen to me."

Fedya looked at him without shrinking. The soft blue eyes looked at him.

"Are you listening to me? We are both creatures, you and I. But I came before you. The Creator created love and the light. When He made men, He began to love them. He said to Himself, 'I wish to send them My most cherished gift—I wish to grant them freedom. I wish for each of them truly to be in My image and likeness, so that they themselves, of their own free will, shall walk along the path to the good and grow toward the light, and not like slaves who accept the good submissively, because the Lord deems it necessary.' And He summoned us, the saints, to Himself, saying, 'Who from among you will be willing to crawl like a shadow upon My earth, willingly, for the sake of men's freedom and for love of Me? Who desires to be despised and persecuted on the face of the earth, never recognized to the very end, for the radiance of My light? For, if there is no shadow upon the earth, men will not be free to choose between the light and the shadow. And thus they will not be as We are.' "

"Thus He spoke. And, detaching myself from the rest, I said to Him, 'I will go.' "

Fedya listened and looked steadily at the brightening image. The speaker continued:

" 'I will go, I will crawl like a shadow upon Your earth. I will crawl that way until the end, like a dog, along the road leading to You, so that everyone will kick the dog aside in order to get to You and be free like You. I will take upon myself the bitterness of curses. But, Almighty One, how can I be certain? You alone know man's strengths! What if I begin to win them over to my side?' "

"I dared to speak to Him in that way, for I had in my soul the shadow of doubt and the suffering of men. And He forgave me, a creature, my first lack of faith in return for my first suffering, and said, 'I Myself will descend to the people to assist them when their strength has faded away. I Myself, in the image of My Son, will go down on earth to them, I will become one of them in freedom and in love, and I will die, just as they will, and will rise again as the first among men. You will recognize Me, and will hover about Me as a shadow. The suffering which you will endure is great, and only Mine and that of men will surpass it. I will send you, of your own free choice, upon the earth in a black garment. Ascend to My throne wearing white, as you are. For them, however, you will remain dark until the Day of Judgment, and about that Day you will not know. Go now.'

"And I descended upon the earth, like lightning . . . I crashed to the earth like a thundering arrow. I am here now. You can see me."

In a white garment, like a gleaming light, a sad angel sat before Fedya. Everything in the room had turned to white. The old yellow walls were barely visible through the pale light; they still could be seen, nevertheless; they were still there.

Fedya suddenly extended his arm to them, to the dear, yellow, vanishing walls.

"You have told me, you have told me . . ." Fedya whispered. "So this means . . . Why did you say it? You have justified yourself to me, you have brought my hatred to an end . . . Does this mean that I no longer need to live?"

The sparkling devil rested his head in his hands and sobbed. But his tears were radiant, gentle, and joyful.

Sharply, like a sword, the familiar understanding of death pierced Fedya's soul. It crossed swords with another—the equally sharp understanding of life.

Suddenly he cried out, falling back onto his pillows:

"Mama! Mama! Mama!"

Someone lovingly and caressingly nestled against the head of his bed; someone enfolded him in a loving embrace, just like his aged mother from Elets, his very own mother, his only one, his everlasting protectress.

"Mama!" Fedya whispered once again, without opening his eyes, and died.

THERE IS NO
RETURN

"The shovel digs in silence,
Unhurriedly digs its hole.
There is no return, there can be
     no return,
Once a wound has crippled the soul!"

At last, everything was cleared up.

Pyotr Mikhaylovich could not believe himself
—after all, he had grown unaccustomed to feeling such joy.

Fifteen-year-old Lyolya came out onto the terrace in the evening and gazed for a long time
at the fading May sky behind the planting machine. She was thinking and could not calm
down.

"They are coming back now. Both Grisha and
Nadya. My Lord, what are they like? How are
they going to look at us now? They are real
heroes. What can be greater than this? Papa
doesn't understand. Papa was only torturing
himself, but I, how I envied them! And I envy
them even now."

She continued to think with bitterness:

"And why am I still small? Why couldn't I go
with Nadya?"

Pyotr Mikhaylovich had been fussing about for three days—
he did not know what to do with himself. He made two trips to
Kharkov. Bobriki, the country estate, where he lived with
Lyolya and his sister Evdokiya Mikhaylovna, was at most two
hours from Kharkov.

Pyotr Mikhaylovich wanted to go and meet his son in Odessa,
but the date of the ship's arrival had not been indicated in the
letter. Moreover, Grisha had written that they should not go to a
lot of trouble about meeting him and that he would come
straight to Bobriki.

Nadya was not coming with him. Grisha appeared to know
nothing about Nadya; at least his letter had said nothing about
her. A separate letter came from Nadya soon afterward.

The war was not yet over; they had just received some terrible
news about Tsusima. For a long time Lyolya did not wish to
believe it and even wept over it a little; however, the news
somehow did not affect Pyotr Mikhaylovich. Only slightly did it
brush against his heart, filled with its own joyfulness. His
children, Grisha and Nadya, who had endured the siege at Port
Arthur and a brief Japanese captivity, his own children had
been spared, his children were coming back! His heart, languish-
ing for a long time with fear for them, crushed with habitual
pain, could now be at rest; it was becoming calm again.

Pyotr Mikhaylovich was a simple and sober man. He loved
his provincial life in a simple way, loved his children with a
steadfast and simple affection. When they had dispatched Grisha
to the Far East, he realized that it could not be otherwise. Even
when his Nadya, the passionate, vivacious, nineteen-year-old
with a sparkling personality, wrote from St. Petersburg that she
had stopped attending the Women's University, had entered a
medical corps, and was leaving for the war—even then he understood everything, was resigned to it, and worried only about
getting money to her safely.

Then those bleak days of despondency, uncertainty, expectation, and despair began to linger on . . . Lyolya went to school
in Kharkov, but often came to Bobriki.

They had many neighbors who would drop in on them, because in that year everyone had one thing on his mind . . .

Now it was over; it was settled. Grisha had been wounded; he had been in a Japanese hospital and had recovered. He was coming home. Nadya was also coming home, accompanying the wounded and recuperating officers.

"Aunt Dunya," Lyolya drew up to Evdokiya Mikhaylovna. "You don't look happy, what's the matter? The heroes are coming back. Just think, our heroes! But you're just sighing."

Her aunt raised up her white head from her knitting, looked at Lyolya, smiled, and sighed again.

"See how cheerful Papa is," Lyolya continued. "Just look at him running around. As if he weren't fifty years old!"

"Well, I am sixty myself, Lyolechka," the aunt said with a smile. Suddenly she added quietly and gravely:

"War is a terrible thing, my dear. A terrible thing."

Once again the old woman's head bent quietly over her knitting.

II

At last the long-awaited day came. Grisha arrived.

He had been home for nearly two weeks now.

Actually, it was impossible to say that he was living in Bobriki —he was continuously taking trips, on horseback or in the *char-à-banc,* not on business either, but to visit his neighbors or Kharkov . . . Besides this, they were always having guests.

Lyolya would gaze at her brother attentively, as would Pyotr Mikhaylovich, and both of them seemed unable to understand something. Although Pyotr Mikhaylovich knew perfectly well that this was Grisha, it would suddenly appear to him that it was not Grisha at all.

He would look curiously at the rather broad-shouldered, not very tall officer with a black bandage tied above his ears, a nimble fellow, and fidgety as a spinning top, talking unceasingly, relating something about Japan, India, his comrades, then again about India, all the time gesticulating in a peculiar manner with his hands—and Pyotr Mikhaylovich would begin to perceive, though faintly, that this was not Grisha. In his thoughts he could not draw a connection between this officer and the dark-skinned, pensive youth whom Pyotr Mikhaylovich had known Grisha to be. That one had calm and lively eyes, whereas this one's eyes were frenzied, rushing, his gaze never stopping. The officer was constantly running about and was always rushing somewhere.

Not one evening did he spend with his family. He could not give a clear account of Nadya. Somehow he barely touched upon it. On the whole he would talk strangely, as though he had forgotten that he had listeners, and would simply appear to be thinking aloud intermittently. As for asking questions, he did not ask the family about anything or anyone, and when they tried telling him anything, he paid them little attention. He would look at something, become lost in his own scattered thoughts or in something else, then would suddenly start rambling on, would begin talking, or would remember some trinket from India which he still had not shown them, and he would bring it in.

"Here, take a look at this *nécessaire!* I'm going to give it to my fiancée. Isn't it a nice one?"

If guests came, he made sure he was the center of attention; he would talk and rush about as usual. It was as though he were one thing, and the guests, including Pyotr Mikhaylovich, Lyolya, and the aunt—all these were something completely different. They led separate lives, never mingling with one another—he was on one side, and they were on the other.

Indeed, many accepted this simpleheartedly—after all, he was a hero, but what were they? He should be completely special, and not do what the others do, and not be as the others are.

Grisha would occasionally give Lyolya a kiss or rumple her hair, which he could not do too well since it was fixed in two long blond braids. He would chatter some kind of nonsense with her, though in reality without noticing her.

Immediately, almost from the first day of his arrival, Grisha began courting the young ladies. He would court them without restraint and in a strange way—he would go after all of them together, in the same way as someone else would go after just one.

There were many neighbors—some even came from the city. All of the young ladies liked Grisha—he was so special!

No one, however, could have anticipated what happened next.

One time Grisha returned home earlier than usual and immediately announced to his family, with a roar of laughter, that he was getting married.

"What do you mean, getting married?" asked the astonished Pyotr Mikhaylovich.

"Just what I said. She's awfully nice. We went on a picnic. Lidiya Ivanovna, the Rakitins, someone else, and Ol'ga L'vovna . . . Yes, we had some good laughs, we joked . . . And I proposed to her."

"You proposed to her? You mean you are marrying Ol'ga L'vovna?"

Ol'ga L'vovna was a beautiful young girl, the daughter of a neighboring landowner. She was a student at the Moscow Women's University. Grisha courted her ardently, and she liked him very much.

"Ol'ga L'vovna?" Grisha said, musing. "Why Ol'ga L'vovna? Why not Marya Petrovna?"

"Who then, in God's name?" Pyotr Mikhaylovich looked about helplessly. "That must mean it's Marya Petrovna?"

Marya Petrovna was another young lady whom Grisha had courted with just as much ardor. She was from Kharkov. Pyotr Mikhaylovich had known her since her childhood—she was small, quite pretty, and unpretentious. Lyolya liked her very much, although she did not consider her very intelligent.

"Manichka!" Lyolya cried out. "But you haven't said two words to her, Grisha! I mean, I don't think she even knows you . . ."

However, it turned out that Grisha had made the proposal to Manichka.

The aunt put down her eternal knitting, looked over at Grisha, and said softly:

"Grisha, have you thought it over? Don't hurt her feelings. It is easy to hurt her feelings . . ."

But by this time Grisha was dashing out of the room, deciding which present to give to his fiancée first.

At the dining room table everyone was quiet. It could have appeared so simple that Pyotr Mikhaylovich's son was getting married to Manichka, a nice, very kind girl. Meanwhile, however, everything seemed to have no meaning; it was strange, not as it should be—and again Pyotr Mikhaylovich did not know how to approach the problem further. Should he go himself to Manichka's parents? Or try talking to Grisha, to find out more of the details, how, when, what? . . .

For a long time now Lyolya had begun to be afraid of her brother; she was even afraid of her own fear.

She got up, removed her shawl from the table, flung it over her shoulders, and went out to the garden. It was a moonless night, and only the light from the stars flickered on the black leaves and the black waters of the pond. It was warm and because of the darkness it was somehow more crowded, as if the walls around were closing in. Nearby, surrounding Lyolya, everything was still alive, familiar, understandable, but there, beyond the walls, lay the unknown. Grisha was beyond the walls, in that unknown.

Suddenly she heard the landrail chirping in the reeds—but perhaps for Grisha, she thought, there was no landrail at all. Perhaps Grisha did not hear at all what Lyolya and the others heard. It was not without reason that in the total silence he would sometimes start, as though listening very intently to something . . . Then he would become his old self again. Where was he now? What was he doing in his room? Was he thinking of Manichka? Could he really be in love with her? No, people who are in love would never say and do the things which Grisha did. After all, when could he have fallen in love? And why with Manichka?

No, Grisha was something special. It was as though he were not here, not himself . . . Then, Lord, where was he?

Lyolya became frightened of the darkness in the garden, of her dark, incomprehensible thoughts. She wanted to understand them and could not.

She slowly ascended the steps of the terrace. A lighted doorway was open. Two people were, as usual, sitting at the round table across from one another—her father and Aunt Dunya. Lyolya wanted to go up to her father, embrace him, ask him about something, say something to him . . . yet she did not know what, and did not dare . . . She then overheard what Pyotr Mikhaylovich was saying either to Evdokiya Mikhaylovna or to himself:

"We forget, yes, we forget all that they have gone through. It is impossible to make demands on him. He still hasn't gotten back into his former way of life. Even his stories are incomprehensible to us. I am very glad that he's getting married. Manichka is a wonderful girl, unaffected . . ."

Lyolya did not hear what her aunt replied. It was apparently something sad and confused. Pyotr Mikhaylovich repeated the same thing, but in his voice there was no confidence, only perplexed timidity.

III

The next day the news arrived that the ship on which Nadya was sailing would be in Odessa in a few days. Grisha was overjoyed.

"Let's see, who will be aboard?" he would rush about excitedly. "Well, Volodin had his leg torn off, but he's still alive, and Ryumka should be there too, most likely—I know it for certain—and probably some others from our bunch will be there . . . You'll see, Lyol'ka, what great guys they all are . . . We can all reminisce together . . ."

Grisha became extremely animated. They decided to go to Odessa together, Pyotr Mikhaylovich, Lyolya, and Grisha. Since

Nadya was accompanying the party of the wounded to St. Petersburg, she could not come home now, so Pyotr Mikhaylovich and Lyolya were to spend only a few days with her in Odessa.

In a minute Grisha changed his mind.

"No, who knows how much longer it'll take you to get ready; I want to go on ahead! I'll check on the rooms at the hotel, make sure they're all together. I'm going the day after tomorrow."

Pyotr Mikhaylovich did not know what to say.

Lyolya became bold.

"What about your fiancée, Grisha—won't you see her? You said yesterday . . ."

"My fiancée? Oh, yes . . ."

He seemed to have just remembered her.

"Oh, yes, that's right! Papa, they're all coming here today. Then we'll get engaged . . . She is really nice!"

Pyotr Mikhaylovich was so taken aback that he even became angry. What engagement? Who becomes engaged in this strange way? Why didn't he tell me plainly? Who is coming? Who does things like this?

Grisha was not embarrassed. He explained that everyone who had been at the picnic yesterday had promised to come, that yesterday they had already congratulated him on his engagement, and that, if Pyotr Mikhaylovich was opposed to an official engagement, it could be done simply, without much ado. Why should it make any difference?

Guests actually did come. Marya Petrovna, the fiancée, came in with her mother, which was unusual and indicated the course of events. The matter was considered settled. Pyotr Mikhaylovich also accepted this to be so, although in a somewhat agitated and distraught frame of mind.

Grisha kissed his fiancée's hand, chattered endlessly about Volodin and Ryumin, then shifted the conversation to India, then went on again about the people he would meet in Odessa.

"So you are planning to go to Odessa? Will you be there a long time?"

"Yes, yes, Odessa . . . Soon I . . . The day after tomorrow, I . . ."

Suddenly he became thoughtful and did not hear what they were saying to him.

After lunch the young people went out for a walk. It was dry and sultry, becoming dark very quickly as a thunderstorm moved in from far away.

Lyolya and Marya Petrovna lagged behind the party. Grisha went on ahead. He was just like before, when he was not yet engaged and when he courted all the young ladies. Today he was laughing a great deal and joking with attractive Ol'ga L'vovna.

Lyolya, quietly disturbed, herself not knowing why, walked alongside Manichka. Manichka was also silent and subdued. She was wearing a sheer blouse; her dark hair had been arranged in a chignon above her neck.

She was about three or four years older than Lyolya, but Lyolya treated her as an equal and even rather condescendingly.

It became unbearable for them to be silent any longer.

"Manichka," Lyolya said, "tell me, do you love Grisha very much?"

The question was somewhat awkward and, in fact, impolite. Manichka, however, failed to notice this. She merely blushed and whispered:

"I wouldn't let myself . . . I didn't know . . . I couldn't have anticipated . . ."

Lyolya nodded her head thoughtfully.

"Yes, this is so unexpected. He hasn't been here long, has he? It is unexpected . . . But we are all very happy," she added with caution.

"I am deeply in love with him," Manichka said hastily and in her simplehearted way. "He is so special. But dear Lyolya! I wanted to tell you . . . I wanted to ask you . . . You see, he is a simple and, it seems, kindhearted person . . . Yet somehow I don't understand him . . . Somehow I'm even afraid of him . . ."

Lyolya looked at her morosely.

"Please don't misunderstand me," Manichka became flustered, "I am very much in love with him, only I can't penetrate him. I can't fathom him . . . Sometimes he speaks so strangely, telling stories about I don't know what . . . Sometimes it frightens me . . . Oh, Lyolya, he is so good, and he has suffered so much. I want to talk to him, to comfort him, but I'm afraid . . ."

"He isn't grieving, why should you have to comfort him?" Lyolya uttered in that same morose tone.

Manichka did not understand her. Actually, Lyolya herself did not understand where this sudden anger at Grisha had come from. It must be the result of her anger with herself, with her own confusion. She remembered how she had waited for the "hero" . . . Indeed, he is a hero. What is bad about him? Yet in him there is something to be pitied, something awful and so strange, something cutting him off forever from Lyolya, Papa, this garden, the pond, and from Manichka—as though he had arrived from a different world.

"There's going to be a storm, let's go home," Lyolya said.

They turned back. The sky had been rumbling for a long time, and now the dark storm clouds, black from the gathering dusk and converging from all sides, erupted in an unbroken roar, massive and deafening, as though the whole sky had been roaring, grumbling, and had been slowly reversing itself. The lightning still struck only rarely, but the prolonged, hollow peals of thunder did not subside for a single moment.

Behind Lyolya and Manichka, far off in the distance, voices of the returning company were heard.

Someone's quick steps suddenly overtook them. Lyolya looked around. It was Grisha, by himself. The pale light caused by the lightning revealed all of a sudden his hatless head of dark hair, the black bandage, and his strange, stony, pale face.

"Grisha! Have you been looking for us?" Lyolya shouted to him, unwittingly quickening her pace, for he had already passed them but had not stopped.

"Grisha! Where are you going?" she shouted once more and, overtaking him, seized him by the tunic. Unexpectedly, Grisha roughly tore himself away from her and again continued walking.

Not knowing why, she mumbled:

"The storm is still far away . . ."

He turned around, hollered something to her, and hurried on.

"What? What did he say? Did you hear him?" she asked Manichka anxiously. "Did he say it was 'unpleasant'? What was unpleasant?"

"I don't know . . . It seemed like he said, 'No, it's unpleasant' . . . or, 'It's unusually pleasant' . . . I don't know. Why did you mention the storm to him? Is he afraid of storms?"

"Why should he be afraid?"

They had ceased to understand one another. They began to hurry. The cannonade intensified; the sky had turned completely black; the storm clouds were gathering, moving toward one another and colliding.

The guests caught up with Lyolya and Manichka only at the house.

"Where did Grigory Petrovich run off to?" attractive Ol'ga L'vovna asked gaily. "He suddenly became silent, turned right around, and left. We thought he was with you."

Suddenly, amid the even rumble, a portion of the sky seemed to be rent by fire and thunder, the earth resounded in reply, and faint thunderclaps hurtled about in the distance.

The young ladies dashed inside the house with a merry shriek.

"This is just a storm, just a storm," Lyolya thought, going up the terrace steps. "Where is Grisha? Is he really afraid of the storm? Or . . . what? . . ."

IV

It was a good thing that Grisha had hurried off to Odessa—when Pyotr Mikhaylovich and Lyolya arrived at the excellent hotel which was chosen for them, they were informed that the ship had arrived the evening before, that the rooms had been prepared for them, and that several officers were staying there with their nurses.

Pyotr Mikhaylovich's legs almost gave way from the expectation of seeing Nadya at that very moment . . .

But there was not that wholehearted, ardent joy which had brightened his soul while he was waiting for Grisha. Pyotr Mikhaylovich was already afraid of something, but of what he did not know.

They met, kissed, embraced each other, all rather hastily. In Nadya's spacious room the young officer Volodin was lying. His leg had been amputated, and he was still very sick. Nadya was caring for him; she was taking him to St. Petersburg. Grisha also turned out to be there, and some lanky officer was sitting by the window. You could not tell whether he was wounded or not— he was cheerful, but all the time he twitched and looked around. Now and then he would twitch and start looking around for no reason at all.

At first Pyotr Mikhaylovich did not fully and completely recognize Nadya. Then he remembered that he had never seen her before in the white uniform and cap.

"The cap makes her face look dark," he thought to himself . . . "and she must have gotten suntanned while she was at sea."

For a long while Lyolya also stared at her sister, in silence, with her eyes wide open. She did not recognize her either. She was so quiet, so quiet . . .

They had no time to talk about anything—how could they, in all this confusion? Then the real commotion began. Throughout the whole day it was impossible to move around in the room. Some men and women, both strangers and acquaintances, would come in with flowers or greetings. Grisha was rushing about with his black bandage. Volodin would lie down one minute, and the next he would hobble and moan around the room on his crutches. Ryumin would click his heels sideways, twitching, looking around, and blinking one eye.

Finally, toward evening, everyone settled down. Tea was brought in. Outside the window, overlooking the inner courtyard of the hotel, stood the dark, hot southern night; the window, however, was half shut—Volodin was afraid of neuralgia.

"Pyotr Mikhaylovich!" Ryumin cried out, monotonously rolling his eyes with their whitish eyelashes. "See what a great fellow our Grisha is! He has a hole in his head, but he's all right! You know, we spoke with him once about the marriage . . ."

"Yes, I remember you telling that pack of lies," the one-legged Volodin retorted from his couch. "Shut up! Pyotr Mikhaylovich, why not move up closer? I will tell you the story myself. They cut me up, the devils, but they didn't do it right. It hurts me, drives me crazy. If it wasn't for that morphine, I'd just die. Nurse!"

Grisha had brought in his small Indian boxes from the country and was pushing them in front of everyone's face.

"Just look what I bought her! Nice, aren't they?"

Pyotr Mikhaylovich did not say anything the entire time. He sat and maintained an embarrassed silence, glancing first at the officers, then at his Nadya.

Lyolya was also sitting quietly in her little corner. She did not move but only looked around.

Pyotr Mikhaylovich had not yet regained his senses. It began to appear to him that a long time ago, not just since this morning, but ever since Grisha's arrival, he had not been able to get hold of himself. He looked once more at Grisha, the nimble fellow—and here he did not appear as the strange, oddly transformed, substituted Grisha he had been in the country. It was just that this was not Grisha at all, but some unfamiliar, savage, distant officer, like Volodin and Ryumin. In this room, with them, Grisha felt at home; he became one with them, and suddenly he began to live their life. He merged with them. And Nadya . . . was sitting there, wearing an order on her chest, with her quiet, somber, expressionless face. Her face looked as though it had been unskillfully carved from wood. In this company she was just like them. Pyotr Mikhaylovich knew that this was his daughter Nadya, but he felt nothing toward this wooden nurse, and he did not believe that this could be Nadya.

Why were he and Lyolya here with them? Suddenly it became quite clear to him that he and Lyolya were two strangers in that room and that those others formed a single unit. However, these considerations had not yet taken the shape of thoughts but were still disturbingly confused feelings.

No one paid any attention to Lyolya. They would suddenly remember Pyotr Mikhaylovich and then forget about him immediately. He busied himself with getting the tea, pouring it out, waiting on them. Nadya did not budge.

"Our newspaper! Our newspaper! Look, I have brought our newspaper!" Ryumin shouted and began convulsively pulling out the gray pages from inside Volodin's suitcase.

"They printed it on the old posters and wrapping paper. Our own Port Arthur literature!"

Volodin sighed complacently. Grisha dashed forward.

"Are those poems of mine in that issue? No, Zalessky's are in there; what a swine! Do you remember the little story I wrote with him?"

"Sure! He couldn't have gotten out of that one. Lucky thing he got the splinter wound that evening; that put a stop to it! What a liar he was!"

"They killed the little monkey then," Nadya said all of a sudden in that same wooden voice, just like her face.

Grisha began yelling.

"Just take a good look at what I bought Ol'ga Petrovna in India! I chose it just for her! She's the blonde. For my fiancée, I tell you, the blonde."

Pyotr Mikhaylovich started from fright. What Ol'ga Petrovna? Was he mixing Manichka up with Ol'ga L'vovna? How would she be a blonde?

While they were examining the small boxes, Pyotr Mikhaylovich said:

"Grisha, you are confused—your fiancée's name is Marya

Petrovna. Were you already engaged while you were in
India? . . ."

Grisha looked around absent-mindedly.

"Oh yes, that's right. Marya Petrovna. Listen, Ryumka, I will
introduce you to her. She is awfully nice! Besides, she is a student
at St. Petersburg's Women's University."

There he goes again! Manichka wasn't a student! However,
Pyotr Mikhaylovich no longer objected.

"What? A Student?" Ryumkin began to laugh. "Very nice.
And I'm marrying the surgeon's assistant. Very soon, too."

Volodin chimed in.

"What's this? My friends,

> 'Lawful marriage
> Is a greedy grave
> (Take my word for it!).
> It is a cold grave!'

"No, I like women of the world better. Life for me means
dancing, poetry . . . You remember what I told you, Grisha, in
the evening, beyond the trench? . . . That was a little before
Vidal'sky was blown up . . ."

"They killed the little monkey then," Nadya said again, not
addressing anyone.

With an effort Lyolya, attempting to free herself from the
vicious circle in which she was entangled, asked her sister:

"Which little monkey do you mean, Nadya?"

Nadya did not answer her, but Ryumin replied casually, still
twitching:

"There was a little monkey . . . One of the Chinese kids
brought it in. It lived with us. Then the chief nurse ordered us
to take it out. Of course, they killed it then. About six men were
killed at the same time, besides the Chinese kid."

They suddenly began vying with each other in recalling who
was killed and when. They would argue. They would laugh,
their mouths wide open, remembering various incidents. Nothing
was important or unimportant—everything had the same value.

Of war itself they did not speak at all. War was something

which existed and without which there could be nothing. War was simply the air they breathed. And the piece of earth where they had all lived together—in the war, just like in the air itself —was their separate world, a special planet all their own. Finally it perished. Naturally, its inhabitants had perished as well. Now, transported by accident to an alien universe, like shadows which had been reunited, they eagerly recalled the days of their lives.

"Yes, indeed, how much you have suffered!" Pyotr Mikhaylovich said, attempting to say something. "How many deaths there were!"

The inhabitants of the lost planet did not even hear him. They continued discussing their own affairs, reminiscing, laughing, becoming angry.

Pyotr Mikhaylovich began once more:

"Yes, we had our share too, while you were in captivity. All kinds of things happened to us! Yes, they did. Then, finally, there was Tsusima. It was terrible!"

Again the inhabitants were not listening. Why should they be concerned with other worlds? Besides, Tsusima was outside the reaches of their planet.

Turning, it seemed, to Pyotr Mikhaylovich, but in reality not caring to whom he was speaking, one-legged Volodin said:

"Now the main thing is that Stessel' was one of us; such a great guy that, by God, it's better not even to talk about him. Now with Kondratenko it's another story. I am simply bound to him spiritually. We were wounded at the same time. The joke was that they got me in the side, down below, but they must have got him straight. In the heat of the moment I couldn't make anything out, and I thought to myself, 'Well, *ganz kaputt* to both of us.' Tha-at's it . . . Those were the devils, all right! They cut me twice, but the tendon grew back. It was so painful that I wouldn't even wish it on a Japanese. If they would only chop it off at once, like they should! No, that Kondratenko—now there was a real man! Nurse, do you remember the story about the milk?"

Everyone remembered the story about the milk. And the one about the oranges. And the one about the little Japanese spy.

They laughed, recited some poems, Grisha and Ryumin sang a duet. Nadya smiled in the same wooden way. When they laughed, however, no one laughed in a funny way or at anything funny. Instead, Grisha would roll his head around; Ryumin would twitch and appear to be looking around. It was as though he were waiting for the usual bang to be heard alongside him, for someone to start moaning, for someone to be carried away—and that was just as it should be, no different. Nadya stood motionless in readiness—maybe they would need her help right now; or maybe it would be only a small monkey and a little Chinese boy—she would not be needed then.

"The hell with it!" Grisha suddenly cried out. "Maybe I won't even get married! What student? Why bother with her? If you want her, take her, Volodin!"

"Leave me alone! I'm looking for a syringe! Nurse, help me! Oh, forget asking her!"

Pyotr Mikhaylovich did not know what to do—should he laugh and pretend it was a joke? Or look stern and surprised? Who was this Grisha? In any case, it was impossible to joke about it. Or was it possible? Surely it was necessary . . . or wasn't it necessary? In the long run Pyotr Mikhaylovich did not understand anything and, gradually becoming infected by the whole thing, he himself began twitching and looking around.

"Maybe I'll just marry this nurse," Volodin declared. "That will give us both a huge pension and money for my treatment. . . . It'll be just terrific; we'll go somewhere together, God willing, okay?"

Everyone was in agreement. That was probably the way they used to make plans together somewhere in the evening, in one of the dwelling places of their planet—that is, if no one got killed before evening. After all, before evening everyone had about twenty chances of getting killed.

Twitching and looking around, believing by now that an explosion could come from anywhere and for no reason, and that he himself could die at this moment, Pyotr Mikhaylovich made one final attempt, speaking in his usual voice:

"Yes . . . you really all ought to rest now. Relax . . . You will get back to normal . . . You will get used to it . . ."

They roared with laughter. Get used to it! What more did they have to get used to? For them it seemed that they had gotten used to everything. Yes, they really had gotten used to it all.

"Do you remember your poems, Volodin?" Grisha bellowed.

"Which ones? 'With a tender reverie, like a veil'?"

"Oh, to hell with your veil! No, don't you remember the lines —'There is no return for anyone'?"

"Oh, yes! I forgot. Wait a minute, they aren't mine, they're Vidal'sky's."

"They finished him off the same day as the little monkey," said Nadya.

"That's right, Vidal'sky's! Who remembers?"

"I do," said Ryumin. "This one is good with music. Even without it . . ."

He assumed a pose and, twitching on one side while looking around, he recited:

"We know, we know, there is no return,
No one can return.
Bullets, bayonet, grenade—
We got used to everything.

We are a closely knit family,
Separate from all others.
Nothing is unknown to us.
Life and death, they are all the same.

We have forgotten the days, the dates,
None of these can come back again.
If I am killed, if you are killed—
We are ready for anything!"

As though it were a song, the rest of them joined in, in unison:

"If I am killed, if you are killed—
We are ready for anything!"

"You know, I will go with you!" Grisha screamed with enthusiasm. "After all, why should I stay here? I'm better off getting married there!"

He remembered Pyotr Mikhaylovich.

"Papa, I have to go with them. They're leaving the day after tomorrow, and that's when I'm going too."

"Where are you going?" Pyotr Mikhaylovich muttered. "What do you mean?"

"I'm going, and that's all there is to it! Ryumka, do you want to run a little with me along the street? I'm suffocating in here."

"Go on," Volodin moaned. "It's so painful. Nurse, where is that syringe? The devils, they still haven't finished cutting me . . ."

Suddenly in a single instant, everyone became quiet, remaining motionless and petrified. They trembled with their usual expectation—and again became still . . . Pyotr Mikhaylovich became quiet along with them, although he did not understand what was going on, or what had happened.

Then he came to his senses.

"Oh, those were . . . wheels rattling along the stones right outside," he said. "I think that was just a bus driving into the yard."

"Oh yes, sure. Wheels," Volodin finally uttered. "Wheels. Oh, that's nothing. We're used to it. Even when there isn't any rumbling, there's always a rumbling in my ears and my head anyway. You just can't get away from the rumbling."

Pyotr Mikhaylovich was about to open his mouth to say something like "You will get used to it," or "You will forget it," but he said nothing.

The room began to stir. Nadya went up to Volodin to help him onto his bed. Grisha and Ryumin searched for their caps. Pyotr Mikhaylovich also got up. Only at that minute did he notice that Lyolya was not in the room. She had been quiet the whole evening in her little corner. When had she managed to leave?

"Good night, Papa dear," Grisha said, adjusting the black

knot of his bandage underneath his military cap. "Good-bye! Volodin, Ryumka, and I are going to wander a little bit along the streets. I couldn't sleep anyway; my legs simply can't stand still."

In his hurry to leave Pyotr Mikhaylovich walked unnaturally fast along the corridor. He reached the end where the door to Lyolya's room was.

He opened the door noiselessly and peered in. It was dark.

"Lyolya! Are you asleep?"

"No, Papa dear. No, Papa."

Her voice was soft and faint.

Pyotr Mikhaylovich entered.

"What are you doing there in the dark?"

He switched on a rather dim light. The room was small and quite narrow. Fully clothed, Lyolya was sitting on the bed.

"What is it, Lyolya?"

He did not know what to say to her. She gazed straight at him with her large, childlike eyes, dark from fright.

"Papa, Papa? What is this?"

"What, my little girl?"

He sat down beside her, feebly and awkwardly embracing her.

"I don't know, my child. I don't know."

"Papa, dear! I realized today. Papa! They are all really insane. Real insane people, the kind they put away in the hospital. They have lost their minds forever."

She did not cry but only shuddered.

"Look, they have come back," she began again. "But did they really come back? Whether they are wounded, or not wounded, whether they have recovered, it doesn't matter; it doesn't matter at all. Everyone of them has been wounded in his soul, but their souls have not recovered. They have not recovered, and they could not recover, and they will never recover . . ."

She was silent, then suddenly added in a low voice:

"And for them it's as though we were insane . . ."

Trembling, she added in a still lower voice: "Maybe we are all insane . . . Both we and they . . . Only in different ways . . ."

In the yard outside the wheels again rumbled with muffled, heavy, and prolonged sounds.

Pyotr Mikhaylovich started, twitched, and looked around.

"Papa, Papa, say something!" Lyolya begged him, "I almost can't bear it! I really almost can't bear it! You are wise, you know; tell me what will happen now? How will it be now?"

But Pyotr Mikhaylovich only trembled and muttered helplessly:

"Yes, they are insane . . . Yes, maybe everyone is insane . . . I understand . . ."

There came a knock at the door—Grisha's shaven head in the black bandage peeked in.

"Lyol'ka, you aren't asleep, I hope? That little red box, one of those which I brought Anna Petrovna from Ceylon, have I left it here? I need it early in the morning. Ah, there it is! Good-bye! And Papa is here? Well, good night, good-bye, sir . . . I was on the point of going out with Ryumin, but I came back, I forgot the box . . . Good night."

He went out without closing the door, walking rapidly and unevenly, waving his cap along the way, and singing rather boisterously:

> "We know, we know, there is no return,
> No one can return . . ."

Lyolya was crying, clutching Pyotr Mikhaylovich, and from crying her shoulders quivered like a child's. Pyotr Mikhaylovich was already beginning to resign himself to it, dully, lifelessly. If they have not returned—they have not returned. If they are insane—they are insane.

They have not returned.

THE ETERNAL
WOMAN

Kokovtsev, a student, arrived from St. Petersburg totally unexpectedly at his mother's estate beyond Terioki. He took them by surprise, like a sudden snowstorm. He came there toward evening on the Finnish sled, in a rather gloomy mood, and had barely finished dinner with his mother and fifteen-year-old sister Lenochka when he called his mother over to the parlor.

There, pacing up and down with his long legs, he immediately started telling her that his wife had left him recently.

"Close the door a little tighter," the mother moaned in a hushed voice. She was not yet an old woman, but had a thin, resigned, shriveled face.

"I am afraid that Lenochka may be able to hear you. Oh my Lord, oh my Lord!"

Ivan Kokovtsev locked the door, drew the portiere, went up to the window for some reason, but did not lower the curtains. From the window a dark blue expanse of sky and snow lay before him; there were still frosts, and the evenings, which were lingering and becoming blue, did not want to end.

"I cannot seem to collect my thoughts," his

mother said once more. "I don't want to believe it. We knew her so well. She had been living with me since she was sixteen, from the time she became an orphan. Believe me, she loved you, and how she loved you!"

Ivan smiled wryly.

"Maybe she did love me."

"Maybe? Have you forgotten the story? Didn't she try poisoning herself because of you? Everything started then. That was when we found out about her love for you. And after that you married her."

"I remember, Mama. How could I not believe that she loved me? You know how much I loved her and felt sorry for her."

"Oh Varya, Varya! Ivan, please tell me coherently what happened? You were still together when you visited me for the holidays. I noticed nothing bad about her then. Did you have a quarrel or what? You lived together for three years, and then you had a quarrel."

"Mama dear," Ivan began. "We didn't quarrel at all. Listen, I must tell you. It all happened in a different way."

He fell silent, continuing to pace from one corner to the other.

His mother followed him with her eyes, caressing with her customary loving gaze his handsome, youthful, though not very young face with regular features, and his luxuriantly thick blond hair. Ivan was her only son.

"She, I mean, Varya, ran off with a tenor," Ivan said.

"What do you mean, a tenor? What tenor? What is all this?"

"There was a singer who came to our house on several occasions. Mama dear, you hardly ever came to visit us in the city, so you knew nothing about how we lived toward the end."

"Oh, my poor child! You unfortunate thing! She ran off with a tenor! Had you had children, this never would have happened. Now that you are finishing your studies, taking your exams, something like this has to happen and upset you. With a tenor! He must be some good-for-nothing . . . I must say I didn't expect this of Varya, I didn't expect it at all!"

Ivan did not hear her, and indeed he was paying no attention to her.

He began his story:

"This is how it happened. Perhaps my Varya was starting to get bored with me. For by now she had been living with me for three years. Toward the end I was studying a lot. Friends who would come to see me didn't seem too interesting to her. By the way, I always told Varya everything. I would talk, and she would listen. However, now that I recall, she would only listen and answer one thing, very concisely, 'I understand.' When I asked her about herself and what she was thinking about, she would give me no reply. Yes, she loved me, I was sure of that. And such a special tenderness grew up within me toward her! She is a cheerful woman, lively, talkative, singing, coquettish, childlike —she certainly is an attractive woman. She always said that she loved me. She declared that she had tried poisoning herself because of her love for me, adding that when someone really loves a person, poisoning oneself is a sign of one's wholehearted affection.

"I was never jealous of her. Little by little she acquired her own circle of friends. Let's leave it at that, I don't pass judgment on any of them. It certainly appeared that something was wrong with all this vanity and shallowness; however, if Varya was happy with him . . . Gradually all of our common acquaintances were left behind—I was with my friends, and Varya with hers. Officers would come to visit her, as well as actors of some kind, musicians, one artist—all unknowns. Varya told me that her voice had been discovered and that she was going to learn to sing. She had always lived in constant dread that I would stand in the way of her freedom, that I would say something, and she looked at me with the greatest suspicion:

" 'I suppose you won't let me.'

"I myself began to be afraid of her, afraid that I might unwillingly forbid her to do something.

"So she started taking singing lesson. There, it seems, is where the tenor made his appearance. Frequently she was not at home. Naturally, we grew further and further apart. When we did happen to meet one another, I would treat her as before, with affection and fear, and she would be very nice to me. She would

speak of her eternal love. She would say that she had the temperament of an actress, the soul of an artist, and the feelings of a
wholehearted woman.

"I had barely managed to convince her to come here to the
country for Christmas. She came and stayed a short while and—
do you remember?—left a week before me.

"When I arrived home, at our apartment in town, the maid
informed me, 'When the mistress arrived this morning, she said
that you wouldn't be here until tomorrow.'

"I didn't undertand and asked her:

"'What do you mean, "today"? She came home a week ago.'

"Suddenly I remembered something, flushed, and added fool-
ishly:

"'Well, all right, perhaps that's so.'

"I went in to see Varya. She sat at the table in her boudoir,
writing something. When she caught sight of me, she hid the
letter. As if I ever read her letters!

"'Where have you been?' I asked her. 'Haven't you been
home?'

"She grew agitated:

"'Who told you?'

"And right then, without waiting for a reply, she hastened to
tell me the whole story, how she had to go directly to Tsarskoe
Selo, to visit a friend, some female singer who was ill, and that,
in general, there had been some kind of tragedy about which she
did not have the right to tell me, since it was no concern of mine.

"'You can't be jealous of me! Oh, you can believe me, Vanya.
Yet you don't understand me. We live by our feelings, by the
fascination of art. You are a bit too rational, you have no hu-
maneness, but I love only you, no one but you. Don't deny me
my friends, since there is much which would be unbearable and
incomprehensible to you!'

"Frankly speaking, not just a great deal, but everything was
incomprehensible and frightening, for that matter. How, after
all, could I stand in the way of human—if it is human—freedom?
Perhaps if I had that feeling of 'possession' toward Varya (this,

indeed, happens to some others in their relations with women, whether of short or long duration), but I never had that feeling toward her.

"So I left her room. She would disappear for entire days, and by then she would never say a word to me, or if she did it would only be about trifling things which were obviously untrue, and she would then cast a sidelong glance at me, as though she were afraid that I would not believe her. She seemed to be eternally agitated, her eyes gleaming. One time she returned at five o'clock in the morning. Afterwards I accidentally heard two women talking about her with dirty sneers and dirty words. They spoke in such a way that I alone could understand that it was about her. There was nothing I could do.

"However, I saw that it couldn't last; it was becoming impossible and unpleasant for both of us. It was I who understood it; therefore, it was I who had to act. On the whole, I began to understand my own extreme stupidity. For, indeed, how many women had I ever known—there had been only Varya. And there had been no intimacy with another woman before or after our marriage. Varya was—as I was accustomed to thinking without deliberating much about it—my 'lifelong companion'; I had become accustomed to think that, above all, both of us were 'people.' But all of a sudden I saw that she was acting in complete opposition to the way I or another person would have acted, and I really didn't understand why or for what purpose she was doing it. Even allowing for her supposedly profound artistic nature, it still would have been impossible to understand anything.

"It was impossible to understand; however, what could I have done to bring everything in our relationship more out into the open? To make her stop being afraid of me? How to make her behavior be more natural?

"Then I decided that it was necessary to act not simply, but with cunning, a cunning that was not too cunning. I decided to act out of pity.

"I went up to her room and, while entering, I said to her:

" 'I know everything.'

"I myself feel that this was sheer foolishness on my part. And what do you think? She suddenly paled, then she rose, shrugged her shoulders, and said:

" 'I know who told you. Well, what about it? What about it? You can't do anything about it. You are threatening me in vain. There is nothing to be done. It is very possible that I love this man.'

"I stood up and sat down again. Until that time my heart somehow had refused to believe what my reason had already come to perceive.

" 'What do you mean, you love him? What kind of love is that?'

" 'He (she gave me the tenor's name) needs me very much. Evidently, such is my fate. I was born an actress. That week I was impelled to live with him at his place . . .'

"You understand, I know this tenor, and I know what kind of love he can give her. Suddenly everything within me became clear, once and for all. I got up and went out. Varya followed after me. I went to my room and wanted to lock it, but she followed me in, although she looked pale and walked as if in fear. She was always afraid of me—this had been the hardest thing for me to bear.

"I gazed at her again and didn't recognize her. I was surprised that I had spoken with her before. I was also surprised at my old, habitual ideas.

"She wanted to say something, but I interrupted her:

" 'Go away.'

" 'You can't undertand anything . . .'

" 'Just go away, for good.'

" 'What do you mean, for good?'

" 'Just what I said, for good, and don't come back.'

"She shrugged her shoulders.

" 'I wanted to tell you that I was leaving. There is nothing to be done. I cannot live at this place, and I don't want to, either. I have to be free, so he is renting a room for me . . .'

" 'Go away, go away.'

"She turned immediately and left.

"I heard her collecting her things together hastily and leaving for good. On the following day she sent for her things and for her passport. She wrote in an unsealed letter, 'I hope you're not so low that you would do insane things and refuse me my passport.' There she was—being afraid again. Of course, I didn't refuse it."

Here Ivan fell silent for a minute, and his mother began lamenting:

"My Lord, my Lord! Who could have thought that she was such a wretched woman. My poor Vanya!"

Ivan looked at his mother in surprise.

"Why is she wretched? What is the matter with you, Mama dear? I don't see why Varya is a wretched woman."

"What is wrong with you? She traded you for a tenor . . . It's terrible!"

His mother was evidently suffering—Ivan was her only son.

"Oh, she never traded me for anybody," Ivan said, frowning with annoyance and occupied with his own thoughts.

"But didn't she fall for that tenor?"

"Why do you say she did? I don't think so. I found out later that she actually lives in those furnished rooms where the tenor does. But the tenor has a very tight schedule. She probably won't be attracted by him for very long. Now Varya has her large and merry circle. She is free. I imagine the others treat her better, more intelligently than I ever did. Only she has a delicate condition. She might even get sick. I want to write and tell her that she can come back to me if she gets sick. I will nurse her back to health."

"Vanya, what's the matter with you? This is actually immoral. Do you want to forgive her for everything? Excuse me, but this shows a lack of character, and it's really unworthy of a man."

Ivan again gazed at his mother with surprise.

"Mama dear, I never thought at all about myself in terms of just being a man. I don't know. I don't want to forgive Varya for anything, because I don't see what there is to forgive. Besides, how can it be immoral? It has nothing to do with people's morality or immorality. Now everything has become perfectly clear to me. In the beginning, according to the tradition, I, too, formed similar judgments. Naturally, I am sorry that all which surrounds Varya is so unseemly, vain, lacking in splendor, and I am sorry that the tenor is not a very good one. It's a pity that she wears herself out so much and that she might even get sick there, but actually it doesn't make any difference. Even if exterior forms had been different, the core of things would have been the same. Everything, always, is approximately the same. I know why I did not understand Varya and cannot undertand her even now. But she is in no way a 'wretched' woman. I don't know what kind of a woman she is (she is certainly not a very happy or successful one), but I know that she is a woman. It isn't necessary to understand a woman entirely. If there isn't even a temporary feeling of possession toward her, then you have to feel sorry for her. If there is a woman who is dear to you, you must give her shelter, feed her. If she goes away, you must let her go. If she comes back, you must give her shelter."

"My Lord, how confused you have become, Vanya. Oh Vanya, my dear! How all this has affected you! Leave her, forget all about this unworthy woman. Get a divorce. You are so young, you can still fall in love with a girl who is worthy of you, who is faithful. You can still be happy . . . You will calm down . . ."

"Mama, can't you see? Can you really be telling me to get married? Feel sorry for her, caress her, give her shelter, let her go, yes. But get married? Are you making fun of me?"

His mother became upset as she perceived a faint sound from outside.

"Vanya, for God's sake . . ." she whispered. "Look behind the door . . . I am afraid that Lenochka is listening . . . It would be terrible if she overheard us. She's just a child."

Ivan opened the door. Two beautiful, dark eyes, intelligent in their own way, righteous, wonderful, yet mysterious, and perfect in their own undying mysteriousness, glanced at him. They were the eyes of a creature whom everyone has agreed to consider and to call a human being, and everyone actually does call her that, trying to regard her as a human being, although from this designation nothing but suffering and pain results for anyone.

The eyes flashed and hid themselves beneath their lashes. Lenochka rose unhurriedly and went out noiselessly. Had she heard their conversation by accident? Or had she been listening? It would have been useless to try to find out the truth. Did she know it herself?

Ivan returned to the parlor and quietly, with a suddenly changed, fatigued appearance on his face, looked at his mother.

"She wasn't there?" she whispered and added in a louder voice, with a heavy sigh:

"No, Vanya. No, my dear child. Believe me, I understand you —you still love this woman, you've been blinded . . . Of course, it is necessary to save her and not let her ruin herself completely. I will go and talk with her. Perhaps I can be of some help to her, but as for forgiving her—no! Believe me, she will even start despising you. To forgive in such cases . . . that is, in this case . . . is simply inconceivable. To trade you, my bright handsome boy, for a tenor! How horrible! Just horrible! It's enough to drive me to my grave. Vanya, do you hear me?"

Ivan raised his eyes, smiled quietly and guiltily, but said no more. He had been talking to his mother for so long about his sorrow and about his new enlightenment that he had forgotten that his mother was—a woman. His elderly, dearest blood relation, bound to him by birth. Yet she, too, was one of those creatures who are given to the world but whom it is not given for others to understand; one of those creatures who are not endowed with a capacity to understand, for his mother, too, was—a woman.

THE STRANGE
LAW

"Hath not the potter power over
the clay, of the same lump to
make one vessel into honor, and
another into dishonor?"

Romans IX:21

He was so well known that I will neither name
the city where he lived nor his profession; nor do
I want to invent a name for him. He was simply
a scientist, a professor. He was not at all old, was
lively and merry in society, and had a quiet,
tender voice.

We became friends at the university, and then
a lasting, peaceful friendship developed from our
comradeship, although we never lived in the
same city. He did not come often to my northern
capital, but it never occurred to me to pass by
that place where he lived without dropping in
on him; this happened almost every year. Anna
Kirillovna, his wife, was a well-educated, energetic woman, very well suited to him. She created
a model school, a so-called commercial one, for
children of both sexes; she ran it well and very
independently. During the summer she used to

From *The Voice of Life*, 1915, no. 4, pp. 3–6.

go abroad to study the organization of school affairs in France and England. To me Anna Kirillovna seemed a real person and a real mother at one and the same time. This combination is so rare!

They had three childern—three sons.

The professor and I did not correspond. We had not seen each other since last Christmas. But suddenly yesterday evening we met unexpectedly here, on the shores of the Neva, in the house of an acquaintance.

Lately I would often drop in to see the elderly Countess Marya Ignatyevna. It was always quiet there, half-dark, and it seemed that a cobweb of sadness, hanging in the corners, shaded the light.

The Countess would be knitting something long, thick, and gray, with her head bent over toward the lamp. Pale Nidochka with her frightened eyes would also be knitting—everything for the war. Sasha, the only son, their joy, had gone off to war. He dropped out of the university—and went off. Everything in the Countess's living room was filled with Sasha, war, and sadness.

There were generally no guests. In addition to myself, perhaps Father Vladimir—a kind, gray-haired priest who did not live far away—would drop by and stay a while; he had christened Sasha and Nidochka and had buried the old Count.

That particular evening he also came. The other guest was— my professor!

We somehow took special pleasure in one another because of our unexpected encounter. It turned out that the professor had come "on business"; he had been endlessly bustling around, had gone off, and had returned only today. He had concluded his "business" satisfactorily and wanted to go home in two days.

"Tomorrow I would have been at your place without fail," he said, grinning faintly, nibbling at his black beard. "But there was no way I could have made it earlier. That's the kind of 'business' it is."

"What kind of business?"

Marya Ignatyevna sighed without raising her head; Father Vladimir also sighed, and Nidochka sighed.

Father Vladimir said:

"What is our business now? We are seeing off our dear ones—to the great war, that is our business."

I suddenly remembered. I had heard only vaguely that the professor's older son Kostya had to pass an examination to become a volunteer . . . There had been some conversations about it, but in passing, casually, a long time ago, as if about something unimportant. I knew little about the professor's children.

"Oh, Kostya! They didn't really take Kostya? Surely he must be past twenty now . . ."

"What's the matter with you, my good man?" the professor gently stopped me. "Kostya has nothing to do with it. He has been a Cossack officer for a half a year now and has already spent five months in the front lines. He is still safe and sound."

"Is that so! Did they take Volya then? . . . That's just nonsense, Volya is fifteen years old . . ."

"Sixteen," corrected the professor. "No, Volya is at home, he is studying. I took care of Vanya, the youngest one. He is thirteen years old, and as a result it was difficult to arrange it. I had to resort to every influential person, and finally I was forced to take him to Warsaw personally. By means of truths and untruths I obtained a position for him with an officer, an acquaintance of ours. How pleased he was!"

I was listening, numbed, and Marya Ignatyevna even began to smile. It was as if it were easier for her because the professor had the same grief, even a heavier one—two sons in the war, and one of them only thirteen years old!

"He is a healthy boy, big and strong," continued the professor. "Suddenly he began to thirst for action. He resembled Kostya. The only thing he could think about was military service, even before the war."

The professor said this with a calm and quiet clarity, as if it were something completely natural, thought through long ago,

and understandable. I, for my part, however, could not get hold
of myself. One had to know the professor and his wife as I knew
them. Their children, it is true, I did not know, but they were
indeed their children! And he himself took his child over there!
. . . What about Anna Kirillovna?

"Their mother must have been very upset," uttered Father
Vladimir, as if guessing my thoughts. "A young child . . ."

The professor smiled.

"Certainly. But my wife understands that there exist immu-
table laws of life, insufficiently investigated, perhaps forever incomprehensible, yet insurmountable—laws of history and of life."

I grew agitated.

"Stop, what laws! Lawlessness, if you please. You are unable
to cope with your own child . . . You yourself took him over
there . . . I don't understand."

"But why should I have to cope with him? Like Kostya's, his
zeal for this particular cause was inescapable. For anything else
they were both completely incompetent. This particular pursuit
is needed very much now. If Vanya was somewhat late in being
born, it wasn't his fault. That's why he is so well developed phys-
ically, strong, and daring."

"Great, great tasks are being accomplished!" Father Vladimir
shook his head.

"Wait a minute," I said, not calming down. "What does 'not
competent for anything else' mean? What, did he study poorly?
And he is your son? What about the middle one, Volya?"

"Volya is a normal child, with a good mind and sound intellectual development. But Kostya and Vanya are subject to the
law. Don't you understand? Well . . . I don't know whether it
is even worth talking about . . . It is sufficient to say that out of
my three sons, all of whom were raised in the same circumstances
and by the very same people, two turned out to be insensitive to
their upbringing, whereas the middle one pursued the most
typical path. Both Kostya and Vanya became equally dull from
each book they read; they weren't interested in anything, ex-

cept possibly the applied sciences. They were the typical 'poor students.' It would have been stupid and cruel to force them to act differently. It is a law of nature, the path of history."

"Again the law? What paths of history?"

"The Lord's paths are inscrutable," Father Vladimir humbly interjected.

However, the professor said reluctantly:

"Yes, it is a strange law. There are such laws and paths, inscrutable, if you please . . . However, their reality is unquestionable."

"What kind of law is it, Professor?" Marya Ignatyevna smiled faintly, raising her eyes from her knitting. "I do not quite understand you. Maybe it is too specialized, and we, the uninitiated . . ."

"Oh, not in the least!" the professor suddenly became animated. "On the contrary—scientifically, it is still unfounded. It is a very uncomplicated thing; I will give it to you in a most straightforward form. The strange law about which I am speaking is the law of the adaptation of mankind to historical catastrophe, and most important, the corresponding adaptation which occurs far *earlier* than the catastrophe, an adaption which, so to speak, has a completely natural and physical basis. The future is known to nature, but unknown to us. Allow me to make it clear: when war sets in—like now, for example—it turns out that the main body of the people, namely those between the ages of twenty and twenty-five, consists of just those individuals adapted in the best manner to this cause, who are best fitted for it, and necessary for nothing else but it. Germany is a clear but debatable example. One can interpret Germany's behavior in this way, if one wishes: the Germans wanted war, and they themselves prepared it within their children. This, of course, is a superficial view—I am not taking Germany alone, or even this war alone—we are speaking about all history. Yes, history itself, or someone who knows its future and the paths of nations, stores in mankind, builds within it, precisely those forces which later turn out to be necessary; history creates people *for* a future catastrophe . . ."

"Stop, stop!" I tried to break in, but the professor was no longer listening.

"My sons, Kostya and Vanya, are two drops in the human ocean which was necessary for the present flood. Vanya was a little bit late in being born, but according to his characteristics, according to his composition, he is precisely this drop in the ocean—he will either merge with the others or dry out in vain. It is the same with the older one, Kostya. Just take a careful look around yourself—don't you see many such drops now? Recall the period before the the the war, recall the barrenness, the languor, the rushing around of the younger generation in Europe—and in Russia, yes in Russia! And this was not limited to any one social stratum—take even the lowest—isn't the familiar phrase 'the hooliganism of rural youth' known to you? They looked for the reason in the social conditions, but there was only one single reason—eternal and lawful—a great battle was brewing, but it had not yet set in, certain forces had not yet found their proper application, they had not yet become a part of the mainstream . . . But the minute they joined in, they became transformed. Kostya and Vanya—are they my children? No, they are children of history, above all children of the times. They were not born for me nor for themselves, but for that world battle which inevitably had to set in. Both of them, big Kostya and Vanya, who was late in being born, beamed with joy, deepened, and changed; they were so happy in repeating those same words: 'We are going off to die for our country.' But the middle one, Volya, watched them quietly and said quietly, 'I will have to live *after* the war.' He was born at the *right* time, not too early, not too late—he was born for himself, for a life *after* the war. That's how it is . . . Such is the strange law of human fates . . . Is it for me to fight with it?"

Agitated, he stood up. He did not notice that Marya Ignatyevna had put down her knitting long ago and was looking at him with the uncomprehending but righteously insulted eyes of a mother. Frightened and confused, Father Vladimir was listening.

"No . . . No . . ." Marya Ignatyevna started, rising a little. "There can't be such a law . . . For war? . . . For . . . No, no . . ."

She put her knitting away and hurriedly, covering her face with a handkerchief and tangling herself in the train of her black dress, she left the room. Nidochka immediately ran out after her.

The professor suddenly became silent and, with a surprised look on his face, followed them out with his eyes. Then he turned his eyes upon Father Vladimir and me.

Father Vladimir shook his gray head.

"How careless you are," he said with regret. "Yes, I do not know scientific laws, but I do see how audacious scientists are in their judgments."

"What did I say to give you that idea, Father?" began the professor, visibly confused. "I have just stated general observations, well known to many."

"It is audacious; these are exceedingly audacious observations. A mother's heart aches for her living son, whereas you maintain he was born for war, and thus to war he will go. Should we really judge who is born for what? This is God's task, not ours."

The professor was silent. His expression was like that of a small child who is guilty but does not know of what.

Closing tightly the flap of his cassock, Father Vladimir added:

"Don't worry about it—I'll go and cheer her up, our little Countess. What laws! A mother's heart knows only one—let him be alive."

"Excuse me, Father," the professor said meekly, "perhaps it was not proper to talk of this here. I didn't know. My wife Anna Kirillovna and I have spoken much about it. And she is a mother. She accepts the world's laws, only she calls them God's laws, incomprehensible, sometimes terrible for us, yet benevolent."

Father Vladimir went to calm Marya Ignatyevna, and the professor and I headed home.

But we did not want to go home. For a long time we wandered together along the quiet, snow-covered streets, while the professor kept on telling me about the strange law of universal providence and predestination. For a long time we discussed the mystery of time, mankind with its childlike cruelty, the entire infantile world, and the incomprehensible, severe, yet benevolent concern of God for the earth.

Sometime I will return to these discussions, to the professor, to his children, to the strange, unfathomable law—to the war.

Sometime, but not now.

MEMOIRS OF MARTYNOV

I have never attempted to write. Of course, I used to write rhymes when I was in school, and then there were reports on assigned topics. But to write some sort of story or tale—no, I have never tried that. Is it really so difficult, though? All you need to do is invent, imagine something, and then write.

Writing memoirs is even easier—you don't have to invent anything. Nowadays everyone writes memoirs—and I thought of writing them, too. Yet if you begin to describe the whole of your life yourself—it becomes impossible! I wouldn't have enough patience. So, having given it some thought, I decided to make a choice—to limit myself to my love stories. They too will be lengthy, even though I will not record everything in them. The plot will be more cheerful, and, most important, I will not run on and on about myself. I should merely state that here we have Ivan Leonidovich Martynov, a man of ordinary appearance, somewhat lanky, coming from a family of the intelligentsia and himself an intellectual, and by profession . . . well, let us say a free-lance philosopher—that will be enough.

From *The Link* (Newspaper), no. 211, February 13, 1927.

The rest is not essential. What I am like—that is not the issue, for this is not about me alone; nor even about those I love.
Love itself is the issue.

SASHEN'KA

This is, first of all, not by any means a story—it is just an episode. Well, let's start right at the beginning.

I was sitting at the table with my books. However, I was not looking at them, but straight in front of me, out the window—the window of our small wooden house—which overlooks the front garden. There was a deep snow and uneven snowdrifts, grayish-white, with faint, starlike tracks of birds. Then a fence, and below the fence, branches of acacia bushes; above the acacias, the cross of our Ostozhenskaya Church and the white, wintry, bleak sky. It resembled the snowdrifts of the front garden, only it was more even. The cross, though gold, was also somehow dull; everything was dull, wearisome, and even strange.

To tell you the truth, it became frightening when I thought to myself—what if it were suddenly to remain this way forever: the sky like the earth, the earth like the sky, the cross above the fence, myself at the window? Everything like this—endlessly?

Yes, frightening . . . but maybe not? Perhaps, if it did not remain this way, it would be still more frightening? Indeed, no one knows what will be. I am only twelve years of age; there is so terribly much of life which is completely unknown. I suppose I might even die soon. I am often ill, don't even attend school—I will take my examinations only in the spring, but I study at home. Well, if I die—that is another thing. And wouldn't it be fine? Then everything would become clear.

About death I often ponder now, not for long periods, it is true, but with a feeling of delight. Precisely because then it will all become clear. Otherwise everything is in confusion; if there is some good to it, nothing comes of it; it is even impossible to imagine what may come of it. Even to imagine!

Well, I decided always to remember this sky with the snow. Although just why, I do not know.

The door burst open. Of course, it was Nadya. Why did she barge in?

I was the youngest. Vova was already a university student, while Nadya had just graduated from high school in the spring. She had a high opinion of herself, put on airs. Oh, how I hated her!

"Vanichka, Ivanushka—you little fool, sitting there like a screech owl!"

"Well, what do you want?"

"Nothing. Go downstairs. Sashen'ka is there."

I felt myself blushing and, as the feeling increased, even my ears turned red. Despite this, I looked sternly and maliciously at Nadya's round face with the dimples on her cheeks, at the rosy-colored pearl necklace (imitation), and asked:

"What, has Gatmazov shown up?"

"Don't talk nonsense—you'd better smooth down those shaggy tufts of hair."

I didn't have shaggy hair, but curls. She knew this and was jealous.

"I'm trying to solve a problem. Get out, will you! Here I am racking my brains over it and you come barging in. It must be Gatmazov. If he's not here with you, then he must be with Vova."

"Well, how should I know where he is? What a silly idea!"

She laughed, deceitfully and odiously.

"You can't solve a problem—very clever, aren't you! Well, I'll send Sashen'ka here to help you. And both of us will cheer up."

"Get out of here!" I shouted and jumped up from the chair.

But accursed Nadya had already turned on her heels and vanished through the door, while I remained in the middle of the room. I stood there as though petrified, my soul harboring terror and inconsolable suffering mingled with rapture.

I know everything, everything. I have loved Sashen'ka for a long time . . . since when? It seems to me now that I have always loved him, even before our first encounter. But, of course, I did not understand anything at the beginning. I don't even remember our first meeting. Oh yes, one evening (a long time ago) we were all sitting at tea—Mama was there, Nadya, and Vova with his student friends (Gatmazov was among them, but I did not suspect anything as yet), and suddenly I looked at Sashen'ka directly opposite me. I looked at his gray-colored student's uniform, at his curly hair beneath the lamp (exactly like mine, only mine is dark while his is golden blond)—and then and there I understood for all time that I loved him, had always loved him.

I must have made a strange face, because Sashen'ka glanced at me, smiled (oh, what he is like when he smiles!), and asked what I was thinking about so intently. I was thinking about my love for him, about everything which had taken place earlier, how he would arrive, how he would speak with his friends and with me; in a word, I was recalling everything—but in a different, new way.

From that time everything appeared in a new light. My love for Sashen'ka was my hopeless rapture. The fact that love is hopeless, as they say, in no way deprives it of its delight. In fact, just the opposite is true. It makes it even more mysterious. Had I not known right from the beginning that there could be no hope here? And what hope? If one could imagine by a stupid miracle that Sashen'ka loved me in the same way that I loved him, well, what good would that have been? What could have come of it? I did not even contemplate such a stupid miracle . . . did not want it . . . and what happened later—I certainly did not want for anything in the world, and still do not. I do not even remember at what moment it all became clear to me, at what point my sufferings, decisively inescapable, entered my life. I was entangled in them, like a fly in a trap, and at the same time I rejoiced. So there you have it—love! I did not want it! Or did I want it, after all?

Sashen'ka was in love with Nadya. I perceived this once when he was speaking with her. His eyes were radiant and pensive (I usually notice everything about Sashen'ka). Later my family began to talk about it, and Vova was joking with Nadya. (My Lord, what wretched people are they who can make jokes about it!) And then . . . well, then there is the main terror—Gatmazov . . .

At first I did not hate Nadya at all because Sashen'ka was in love with her. I could not care less about Nadya. But when Sashen'ka's eyes began glowing, so that love sparkled in them, I for some reason felt closer to him.

Gatmazov was incapable of love. Nadya—also. Therefore . . . this whole affair flared up between them. Bursts of laughter, various compliments . . . Gatmazov had such shoulders (even under his gray student's uniform!), such cheeks, a stubby little moustache, oily cherries for eyes, and a voice as thick as Malaga —indeed, his entire appearance gave the impression that he was made precisely for courting. He was pleasing to young ladies like Nadya. And Nadya herself began to like him.

Let her like him. They are both accursed. But . . . Sashen'ka? His eyes have become so very sad. His face has grown pallid. He comes over nevertheless, but sees that Nadya wants to get rid of him in favor of her Gatmazov.

Should I kill Gatmazov, or what? Or Nadya? For Sashen'ka's sake I would not regret it, but would it have any meaning for him?

When I stood in the middle of my room—in rapture, because there, behind the wall, was Sashen'ka, and in terror, because Nadya wanted to get rid of him again and actually may have even sent him up to me—I was simply being crushed beneath this unbearable weight. What, then, did I want? For Nadya to cease liking Gatmazov and begin liking Sashen'ka? Or for Sashen'ka to become unable to love anybody, just as . . . these two are unable to love?

No, I don't know what I need. I don't understand. It would be good to run away . . . to die . . .

But I did not die, and did not succeed in running away, for there was a knock at the door, which opened halfway, and at the threshold I beheld the very tall, very slender figure of Sashen'ka. I saw him not with my eyes alone; I sensed him with my whole being, and I felt limp and inexplicably withered.

"Vanichka, isn't the problem going all right? Come on, let's have a look at it."

He spoke in a low voice, as always, and it appeared as if he had forgotten the strange, distracted smile on his lips. He advanced toward my little desk by the window. Since it seemed to me that all was lost anyway, I moved behind him and also sat down by the desk. Sashen'ka did not ask more about the problem. It was as though he had forgotten about it and about me. He stared out the window as I had when I had been alone not long before. Then, together, we looked out at the snowdrifts in the front garden with the bird tracks, at the fence with the acacia branches, and at the hazy outlines of the cross atop the Ostozhenskaya Church in the white, murky sky. But I was no longer thinking about anything. More and more I became filled with a mixture of despair and delight, and finally my feelings became almost impossible to restrain.

I then turned my eyes from the snow and gazed at Sashen'ka's face.

His face was peaceful, with that same smile transfixed on his lips. What did I see in his face? I did not know. I did not know what I would do or say at that moment, and I began speaking— as though it were not I. I remember all this only approximately; now it even appears as something nonsensical, incredible. However, at that time it was probably the most natural thing to happen.

I spoke in a whisper, a menacing whisper:

"Alexander Alexandrovich. This is impossible. I know. I love you. Look at me. I know, I know. I love you. Look at me!"

He started, as though he had just awakened, wished to say

something but did not say it, and silently, with an astonished gaze, looked me straight in the eye. I proceeded further, whispered quickly, not remembering what—it was as though I were not even there:

"All this is not worth it, and that is why it is impossible. There is so much to life; it doesn't matter at all that your future is unknown; everything, however, will be as you wish it. They don't know, but you know, and I also know. I love you because . . . well, because of nothing, I simply love you. This is terribly important. And that it is you—this is also important, and that it is you alone. Those other people there are insignificant. She doesn't understand."

For some reason I then added (something which I had never before considered):

"She will understand later, sometime she ought to understand, you will see. You will see, all will be well, splendid. I don't know how, but it will be. *I* know. I know everything! I know everything. Everything."

No doubt, if one were observing it from the outside—this would all appear quite comical. A disheveled urchin in a frenzy assures the tall, lovelorn student that he "knows everything" . . . what, exactly?

But the student was not looking at it from the outside—and he did not laugh. I saw how the very corners of his eyes swelled with tears, and beyond that I saw nothing, because he grasped my head with his arm and pressed me to him, to his jacket. It was there in the darkness, where it smelled of cloth, that I wept —inaudibly—happy, all-solving, all-dissolving tears, as I would later weep only in my dreams.

What then?

After this Sashen'ka immediately stopped visiting our house— as though he had cut himself off. I not only did not grieve, but strutted about as though it were my name-day party. It was even good that way, and necessary, so that "all turned out well." Later Vova once remarked:

"Sashen'ka has transferred himself to St. Petersburg! I saw him before his departure—he was very gay and, can you imagine, Nadya, he asked me to convey his kindest regards to our Van'ka. But about you—not a word!"

Hateful Nadya only shrugged her shoulders. In a year she married her Gatmazov who, after another year, dropped her. So much for her!

As for Sashen'ka—only after a long time did I understand with clarity—he had been on the verge of suicide that day, and I had rescued him. That is, of course, not I—it was love itself.

SCANDAL

"I cannot believe my eyes! This young man—is this Vanichka? I remember a small, sickly boy . . . And suddenly before me stands a young guardsman . . ."

"Yes, he has grown tall," said Mama, sighing. "He has finished his studies satisfactorily at the high school, thank God, and in the fall he will enter the mathematics department. He even wants to enroll in the department of philology; I don't know what will be. I wonder . . ."

Mama was always in sour or panicky moods lately.

Our conversation took place on the circular balcony of our dacha, an ancient little manor house where we had been spending the summers for many years, ever since I can remember. We considered it practically our own. On the estate there was also an actual manor house—a palace with white columns, almost always deserted; the owners rarely came to visit it. It was connected to our wooden house by an enormous park and could not be seen because of the trees.

I did not remember this woman at all, this Magdalina Kirillovna, who assured me that she remembered me as a "sickly

From *The Link* (Newspaper), no. 215, March 13, 1927.

boy" and that now I resembled a guardsman. I knew vaguely that she was some sort of distant relation of my mother, or something like that. I heard (all this very recently) that after her divorce she left Russia. She had spent six years in Paris, but had now returned to Moscow on business. It was very warm at this time of year (July), and Mama invited her to stay with us for a while.

Our house was large, now that there was no Nadya or Vova, only myself, Mama, and the eternal Uncle Odya, Mama's eldest brother, a retired general. He was already beginning to fall apart and walked crookedly. Most of the time he was rigidly, almost threateningly silent, and naturally he hardly understood anything.

Our visitor leaned with her round, bare elbow against the railing of the balcony.

"Oh, how I like your 'wilderness!' *Cela me repose.* How charming this little green clearing is, leading downward, and these century-old trees in the park beyond it." "Vanichka," she turned to me, "you must show me everything, everything . . . Certainly you must take many walks?"

"He is on horseback all the time . . . his new pastime," Mama said. "The manager gives horses to these youngsters only for the purpose of making mischief."

Magdalina Kirillovna nearly jumped up.

"Oh, how marvelous! I adore horseback riding! I don't have a riding dress, but here in the wilderness one can do as one pleases. Vanichka, will you be my escort?"

She looked at me once more with those dark flashing eyes (I did not know that they were all made up), which I had noticed and which had already confused me. I felt that I was blushing again as I mumbled:

"I think there is a lady's saddle . . ."

"I have grown unaccustomed to the old-fashioned lady's type, but there's no harm done, I'll get used to it again! Agreed, Vanichka? And we won't postpone it, tomorrow we'll make the arrangements. You know I'm not afraid of any horse, not even the young ones or the very meanest."

I was vexed at my own stupid confusion; with an effort of will I dismissed it and said with deliberate overfamiliarity:

"Oh, I suspect that you are an excellent horsewoman. I'll be happy to be your escort! Today I'll see about the saddle. You'll have a wonderful horse . . ."

Though I was already far from the balcony, my acute sense of hearing allowed me to catch the words of Magdalina Kirillovna: ". . . your Vanya is charming . . . how handsome . . . those tanned cheeks and . . ."

I did not hear my mother's reply. And I was not interested. I suspected that I was handsome; however, the words of Magdalina Kirillovna filled me with agitation. This woman, in general, excited me, though I did not find her attractive. She was in no way pleasing to me. Not stout, but too heavy, in my opinion. Her dark red hair lay in rather stiff waves, and she had a strangely pallid, even face. Granted, her scarlet mouth was beautiful. All the same, however, this was not the point. She disturbed me with her every movement, every gaze, every trifle— with her Parisian dress, strangely gathered up; with her face, small like a cat's; with the fact that from her room upstairs, whenever I would walk past and the door was half-opened, I would be overcome by that new, sultry, and sweet aroma. She exuded the same disturbingly sweet fragrance even while in the fresh air, outside on the balcony.

Of course, from the very first I asked myself directly—"What if she suddenly wanted to seduce me?" The second question— "Do I or don't I want to be seduced?"—I had not answered yet; I was still preoccupied with precisely that second question.

Something must be clarified here.

The thing was that during the seventh and eighth grades I had not studied at home but at the high school, and although I did not make friends with anyone in particular, these winters had brought about a change in me. I had abandoned all my own, so to speak, sweet dreams ("heavenly almonds"). I acquired a realistic outlook on things. But the strangest thing of all was that, although I had abandoned these dreams, I had not actually

abandoned them; they had somehow slipped back in, like contra-
band, and existed in perfect harmony with my realism. I then
noticed for the first time that everything within me was dual.
I vaguely felt (and was not mistaken) that this was perhaps the
same with everyone. But, sparing no effort, I tried to unravel this
strange situation, tormented myself over it, and attempted to
reduce it to mathematical formulas (I was very fond of formulas);
of course, nothing came of it. Thus, this unresolved "duality" of
mine remained.

I would play pranks with the housemaids, with the wenches
who tended gardens in the nearby districts, and I played these
pranks quite plainly and too coarsely; once I even got into a
cabin with these girls (however, things never did reach the final
phase). Yet at that same time, at that exact same time, I would
wander along the park on moonlit nights, thinking of something
obscure and lofty, almost about the young lady with long, light
chestnut braids reaching the edge of her skirt, whom I would
sometimes view from afar in the grove. Not only did I not want
to make her acquaintance—I did not even want to find out her
name, or who she was. Furthermore . . . I composed poems.
Strolling along the moonlit paths of the park, I would repeat
these poems, and they appeared beautiful to me . . .

To this day I recall one poem, my favorite, and perhaps it was
characteristic of both my struggle with that twofold confusion
and my thoughts about love at that time.

> My severe spirit, do not oppose
> My love, my poetry.
> I will not betray my living heart—
> Love is poetry. Poetry is love.
>
> All is indivisible,
> Sorrow, and mystery, and sin,
> And all is intertwined with love—
> Poetry is love. Love is poetry.

Magdalina Kirillovna fell into these moods of mine like a
stone. I felt at once that with her, most likely, there should be

no playing pranks. But . . . didn't I like her at all? Our Domnyashka with the light brown curls, she was the one whom I really liked . . . Indeed, where could I place Magdalina Kirillovna? Certainly not with the young lady in the grove, nor could I associate her with my poetry—that would be ridiculous! If it were love, one could not help but think of trivialities, banality: indeed, an aging woman, and I—a fresh young boy; well, really . . . At this point I plunged into the depth of my realism, but then suddenly I was able to compose myself, for, in the first place, there has been nothing so far; perhaps she does not even think about it? . . . Second, I do not know how I would behave with her anyway, if? . . . Third, she excites me, this is a fact (and much more so than Domnyashka, whom I like), and that she called me "handsome" also pleases me.

Having pondered awhile, I decided that I could not care less about what was to be—it would turn out all right. In due time we would see.

I eagerly made provisions about the horses and the lady's saddle, and we began to go out riding almost daily.

Magdalina Kirillovna was really a good rider and had a graceful hold upon the horse; however, she appeared heavier because of a bodice which was too tightly laced. Moreover, in the bright sunlight I observed that the evenness of her complexion was caused by a thin layer of something on her skin, and that her eyes were outlined with bluish and brown lines. This, incidentally, did not change anything. I liked her just as well and was just as excited when, for instance, we would ride slowly, close to each other, and she would suddenly place her gloveless hand upon the pommel of my saddle. She would chatter a bit, often looking at my face, but I was not listening. I thought of my excitement, about the fact that she had noticed it, and this would excite me all the more.

The third or fourth time Magdalina Kirillovna seemed nervous, as though upset by something. She did not laugh and did not even once place her hand on my saddle, yet all the while she seemed to be looking intently at me. It was hot, and we soon returned. But in the evening when we had finished our tea, when Domnyashka had led Uncle Odya up to bed and Mama had retired, Magdalina Kirillovna said abruptly:

"Vanichka, would you like to go for a short run, perhaps along this little path, up to the large maples? It's a pity to go to bed—it's so cool, and there is such a moon tonight!"

The moon, to be sure, was immense, copper-green, so common during those summer nights. It did not affect me—lately I had been preoccupied neither with the moon, nor with any sort of dreaming, nor had I been writing poems. Not that I had forgotten them, but for a time I had hidden them securely in some drawer and locked it.

I rose at once, however, and offered my hand to Magdalina Kirillovna.

We descended the stairway of the balcony and walked along a side path.

My companion was arrayed in something light and blue, draped from head to foot in a manner contrary to her custom. She walked slowly, in silence. Approaching the bench beneath a nearby maple, she said softly, "Let's sit down." We sat down.

"Are you a romantic, Vanya?" Magdalina Kirillovna said suddenly, even, perhaps, with a sigh. "Do you like sitting this way, looking at the infinite evening sky, at this indifferent moon? I can dream for hours . . . about what? I myself do not know. But maybe I do know. Where are you being carried on the wings of dreams, my dark-curled page?"

I looked at her in astonishment. Her face was raised toward the moon; the scarf on her head appeared gray. Her face did also.

"Aha," I thought. "So this is what you're driving at! No, you will not be successful in this. This is not the place for you."

At this moment she did not even excite me! I even regretted my former excitement. Hastily, with a certain rude impudence, I said:

"Imagine, oh beautiful lady, your page is not at all a romantic. He doesn't know how to dream, and the moon often seems to him merely a brass wash basin."

"Oh, I don't believe it, I don't believe that you don't know how to dream," said Magdalina Kirillovna, much more gaily, however. "All the youths in the world dream . . . at least, about love."

"This means that I am an exception. To dream, and about such things . . . Life is so beautiful in its simplicity, don't you think?" (At this point I moved nearer to her.) "One must seize the gifts of life, its each and every minute, not wasting time on any such dreams. Why do I need the cold moon when there is a hot sun?"

In order not to disturb the tone, while selecting these trivial expressions, I took hold of Magdalina Kirillovna's hand. I did so rather abruptly—I had not intended to—but it did not matter. She did not release her hand. Feeling it necessary to continue, I slowly raised her hand to my lips and kissed her palm. It was soft, warm, and had the fragrance of something familiarly sweet. Involuntarily I kissed it, again and again. Magdalina Kirillovna pressed herself to me for one moment, but then immediately stood up.

"So this is what you are like, Vanichka . . . enough, enough, oh secretive one! So you love the sun more than the moon! But I love everything, all kinds of things! Well, tomorrow we will again go out riding in the sunlight. I don't fear the heat. But now we must go home. Anna L'vova is not sleeping and perhaps is awaiting our return."

At this time she was speaking in her usual voice, without the sultriness induced by the moon's presence.

I did not know what to think. The next day I rode somewhat stupidly. The heat was exhausting. I had spent the night poorly —a sharp, familiar agitation would seize me momentarily and then fade away. When I glanced at her (I did not look long), Magdalina Kirillovna also appeared excited, or generally different.

"Let's not go far," she said. "Past the felling there's a path into the forest, along the stream."

It was very hot to ride past the felling. Nevertheless, the path wound evenly, and we kept a lively trot. Magdalina Kirillovna's capricious bay horse Laska was frisky, friskier than my Chestnut. When we turned into the forest and proceeded slowly, we were overcome by a spruce-like fragrance similar to an apple tree's, warm and moist. On the right, the brook, surrounded by bushes, was babbling. The place was very remote; the forest extended for miles. We soon passed through the spruce forest and entered a forest with mixed trees; the woods became denser as the path narrowed.

"You know, Vanya," Magdalina Kirillovna said suddenly, in a faint voice, "it is so beautiful here, but I seem to have overrated my strength."

"We can rest. Right here, beyond the turn, there will be a small clearing. Below the hillock . . . Would you like?"

I helped her down from the horse and carefully seated her on the moss, on the soft, fallen leaves. She leaned up against the solid tree trunk and closed her eyes. I tied up the horses and sat down beside her.

"Aren't you all right?" I murmured, perplexed, embracing her shoulders.

Is she about to have a fainting spell?

But she instantly gave herself to me, found my lips with her own . . . and it seemed to me that I was actually disappearing somewhere, was perishing, had already perished. For how many seconds did this kiss last? The sensation was so strong, so boundless that it even became destructive. Breaking loose from one insanity, I lapsed into another, suddenly losing my senses in a new way. With overpowering repulsion I felt her bosom on my chest, felt the smell of hot perspiration through the scent of perfume, felt all of her excited weight upon me. I half-felt, half-saw her eyes drowsy with desire, her short, cat-like face with its insane smile—a grimace on her lips as they were reaching mine for another kiss. I ceased making excuses for myself, indeed I could not—I had become bare physiology . . . as she had also.

Since, however, I was a human being, a young boy, I certainly behaved like an idiotic youngster.

"Leave me alone!" I shouted in a trembling voice, releasing her hands from my neck and jumping up. "You ought to be ashamed. You're an old, promiscuous woman. Just look at yourself! I have never, not even for one minute, liked you. Never! I say this not from virtue, I don't give a damn for it, but I find you repulsive! Repulsive!"

I could have added anything I felt like saying, even "I'll tell Mama on you!" I could have cried at the top of my lungs like a five-year-old—all this was possible. It seemed that I even stamped my feet. She arose, pale, went past me, her lips pressed together tightly, going over toward the horses. While passing, she appeared to make a motion with her whip, as if she wished to strike me . . . but she did not strike. (I was sorry afterwards that she had not, for I had deserved it.)

She untied her horse, mounted rather lightly, tearing only her veil—it had snagged on a branch—and immediately took to a trot along the narrow path. In the meantime I stood in one place and looked, without comprehending.

Comprehension came much later.

I began to cry and blew my nose for a long time, sitting on the hillock all the while. I then descended to the stream, washed myself, immersed my whole head in the water. Then I noticed that my horse was not there. Of course, while untying her own, Magdalina Kirillovna had accidentally untied Chestnut, and he must have followed her home.

What will they think at home? What will she say? What, in general, will happen when I arrive home?

But for me this long journey on foot through the forest in the gathering evening had been very beneficial. This was exactly the time when I came to my senses at last and understood the entire extent of my shame.

Well, I did not exactly understand it, how could I? But I sensed many things intuitively. I could succumb to the temptation of Magdalina Kirillovna or I could not; I could feel her repulsiveness, but to behave as I did, to say to her all that I had said, that I could not do. A man cannot. He then insults not the woman but the "feminine" in general. Besides, he loses his "masculine" honor.

The shame of losing this masculine honor gnawed at me, indeed devoured me, as I made my way homeward along the virgin soil, stumbling against the tree stumps, getting tangled in the piles of underbrush.

In the courtyard by the porch, enveloped by twilight, I encountered the housemaid Domnyashka.

"Oh, master," she began to chatter, her eyes shining slyly (she obviously sensed something), "how frightened we've been, your horse comes back to the estate by itself; the steward arrives; it has to be an accident, they said, but then, thank God, the lady returns, awfully tired, her clothes torn, and she explains everything to your Mama. Your Mama comes out to the steward and tells him everything, meaning that the event isn't important after all, and that all is well. The steward wanted to go find where you had disappeared to, but your Mama said it wasn't necessary, that you would come on foot. And now look how late you are . . . haven't had a bite to eat . . . Your Mama and the General have been waiting for you in the parlor, and the lady is in her own room, not feeling well, and I've heard that she has to go to Moscow tomorrow . . ."

Not hearing the rest, I entered the parlor at once. There a tall lamp was burning (it was lit only on solemn occasions). On the divan, sitting up straight, was Mama, her hands resting on her knees, and next to her, in the armchair, sat the General. His face was menacing.

I stopped at the threshold.

"Come here," said Mama, "and close the door."

There were three doors in the parlor, so I closed them all and went up to Mama.

"You are a hooligan," she said. "You should be tied up, locked up . . . You have dared, in your mother's house . . ."

I still did not understand. I was still thinking my own thoughts. Had Magdalina Kirillovna, in fact, told her? . . .

But the General, fixing his gray eyebrows upon me, muttered in a threatening manner:

"You have dared . . ."

In a moment it all became clear to me. A fit of ridiculous laughter constricted my throat. I held it back, of course. I had to consider quickly what must further be done, and I almost did not hear my mother's sobbing voice:

"She came back, raving . . . her veil was torn . . . I forced her to tell me the truth. This unfortunate woman, barely escaping the hands of a violator . . . And who is this violator? Who is this profligate? My son!"

She became breathless and then suddenly added, less pathetically:

"Now she will spread the news of this scandal across the whole of Moscow . . . It will be impossible for me to show myself anywhere . . ."

I had already formed a plan of action. The plan was desperate, but I felt in myself an unusual strength. I had been unwittingly delighted by what Magdalina Kirillovna had invented. How clever women are! Never would I have thought of such a thing! But indeed it was the right thing.

"Mama, listen. This is a serious misunderstanding. Magdalina Kirillovna is a very nervous person. She imagined God knows what; I didn't have time to release her veil from the twig—she galloped away as if possessed . . . I won't hide it, I almost did court her . . . But Mama! Is it like me to . . . ? Yes, it would have really been ridiculous if it weren't for your grief, and that of Magdalina Kirillovna, whom I deeply respect!"

In my voice was such sensible firmness (at the word "ridiculous" I grinned slightly), that Mama stared at me in confusion. But I continued:

"I can explain this to Magdalina Kirillovna herself in two minutes. How can she endure such a misunderstanding! You will see . . ."

"Oh no, no, don't go to her!" Mama cried out, noticing my

movement. "She will be in hysterics, and I had enough trouble calming her down with tranquilizers."

Uncle Odya, the General, who had fallen asleep, also emitted a threatening grumble.

But by now new strength was beginning to take possession of me. Shouting to Mama, "Sit here, wait a moment, you will see!" I dashed like a whirlwind up the staircase and literally thrust myself into Magdalina Kirillovna's room. The most genuine violator could not have done much better. With the slightest bit of reasoning I would certainly have hesitated to undertake my plan with such turbulence. Is it not natural to be frightened when a person who has just been slandered breaks into a room like that? Is it not even natural to think that I would most likely appear in order to heap new insults upon her?

There was, however, a different involuntary reaction; it was irrational. Dashing in, I fell to my knees at once in front of the sofa where Magdalina Kirillovna was lying. At once I grabbed her by the arms, kissed them, and then embraced her, jabbering incoherently:

"Forgive me . . . Forgive me, dear, kind . . . I was mad . . . Your kiss drove me insane . . . I have died, I have perished . . . Dear one, my life, my happiness . . . Did you actually see through it? . . . My enchantress . . . Forgive everything . . . Forgive, forgive me . . ."

We kissed again, it seemed, but I no longer sensed these kisses; I felt neither destroyed nor repelled. Maybe she had not noticed this, because, in fact, our kisses were not indifferent ones—only filled with a different excitement. Yet to this day I do not know whether she believed me then or not. Perhaps she pretended that she believed? But was this pretense for me, or for herself as well? Did she really want it that way for herself?

In the midst of the kisses I even recall assuring her that without her "I could live no longer" . . . Casually, though rather firmly, she remarked:

"Nonetheless, I must leave tomorrow for Moscow . . ."

I did not object; I only began saying with great haste that

I would be going there myself, that we would see each other there, and that it was already settled, was it not? She would not send me away? She would not forget?

She was smiling. But I saw little of her—all this happened very quickly, and the important thing that I remembered was a strong smell of Valerian drops coming from her and filling the entire room.

With Mama, of course, everything was taken care of—she did not go into detail; there was no scandal—thank God for that! Uncle Odya slept through everything. And what they chattered about in the kitchen, who cared?

It goes without saying that I did not show my face in any part of Moscow until September. I rested well. At first, whenever I recalled this story, I would think with a sigh of relief that anyway, as far as I was able, I had made amends for the sin against my masculine honor.

HUMILITY

St. Petersburg.

To recount why I transferred from Moscow University to St. Petersburg would take a long time, and it is not even important. Mama remained in Moscow with Uncle Odya, the General, who has by now completely fallen apart from old age.

I am living by myself in a small but very comfortable apartment. I have been studying quite a lot and enjoying myself a great deal. Companions are numerous; I have many good friends, too.

In our circle I have achieved a degree of recognition. I am called—and I call myself also—the "confirmed idealist." In jest they call me "Romeo without Juliet" and, in addition, "Brother John." But the latter is not witty, since I am a monk in the very

From *The Link* (Newspaper), no. 217, March 27, 1927.

least sense of the word. I am very elegant, I love a good table and handsome things, and I engage in sports. Moreover, all my chic lies in the fact that, although I am an "idealist,' I refuse nothing, neither a small party given by one of my acquaintances, nor a drinking bout of the most unidealistic sort. Neither shying away nor hiding, I, a "confirmed virgin," fearlesssly squandered this virginity of mine in the most inappropriate places. The happy quality of being able to drink—on occasion no less than the others—without becoming inebriated, has helped me very much. I did not reveal my convictions to anyone, did not preach anything; on the contrary, I laughingly entreated them by no means to imitate me, because my "convictions," I said, were well suited to me alone, and for another person they would be of no use. Nonetheless, I certainly could not resist the occasional feeling of my own superiority, somewhere in a cramped, musty back room in the middle of the night, while gazing at the red faces all around me, at perspiring hands extended toward bare shoulders or the legs of shrieking wenches. I did not permit myself to condemn anyone. I would only display a look of tender regret, nothing more. And my friends would not even notice that—*ils avaient autre chose à faire.*

My closest acquaintances were Nivinsky and Dorn. Different in everything—from outward appearance, manners, and character, to social position—both were considered, however, the ringleaders of our merry circle, the leading masterminds. Nivinsky was a heavyset, cheerful sort of merchant, bent on high style, wanting everything to be in a more refined fashion, the girls to be more expensive. The tall Baron Dorn, on the other hand, had a more mundane style, not from miserliness, but simply because the lower and the more base our escapades, the sweeter they appeared to him.

It was usually agreed that we would begin our activities in a more grandiose manner, on the highest level, for Nivinsky's sake, but toward morning the entire company, in order to please Dorn, would revert to the lower depths favored by him. By morning, of course, the others, including Nivinsky, could distinguish very little.

Neither of our main debauchees went without me. Roaring with laughter, they claimed that I "set the tone" for the whole company, and that in it "everything is pure because here we have an idealist." Underneath the joking I felt some kind of enviously respectful attitude toward me, which was certainly pleasant. Only once did Nivinsky utter an indecent and unforeseen vulgarity. But this happened amidst drunken tears; besides, he was in such a state that I didn't pay any attention.

At Christmas, after a brief recess (from studying!), we decided to do some carousing.

There were about six or seven of us. As always, we began at that time in the spirit of Nivinsky. Somehow everyone was scurrying about, constantly moving from place to place. Perhaps Dorn was rushing them. But although he was rushing them and we did not remain anywhere for any length of time, we still did not succeed in reaching Dorn's real hangouts.

As a result of this rushing, and from the continual jaunts into the cold air (the night was severely cold), the wine especially went to everyone's heads—seldom did I feel so much the only sober man among the drunks.

Along the road we burst in, almost by accident, to one of the shabbiest little houses on the Fifteenth line, by Maly Prospect. Neither a very clean nor a very dirty house—somewhere in between; it seemed that our group had already been there.

They burst in, to "warm up," but suddenly everyone, even Nivinsky, began to protest violently, "Why go out again into the frost? Why don't we remain here for the time being; what more do we need? Isn't there enough wine here?" Youthful, tow-haired Ladin even exclaimed, "We keep on carousing around, and everywhere there are only castles in the air! It's time to put a stop to this, for the sake of what is most vital!"

Drunken approvals rang out; the speech was taken to heart . . . or to the imagination. Someone even said, twisting his tongue with difficulty, "Of the convinced among us . . . there is only one idealist . . . But we are convinced . . . realists . . ." (He did not say "realists," but another word, which everyone liked as well.)

We were all dressed in civilian clothes, but the proprietress, a withered old German woman with her jowls hanging on her neck, Madame Ameli, surmised right then and there that this was a company of students, and that they were rich ones, besides. There were not too many patrons in the hall; moreover, they were not up to our standards, but probably of the middle class, and we immediately became the center of attraction. Bottles were brought in, a music box began to play (they were still using music boxes instead of gramophones in some establishments), and the young ladies of the house started dancing.

There were a fair number of these ladies. As to what they were like—I didn't notice. The fellows in our party, meanwhile, were getting more and more carried away. Laughing boisterously, they would catch the ladies by the edge of their skirts or else by their legs. Amid shouts, however, they made their selections and sneaked off in pairs.

"Idealist! Brother Johnny!" roared Nivinsky. "I have no courage, although the devil himself inspires me! Point out to me which one is the best! You can see better than I. And choose one for yourself, to instruct her in the quiet of your cell, so you won't lag behind the company. Which one . . . for me?"

"Take this one!" I said, grabbing by the hand the first one to come my way; she was standing by the table.

"M-marishka? Oh, to hell with her! She is too skinny, curse her. I'll have the velvety one over there!"

He got up and, tottering and looking back at me, walked over to the velvety one.

At times, in cases similar to this, I loved to show that I did not like to disturb the company, to "lag behind." I would choose a girl, lead her up to her door respectfully, advise her either at her door or behind it to use this time for a rest, to take a nap for twenty minutes or so; I would pay her generously—and then leave. The company knew this and undoubtedly esteemed such a comradely gesture.

"Are you Marishka?" I said to the girl whose hand I continued to hold. "Let's go."

She answered nothing and walked on ahead. Indeed rather

slender, she had dark hair falling in gentle waves; the nape of her neck was thin.

Her door was almost the first one along the corridor. Marishka opened it in front of me. At this time some people were still walking along the narrow corridor, and I slipped behind Marishka's door. And why shouldn't I enter her room? I remembered visiting some of them. I would not bother her. Perhaps, it would even be better to wait here than in the hall.

The room was an ordinary one, not very large. Across from the bed, over by the window, there was a table, and upon it a rather dim lamp. By the table stood a filthy-looking armchair. Marishka was fussing around the bed, taking off her clothes.

But I, as comfortable as possible, sank into the armchair, stretched out my legs, and began to smoke.

The wine had not intoxicated me. I have already mentioned this. But, in any case, it had affected me, and in an unusual way. If it had not affected me in any way, perhaps I would have left our company a long time ago. It is fatiguing for a sober person to be continually in the company of drunks, although at the same time it is also amusing. Many things appear to be very unsophisticated. A sober person may enjoy observing the others, watching what they are doing, realizing all the time that he is not like them. But by itself, even this *à la longue* could become boring for him. I had something else to amuse me.

I noticed that sometimes wine inspired a particular mood in me . . . or a condition. Wine acts not as an intoxicant or as a dulling influence, but as an enlightening one, as it were. I felt all of myself bound in one tight knot; I felt—and it is difficult to explain—almost elasticized, ready to spring, and transparent as well. Everything inside me was also becoming transparent— as though a dull, moist decal were beginning to slide off its picture. And it appeared that it would slide off at any moment . . . I was ready, I was waiting for it. The wine had turned me *as clear as crystal*—my feelings and thoughts, made transparent, had been completely prepared, for what I did not know, but for something which did not usually take place.

This mood was disturbing, but I loved it even though it was

transitory. It was produced not by the wine, but . . . I did not know by what. Of late it had been this wine which would "crystallize" me more often.

I was engrossed in thought, smoking, and I practically shuddered when I heard an insistent, rather vulgar whisper beside me:

"Well, what about you?"

Two dark, round eyes were glaring at me from Marishka's bed.

"Oh, yes!" I stretched out in the armchair, lit a fresh cigarette, and with a cautious tenderness began to utter my customary words to the girl, "Use this time for a rest . . . be calm, I will pay you well," . . . and so forth.

She listened, sitting quietly, and looked at me all the time with her round eyes.

"Go to sleep!" I said. "You will have many more customers."

No, she did not understand.

"And what about you?"

"Nothing about me."

With some impatience I explained to her that I did not "indulge in such things," that I only went around with my comrades to amuse myself and nothing more, that I was not "like them."

I tried to speak in accordance with her mentality, but she did not understand.

"How are you not like them?"

Her unblinking eyes were directed at me, the eyes of either a child or a young beast. The penetration of her gaze aroused my anxiety.

"Oh, you don't understand? Then listen to this."

And I, not only not humoring her, but purposely selecting those expressions which were totally foreign to her, began to explain that I was a "confirmed idealist," that I was a "virgin from principle," though not an "anchorite," that I was not afraid to betray my principles in any place, including a locale such as this squalid refuge here . . . For a man of such serious convictions it is sufficient to have just a little will power . . . My colleagues are good enough chaps, but they are not very discriminating. However, I do not pass judgment upon them. If the young lady fails to understand, it is not my fault. I am giving her all the necessary explanations . . .

I continued to chatter for a long time, leisurely crossing my outstretched legs, and smoking. Not once did she interrupt me —she merely kept on looking straight at me, not batting an eyelash, with her disturbingly fixed gaze.

Finally, I, too, fell silent and also began to look at her, at her wearied face with the sunken cheeks, at her frail bare arms, at her entire small body, huddled in the corner of her wide bed.

Our strange silence lasted for several seconds.

Suddenly she uttered:

"What a scoundrel you are . . ."

And then again, once more, with quiet assurance:

"A scoundrel is what you are . . ."

Her words went right through me—into my crystallized, prepared soul—no, not into my soul but through my entire being. The decal's faded paper had slipped off.

I sat on the edge of the wide bed and kissed Marishka's thin arms.

And so, on that night, with a humble little prostitute I humbly lost my virginity.

THE MOUNTAIN CORNEL

. . . Sometimes it occurs to me—was it not in vain that I decided to write such strange memoirs, of love stories? If only I were a celebrity, or if only my love stories were in some way unusual! But I am an average man; those whom I loved and who loved me were likewise; besides, writing is not my specialty—I can only relate in a simple manner that this and that took place.

From *Russia Illustrated*, no. 17, April 23, 1927.

One thing is comforting—the issue here is not the person but, as I have already said, love itself. Love itself is so far beyond the "average" that whenever it touches someone with its feather, even slightly, everything becomes different. At this moment, if we are to believe Vladimir Solovyov,[1] "both the Heavens and the nether world" begin attentively to watch over that person. And his human essence, his inimitable self, reveals itself.

My love stories, of course, resemble the stories of many Ivan Leonidoviches, Petroviches, Sergeeviches . . . But let Ivan Petrovich take note of how he resembles me and how he does not, and he will come to know himself better. I could have listened with pleasure to the love stories of the Ivan Petróviches if they had recounted them honestly, as I have done, for I am very much interested in all people . . . both the unusual and the usual.

The story which I will relate is perhaps not a story at all . . . it depends, though, on how you look at it.

I was sitting on a long veranda of the kursaal, not far from the spring in the park, with my new acquaintance, Nikolay Danilovich. Midday was approaching; the park was deserted.

I was a dandified, rather handsome St. Petersburg student. I happened to come to this mountain resort—a provincial wilderness!—rather unexpectedly. I had an argument with Nina . . . it wasn't that we argued, but something like it . . . (I doubt that I will relate this story about Nina, for it is not very much of a "love story.") In the course of our conversation I said that I was becoming bored with Yalta, and if she made any more scenes I would leave. Moreover, Nina's husband was expected to arrive in Yalta in ten days. Nina said to me, in her inane womanly fashion, "You shall not leave!" Early the following morning I boarded a ship and left . . . went as far as possible, with a feeling of freedom and satisfaction. I chanced upon this place, and I liked it here very much. So I let Nina brood over it at her leisure. Nothing will happen to her if she waits. For the time being I was preoccupied with something else.

1 Solovyov, Vladimir Sergeevich (1853–1900). Famous and influential Russian religious philosopher, poet, and critic. He greatly influenced the *Weltanschauung* of the Russian Symbolist poets.

"Oh, so you are acquainted?" said Nikolay Danilovich, looking at me cheerfully.

"In the rotunda, at the children's party, they introduced us . . . it was her brother, I believe."

"The eldest? Or was it Mitya? Oh, that one is a good-for-nothing. A lanky fellow, still stuck in the fourth grade. You know, her entire nature is revealed by this: she would attend a children's party, just for half an hour, but for nothing in the world would she dance on a Sunday! Take a look at our local young ladies—they do nothing but attend concerts; they don't walk one step further than the main avenue—yet they're surrounded by escorts! Ol'ga Gvozdeva, for example, now there's a coquette! Yet what about her, you may ask? She's not at all interesting."

I did not find Olya Gvozdeva interesting, but she seemed amusing to me, just like this whole flock of provincial young ladies. The one whom we were discussing did not hold my attention at all.

"The local youths certainly don't consider her interesting," Nikolay Danilovich went on. "But what do they know! If a girl is modest, keeps herself at a distance with a book in her hand, doesn't laugh out loud, doesn't flirt—they wouldn't notice her, even if she were a raving beauty . . . Now, this is the second year she's come to the resort, and I can tell you frankly—she is the most beautiful of them all."

"You are indeed in love, Nikolay Danilovich! Had I only known it! They introduced us in passing . . . and I didn't even succeed in getting a good look at her."

"I've loved her for a long time," Nikolay Danilovich confessed. "And somehow things still haven't turned out right."

He pinched his round, ruddy beard and became thoughtful. He had trusting, meek, blue eyes. I asked him sympathetically, "Why haven't they turned out right?"

"Well, you see . . . it was also because of me. I haven't been very resolute about the whole thing. She is no conversationalist, and I myself can't approach people very well. There are also some other considerations: she's nineteen, whereas I'm already thirty-four. Her family is very distinguished in this area, although they're not wealthy; they live in Tiflis. But here, it is wilderness, there's music and everything of the sort—during one season only, but the season is short, and I'm a whole ten miles from the place. Besides, what am I? I am only junior manager of the Grand Duke's estate, where no princes ever stay . . . and that's all there is to it."

"Really, what nonsense this is! You even contradict yourself. If she keeps apart from the others, why should she mind the wilderness? Only her love is important."

"Her love! But does she love?"

I almost burst laughing, but he was so kind, so sincere—even to the point of *naïveté*—that I became sorry for him.

"Don't be afraid. Look, I'll meet with her again . . . I'll make you a fair prediction—maybe she's loved you for a long time . . ."

Nikolay Danilovich's face lit up with a smile. He drew near to me and began to speak in great haste.

"I'm waiting for her to pass by here. After breakfast she often sets out for this place, the ravine. You're not aware of it, but these local girls, these southerners, especially from distinguished old families, are often secretive, but quick . . . Unfortunately, it's time for me to leave now—the horse is ready at the lodge. I wanted to see her today for a moment; tomorrow I must be off for the Atskhel sawmill, and I won't return for three or four days . . ."

"You wanted to have a chat today?"

"No, what are you saying!" Nikolay Danilovich became terrified. "I might not even dare approach her. Or I'll only say hello. What are you saying! I just want to see her."

He was a touching sight, this strong, heavyset gentleman with the kind face. And his love was obviously just as strong; by virtue of its strength, it was timid as well.

I liked him. I also liked the park, the veranda surrounded by the wild grapes, and the sky. How clear and soothing it was! What foliage, what coolness in the ravines, how loudly the mountain brook babbled on, just like silk! The warm paths up above, on one side of which there was a cliff, whereas on the other—a feathery sea of green tree tops reaching the very edge of the sky . . .

I also loved the unassuming kursaal and the darling, coquettish, young ladies dancing to the music with their escorts—overgrown high school students. How did I not notice Nikolay Danilovich's Beatrice, Sonichka Enikadze?

"There she is!" Nikolay Danilovich whispered loudly and sprang to his feet.

He had noticed her earlier, but I saw her only while she was walking along the veranda, on the shaded side; she had to pass us in the park.

She had dark, smooth hair. She was without a hat, wearing a blue dress with small crimson flowers on it and holding a scarf and a book in one hand. Over her other arm hung such a long braid that if she had not tied it up, its brown ribbon would have reached below her skirt hem. Downcast lashes fell in black half-curls upon her dark, fresh, unrouged cheeks.

Nikolay Danilovich jumped up and stood as though rooted to the spot. I was about to leave, not wishing to disturb them. But seeing that perhaps from indecision he would not approach her at all, I also rose. When she approached us, we moved forward together.

"Sofya L'vova . . . Good morning . . . Oh, did I frighten you?"

She was not frightened, however. She raised her lashes; her fresh face turned a delicate scarlet.

"Can it be that you're going for a walk?" Nikolay Danilovich inquired rather stupidly, clearing his throat. "How unfortunate I am. I'm going home right now. It's so charming in the park at this hour. But you always love to take walks by yourself . . ."

"Oh, no . . ." she said in embarrassment. "I really don't go very far . . . Just a short way into the ravine . . ."

"So then, will you permit me, the next time, to infringe upon your solitude?" insisted the emboldened (due to my presence, most likely) Nikolay Danilovich. "How very unfortunate I am now, for the horse is out there at the lodge, and tomorrow I'll be off for the sawmill . . . such misfortune!"

Without smiling, Sonichka flushed and obviously did not know what to say. She whispered, "Certainly, I always . . . I never go very far . . . I have one favorite little bench there . . ."

"Perhaps today you'll permit me to accompany you to your little bench?" I said suddenly. "It's very annoying that my friend must hurry this way . . . It's such a lovely time of day . . ."

While saying this, I cast a knowing glance at Nikolay Danilovich. I received his grateful look and vigorous handclasp at parting. He understood that I wished to help him.

Sonichka and I then retreated into the verdant depths of the ravine. First the murmuring, then the hum of the stream could be heard as it hopped along the stones, not breaking, but only rippling and ruffling the silence with its gentle waves. It smelled of warm moisture and of mildly penetrating mosses and herbs. I looked at the dense shadow of Sonichka's lowered eyelashes, at her fresh, half-childish little face, and it seemed to me that this softly swaying grassy aroma came from her, from her blue frock.

I was saying something trite, of no significance, for I had decided that she was a shy girl, and that she must first of all be allowed to rest from her embarrassment. But when we reached "her" bench—below the cliff's projection, as though beneath a vault—I saw that my companion was not shying away very much. She often raised her lashes. Her eyes were beautiful—dark, without the slightest sparkle. Were they timid? I do not know, but they were incomprehensible.

She even smiled. Once she even laughed, displaying a row of very even white teeth. I attempted to speak about Nikolay Danilovich, but she stopped smiling, as though she had closed herself off. I again began relating some trivial thing. I asked her what she was reading. She showed me, although I had already noticed myself—it was the verse of a contemporary poet, not a very good one.

We strolled for about two hours.

"I'll take a detour," said Sonichka, as we approached the main pathway. "There will be music very soon, and I'm not in the mood for it. But you go to the music."

She extended to me a small suntanned hand, her luxurious braid wound around her wrist. I was about to tell her that I hoped soon to repeat our "marvelous" promenade . . . or something of the sort—when she suddenly added (and, I admit, it startled me with its unexpectedness):

"Come to the same bench tomorrow."

She said it so simply, without smiling, without embarrassment, and left so innocently nodding her head to me, that at first I wondered—had I heard correctly? And then—didn't I have a poor imagination? Didn't she say this in a childlike way, just as children would say, "Can we go for a walk tomorrow, too?"

In any case it was time for me to become accustomed to the incomprehensibility of women. It had astonished, agitated me for a long time. But hadn't I decided, hadn't I promised myself never to let anything surprise me, always to expect anything, and not even to attempt to find a solution?

The decision had been a wise one. Only I myself, alas, had still not attained wisdom. I had only had a presentiment of it, but I still did not know what is—for us—the eternal secret in a woman; it is useless, though, to try to define it, because it constitutes the same secret for the woman herself . . . And the best thing of all is not to think about it.

The next day I set off, naturally, for Sonichka's bench. Although I arrived early, Sonichka was already there.

She wore her blue frock and a scarf, but she was without a book. The patches of sunlight again flickered through the thicket, and there was the same smell, still more penetrating, grassy, moist, and warm. Sonya was even more charming today, as fresh as a tall bluebell in the grass.

I could not even find anything to say right away. I silently kissed her hand (she was not surprised) and sat down beside her. I then began speaking—not very coherently, but ardently—about the sun, the verdure, about the stream whispering over the stones, about the fact that these things seemed to me real and living, and that I had never seen anything like this before, never had felt anything so intensely.

She did not interrupt me, looked straight in front of her, not lowering her eyelashes. Not only did she not lower them, but even turned her quiet gaze upon me, when I began to tell how she resembled all this fresh summer enchantment. I also mentioned the bluebell to her.

Suddenly I interrupted my own ardent speech. I paused. What was this? . . .

"Let's go for a walk," said Sonichka. "Only for a little while. Today I must go home early."

Using the slippery green stones, we crossed over to the opposite side of the stream and headed toward the mouth of the ravine.

Trying to change the tone, I told her about St. Petersburg, about this thing and that . . . However, she listened with her former seriousness and attentiveness. She then said:

"You're probably very lonely there . . . However, one feels lonely everywhere . . ."

I inquired how she lived, whether she had any friends . . . But all the while for some reason I was afraid to depart from my flippant tone, which somehow was not coming across too well.

"You're a shy girl, always carrying a book . . ."

"No, that's not so . . . But then, what friends would I have?"

For one second I remembered Nikolay Danilovich and then immediately forgot him. At the gates of the park, while saying farewell, I myself asked this time:

"Will you come tomorrow?"

The charming, incomprehensible eyes looked at me in surprise:

"Of course."

I glanced around—there was no one there—and again kissed her hand.

"And if you wish . . ." she suddenly added, pensively, "over there, by the lower park, there is a path leading to the mountain, into the forest, over to the brickyard; the yard will remain below us . . . Do you want to go there? It is also a favorite place of mine . . ."

We resolved to meet at the lower park.

I arrived home in a cheerful and terribly lighthearted frame of mind. I was surprised at nothing, thought about nothing, everything was splendid. Before me lay an endless succession of wonderful days, a whole line of fragrant promenades with Sonichka. It is really ridiculous for people to think and worry about things: we only need to approach life simply—and how pleasant it can be!

A little later I proceeded to the kursaal, courted the young ladies, even showered Olya Gvozdeva with half-compliments or half-impertinences (it was acceptable here, according to the fashion). However, I did not remain long, and returning to my room on this pitch-black night and hearing the voice of the water from the darkness, I wanted all the time to catch sight of the stars through the indistinguishable branches. For some reason it was important for me to catch sight of even one. Approaching the hotel, I saw many of them, huge, simple ones—and became comforted.

A mountain path. Sonya's white scarf. The green waves of lavish tree tops along the precipice—as though flying above us. The sun, the sun . . . its gently sloping rays slide along the green sea. Cornel bushes, tall, dense, and dark. Beneath them, parched by the sun, raspberries—red, fallen berries. They taste good only when the sun ripens their tender bodies through and through, rocking them in the moss, in their warm cradle.

Beneath the cornel bushes it was as if we were in a hut. Her dark girlish cheek, her lips, innocent and scarlet, like a sunlit cornel. I bent down, lower, closer, still closer . . . Was I really kissing this tender cheek? Yes, perhaps . . . It seemed that, yes . . .

All at once the trusting arms embraced me; her braid, pressing against me, tickled me; I could see her lustreless eyes—were they incomprehensible? Comprehensible? Passionate? Innocent?

"I will love you so much . . . Will love you so much . . ."

Who within me suddenly disengaged these embracing arms? I arose and lifted her up. She raised herself submissively, pressing her dark head toward me with a childlike trust. I had to put my arm around her shoulders, and thus, together, we headed downward. In silence. I quickened my pace, supporting her light body.

When the first houses came into view, I discreetly released her arm and looked at her. Her downcast eyes were almost closed. What profound happiness was reflected on this face . . . Suddenly (from the lower park) the music pealed out, scattering along the mountains like brittle glass.

"Tomorrow . . . will you come to see us?" Sonya asked.

She raised her eyelashes. Her beautiful eyes were suffused with radiance and tears.

"To your house? Yes, yes, of course," I muttered. "I shall come tomorrow. I shall come without fail."

Hurriedly and becoming flustered, I repeated, "Tomorrow, to your house, of course . . . Yes, yes . . ."

She wanted, it seemed, to smile but she did not—the radiance of her tears was filling her eyes all the while. Not far away a wicket gate banged. I was, therefore, unable even to kiss her hand. Sonya tossed her white scarf onto her head and quickly slipped down the lane. Her home was there.

I remained behind.

"Dear Sofya L'vovna" . . . No . . . "Dear, sweet Sonya" . . . No, simply, "For the love of God, on my knees I am begging you" . . . No, it is better to be more blasé, "I do not know, I am not sure, that I love you as you deserve. I must leave, by myself" . . . What—by myself? What nonsense, nothing is necessary. Only go to her and say . . . oh, no, I would be like Lermontov's *Hero of Our Times*.[2] I knew that I could not do that.

Only toward morning did I fall asleep. A familiar voice roused me:

"Please forgive me for bursting in this way. I thought . . .

2 Ref. to Pechorin in Lermontov's novel *The Hero of Our Times* (1840).

since it is already late, I thought that we would have lunch together and later go for a walk. Fortunately, I have finished my business at the sawmill earlier . . ."

Nikolay Danilovich! I remembered everything. The radiance and tears in her eyes . . . I felt a cold malice toward Nikolay Danilovich.

"Oh, my dear fellow," I said in a hypocritically sorrowful tone (surprising even myself). "You are lucky, whereas I'm unfortunate. I've received a telegram—I'm due to leave today at four! This is not important, though, and I'm leaving you my blessing."

"Oh, really? What a shame! But . . . what kind of blessing?"

"She . . . if she doesn't love you yet, then she is prepared to love. Only be very, very cautious. She is a shy girl; take your time. You could spoil everything."

Nikolay Danilovich sank into a chair.

"It is true? Oh, how am I to thank you . . . The important thing is that I can hope; I am a patient man. It's a shame, though, that you're leaving. Anyway, we still have time until four o'clock to have lunch in the kursaal and go out together . . ."

Convincing him that I still had to get my things together and pack, I managed to get rid of him. He promised to be at the station by four—to see me off.

However, I left—not at four, but on the three o'clock train.

And certainly not to Yalta—to the devil with both Yalta and Nina! I went straight to St. Petersburg.

WHAT IS THIS?

I am in an anguished state.

Had I understood a bit earlier what was happening to me,

From *The Link* (Magazine), no. 1, July 1, 1927.

perhaps it might have been possible to prevent some of it, or would it have been impossible? But I had not understood it; that is, I had understood it God knows how . . . with a smile. I had considered it from its comical side. (I am very conscious of my own comic nature.) However, I soon discovered what exactly constitutes a tragicomedy or even a comico-tragedy. Something else, besides, was revealed to me . . . but I have not to this day found the words for it.

I will relate it from the beginning. In the summer, at Tsarskoe Selo, I made the acquaintance of Anna Nering, the daughter of our university professor, and by September I began to frequent their home as her fiancé.

It was, by all considerations, early for me to marry, but what young man in love thinks of this? Very likely, it was early for even Anna to be married—she had hardly reached her eighteenth year. At first sight, however, she might easily have been taken for older, for she was so tall, strong, had such a confident manner, and such . . . not exactly gracious—this word is not suitable at all—rather, "intelligent" movements.

She was a student at the Women's University, but devoid of the typical traits of either an old or a young female student. True, she played sports . . . but was even this so typical for a new girl student? Yes, Anna loved sports. In fact, we first met on a tennis court in Tsarskoe Selo.

Speaking for myself, I do not remember when I proposed to her, or even if there was a "proposal." Somehow it turned out that we began to discuss our wedding and our married life as though it were an established fact and could not have been otherwise.

We argued frequently, though always about irrelevant things. She was often victorious. But of our love for one another we had no doubt.

And what was there to doubt? I did actually love her. Spiritually? In truth, I am unable to make such distinctions in love; that is, here is the soul, and there is the body. To love means to love, and that's all there is to it. Perhaps one does not consider it in such a light; one approaches it from a different angle . . . yet one ought to love the entire person without regard to reason.

I would not say that Anna inspired in me an intense, all-absorbing passion, but a passion there was, and a very strong one. I felt that Anna was—necessary. She responded ardently to something within me—by her voice, a low contralto, the luxurious auburn waves of her hair, the "intelligent" movements of her muscular body, and even by her steadfast obstinacy during our arguments.

I saw that her attitude toward me, although peculiar in its own way, resembled my attitude toward her. She was the one who first kissed me—not expertly (after all, she was only eighteen!), without any joy but with an awareness of her power over me, and I felt that this kiss was "ours." And then, always—not often, it is true—it would happen that she was first to embrace me affectionately and imperiously; she would bend my head over and kiss me. Not that I did not dare to do this—why shouldn't I dare?—but I liked this particular movement of hers toward me, awaited it, and reciprocated it passionately.

I am not a weak and timid man, but in this girl, in her entire being, there was something which gave me an acute delight in being submissive to her, in following her. Capricious feminine domination is well known to me. Anna lacked this quality; however, there was something direct, unaffected, and natural in her, and thereby alluring. We were fiancé and fiancée; at times, strange as it seems, it was impossible to determine which one of us was the bride and which one was the bridegroom.

I was subject, moreover, to fits of rage. I would suddenly refuse to yield, would argue vehemently, almost with irritation, and was joyous when I would gain the upper hand. But we never reached the point of a serious quarrel—Anna had an even temper and was not at all prone to sulking.

The professor (not one of the most illustrious) was an old man and an eccentric, paying little attention to anything. Anna was indifferent toward him; she was close to her mother.

In the evenings, at tea, the three of us would sit together;

only rarely would the professor come in, in his dressing gown, goodheartedly joking, "I have come to pay a call on my Annas and the young gentleman . . ."

He called his daughter "Anna the big," and his wife, "Anna the small." My Anna took after her father both in her stature and her red hair (the professor's was turning gray); indeed, she did seem big next to her mother. Certainly not everybody would have believed that this slender, dark-haired, pensive woman was Anna's mother. At our first encounter I thought to myself—isn't she her stepmother? Isn't she the professor's second wife? But it turned out not to be that way.

"Do you find Mama youthful?" Anna once asked me. "And isn't it true that I don't resemble her at all? Everyone says so. Oh, Mama leads such a life of her own that it appears she will never age . . . I have her portrait as a young girl. Exactly the same, only her dress is different. And she was even younger than I when she married!"

I was very fond of our evenings at the tea table. If the conversation lapsed into an argument with Anna, Anna Romual'dovna more often would take my side. Since she was a woman of a few words, she would only shake her dark head, smiling, and say two or three words, very simply and precisely, blushing like a small girl.

One time—it was in winter, and our wedding was to take place in February—Anna and I had a bitter quarrel. I won the argument, and she fell silent. However, feeling myself in good form (a fit of rage had overtaken me), I continued to speak. From the original subject of the argument—some book or other—I jumped to discourses on more general topics, almost lecturing on the philosophy of art, and finally on poetry . . . Anna listened, knitting her brows. In the heat of inspiration I looked at Anna Romual'dovna, and involuntarily stopped—her face was so beautiful. It was all-attentive—there was a questioning in her glance, and in her parted lips there was something childish or girlish. Of whom did she remind me? Whom did she resemble? Only after a moment my favorite painting of Murillo [1] stood before

1 Murillo, Bartolome Esteban (1816–82), Spanish painter.

me—the delicate oval of her rosy-swarthy face, the dark locks near her ears, and the attentive half-puzzled look in her widely opened eyes. How it always penetrated me—this look!

On the way home at night, sunk in thought, I remained standing for a short time near the Summer Garden, gazing at the trees in their fur coats, blue in the moonlight, and at the blue, snow-covered expanses of the Marsovo Field. Somewhere runners were screeching sharply, and I could hear the crunch of sporadic footsteps. A strange languor overpowered me. I thought of Anna . . . Romual'dovna? No, of Anna. Yes, and Anna Romual'dovna as well. Of both of them?

My languor passed in a few days. Everything within me was becoming more intense, more oppressive; at times it even gave rise to irritations. I became nostalgic and, as I like to be frank with myself, I asked myself honestly—perhaps I am not in love with Anna, but with her mother?

Yet so strongly and so ardently did I feel Anna's presence that it was as clear as crystal—I was indeed in love with Anna.

However . . .

It was late. I was sitting in my study, smoking, when it occurred to me for the first time that I was in love with *the two of them.*

I was beside myself with laughter. With the two of them! What kind of whim was this? "Marya Antonovna! Anna Andreevna!" [2] With whom, then, shall I retire to the refuge of the streams? [3] Certainly with Marya Antonovna, since Anna Andreevna—alias Anna Romual'dovna—"is to some extent married . . ." [4]

I felt that I loved them with equal intensity, and I loved one stronger than the other only when I would mentally reject the first one in favor of the second. I would then love more strongly the one whom I had just rejected.

I laughed, I jeered at myself, but I can say in all sincerity that not everything was funny here—my pain was not funny at all, nor was the intense, sudden burning of this twofold love. It was

[2] Ref. Gogol's play *The Inspector-General*, Act IV, Scene XIII.
[3] Ibid.
[4] Ibid.

the most real burning sensation, which I knew neither how to cope with nor understand.

I was only happy . . . no, not happy, but I enjoyed a slight respite from suffering when both of them would sit with me in the evening, both Annas. However, even then I would become reflective at certain moments, lost in thought, would not hear the questions.

Anna would embrace me in the anteroom as before, and I would respond avidly to her kisses. This would be a moment of oblivion. But hardly would I leave, when Murillo's eyes would be looking at me, and I would drop off to sleep with a feeling of pain, of betrayal, for "her" . . . and for myself.

Naturally, I thought all the while that this was an empty whim, a fantasy, a delusion which would soon pass. But it did not pass, and I was becoming more and more irritable. At this point I no longer started arguments with Anna but moved directly into quarrels. Finally it happened—one evening Anna, without answering me, arose, pale, and quickly left the room.

I gazed vacantly after her and vacantly began to leaf through some albums which were on the table, when suddenly Anna Romual'dovna appeared at the door.

"Why don't you and Anna live more peacefully?" she said softly and hesitating a little. "If, perhaps, you don't . . . that is, if she isn't . . ."

I mumbled, "No, no." We both looked at each other disconcertedly. I remember perfectly well that she had a disconcerted look about her.

"If Anna doesn't want me to come, then I won't," I said at once (and unexpectedly for myself). "When she wishes, she may call me."

Without saying good-bye, understanding little of what I was doing and why, I turned away, unhurriedly put on my overcoat in the anteroom, and went home.

Thereafter I began to stay at home permanently, in a torpor. What was I waiting for? What did I intend to do? What did I want?

Nothing. Nothing. Perhaps if I were to search my memory and describe in words my desire which was then inexpressible, it would be expressed thus—that Anna should come; that I would tell her everything; that she would understand it all and decide for me what was to be done in the future, and I would just submit to her. But I knew too well that this was impossible. Such absurd, impossible desires we are instinctively afraid to make into thought.

Of course, an ordinary thought, a most natural one, preyed on my mind—to leave both of them. Yet somehow this thought was not within me, but around me, as it were. I saw it from one side, as if it were someone else's. Such an escape would be very suitable for another in a similarly hopeless situation, but . . . not for me.

Winter twilight. I did not even remember whether it was dawn or dusk, or which day it was.

I put on the lamp, but then put it out. For what purpose? I lay on the wide divan anyhow, among the wearisome pillows, in a dull frame of mind, doing nothing, not even desiring to smoke.

What a repulsive silence! And in the apartment (for I lived alone), and behind the bright lilac four-cornered windows, it seemed there was the same silence. My windows were high up; they contained nothing besides this regular, even, lilac quality. And I could hear . . . but what really could be heard from below, from the wintry street, even though the corner of Mokhovaya Street is such a busy place? Nothing could be heard. So there it was—simply this wintry, snow-covered, murky, lilac silence.

Nevertheless, it was repulsive. Stifling. Oh, how I longed to hear a sound! I want, I want, I want a sound . . .

A sound came. A short ring of an electric bell.

With an unusual swiftness I jumped up from the divan. No guessing, but certainty—this was the important event.

"How good it is . . . that I have caught you in. I must have two words with you . . . just for a minute. I can say it here . . ."

"What are you saying! Come in. Do come in."

I took her by the hand and led her into my study through the dining room, which was still lit.

She walked obediently, gazing at me with frightened eyes from under her fur cap, and obediently seated herself on the divan where I asked her to sit. I was on the point of putting on the lamp, but I felt sorry for her dear face—it was entirely in the light of the lilac windows, such a lively and indiscreet light. And she, as though having guessed, said timidly, "Very good, indeed. It is still light. I will be going right away. Just two words."

She stopped. I was silent.

"Only two words. To find out. You said, 'She will call.' But how can she call? I did not tell her. Just think, if she loves you. Furthermore, it was all because of some trifles. If you do love her . . . or, if you do not love her . . ."

I fell to my knees on the carpet and embraced her knees.

"I love, I love . . . I love you . . ." I whispered in a frenzy, kissing her dress. "I love you . . ."

She cried out faintly and made a weak motion . . . but I was already holding her arms, kissing her pale, tender face which smelled of the fresh cold air, kissing her frightened eyes, and I saw how the fear reflected in them was slowly subsiding, how her lashes were growing heavy . . .

Everything in novels proceeds swiftly, smoothly, simply. In life it is infinitely more complex, more awkward, more trivial—even funnier. But in our case it happened as it does in novels—with a nonexistent simplicity and irresistibility. For she must have felt this irresistibility and, thus, did not oppose it.

Her face, suffused with tears, was upon my shoulder. A soft whisper, confused, bewildered, and submissive:

"You love me? . . . I love . . . oh, what is this . . . what is this?"

She cried, burying her face in the pillows.

It was by now completely dark. I put on the lamp, lowered

the lampshade, then returned to her and caressed her trembling shoulders.

"Anna, my love . . . Don't cry. Do you hear me? Don't cry, my beloved."

Obediently, she turned her face toward me and whispered:

"What is there to be done now? What is to be done?"

I knew what was to be done. Embracing her, comforting her like a child, I was thinking not of her, but of all of us. I knew that what would happen was inevitable, as inevitable as what had happened before.

I loved her, my little Anna. I loved her at that moment with the entire fullness of my love—for her. Now I had not merely a presentiment, but knew that I needed her. Her innocently resigned body, her surrendering, puzzled eyes filled with a quiet light. Yet . . . I loved the other Anna as well. I had never loved her with such pain and sharpness. Never had I so longed for her to lay her head on my shoulder, to weep as little Anna was now weeping before me, or to feel her comforting hand on my hair. Yes, indeed, my other Anna—yes, indeed, I needed her too.

But next to Necessity stood Impossibility. I—was one being, and my love—was one being, and both Annas within me—were one being . . . But only within me, only within me, alas!

"Anna," I said, "you do understand, you do understand . . ." (She nodded her head, but I knew she could understand nothing, just as the other Anna would not understand. Did I myself understand?) "You will understand that we need time now. We must soon . . . part, never more to see each other. I will write to Anna. Don't fear, she will see that I am unworthy of her. She will forget, for she is so young. I will go away, will write to you. And when it is forgotten, after some time . . . Do you understand?"

She understood, she assented, but again began to cry, without, it seems, being aware of it. Tears streamed from her dark, wide-open eyes.

I no longer recall what else I said to her, how I consoled her, which words of tenderness my love was able to find. Certainly I was not lying. I lied only about external things, shrouding them in falsehood, which she was in no way able to comprehend. A lie in love is sent as a gift of mercy, as a garment for shielding the cruel and incomprehensible truth of Love. For can the human gaze endure its nakedness?

Indeed, I myself could not endure it.

I remember, as though it were yesterday, the hours which I then spent alone in my study. The last, poignant sensation of happiness—certainly I did love the one who was there at that time—and the last, poignant sensation of pain, of longing for another, the one who was just as necessary, the one who was likewise loved by me. And beyond my happiness and beyond my pain there was the shroud of Impossibility, which I accepted at last, bowing my head before it—yes, I must leave them both.

It was there, at the same moment (oh, how strange is man!), that the coarse, petty devil, in stupid self-derision, was still twisting about—he was again leaping, as in [Gogol's] "Fair." [5] Again he guffawed; again there were "Marya Antonovna" and "Anna Andreevna," and their "So, you are in love with her?" Again he whimpered, "So, what does all this mean? One is not enough for you . . . You need two at once! And now you are planning, exactly like Ivan Aleksandrovich Khlestakov, to take leave of both of these women and head for the next county? Let's assume, it is not quite so, for you have lingered with one of them for a little while . . ."

Ugh, even at this moment it is oppressive and frightening to think about it, yet not shameful. For even at that time I felt that, although there was no way of knowing what this twofold love of mine was, and although even later I was unable to find the necessary words and never did, there was nothing shameful in it. Unless, of course, you would look at things as the devil would; that is, from his single, devilish, petty side.

I wrote to Anna, adorning my love with the same merciful,

[5] Ref. to Gogol's "Sorochinskaya yarmarka" (1831–32).

tender garment of falsehood which is sent to us as a blessing and a respite. Then I left—for a long time.

I never met either of them again.

YOU—ARE YOU

I began my recovery from a severe illness on the first day of the holidays. For convalescence I went to the most festive country, to the gay, "azure" south of France.

I was already quite well, by the way. Or almost completely well, for I still felt that every day new strengths were developing and increasing within me and that, parallel to them, a joyful gaiety was growing in my body. Just as in childhood—thoughtlessness, a pleasant tremor from within, and you want . . . well, you don't exactly know what you want, except just to run, to run forward throwing back your arms, to laugh, to have the wind beating at your face.

A slender and youthful-looking man (for after the illness I actually looked about twenty years old), I nevertheless appeared too lanky. What would the refined English ladies have said if I were suddenly to go darting along the promenade like that? So at first I was forced to substitute a bicycle for running, but later I rented a small car by the week—a Renault—and went out on my own, at times like a madman, simply in order to go tearing along.

I lived in Menton's Palace Hotel, but it would be more proper to say that I lived everywhere—in Nice, in Monte Carlo, and in Cannes. All these places, it seemed to me, constituted one endless, delightful beach with the same fashionable ladies. I was in love—oh, of course—only I didn't know with whom. I still hadn't decided, and in the meantime I was in love with everyone.

From *The Link* (Newspaper), no. 225, May 22, 1927.

The casino did not entice me at all. Excited by the lights, the movement, and the constant presentiment of some unknown, mysterious joy—why should I listen to the monotonous flashes of dice in the stifling semidarkness? To Monte Carlo I definitely preferred the flowers and the palm trees of the park, and, in the evening, the glitter of the Café de Paris.

I became entirely immersed in the whirl of carnival days. I wanted to be everywhere at once—in Cannes, in Menton, and in Nice.

I traveled everywhere, took a look at everything, and dashed along the streets strewn with confetti. I became mixed up in a crowd of masks, although I was usually by myself. They talked with me merrily, and I chattered with them. Once, toward the end of the day, tired and in high spirits, I somehow found myself in Nice (the noisiest and merriest of all of them!) and decided to have dinner . . . but where? Well, what about this restaurant, near the square? It would still be possible afterwards to attend the ball . . .

In front of me a happy group of maskers entered the restaurant. As always, there was Pierrot, the gypsy, the canteen-keeper . . . They sat down at a large table not very far from me.

I noticed that not all of them were in costume—a few ladies and gentlemen were dressed in everyday clothes, with masks only.

They were enjoying themselves. I regretted that I was sitting alone and began to wonder what would be the best way to make their acquaintance. Surely I would fit in with this company . . .

Little by little the masks were removed. The two in the dinner jackets were of a rather venerable age. The others were young people. The ladies—oh, certainly not very strict in their conduct, this was immediately evident—were all small in stature. One, in pink, had thrown off the downy cloak from her bare shoulders and arms, but did not remove her mask, which was also pink. For some reason I cast my eyes upon her frail, slender arms and on her eyes, which sparkled through the pink velvet. They also looked at me, those eyes.

Then she slowly lifted her mask . . .

As soon as this happened, I understood why I could not tear myself away from her—I was in love, yes, in love, with her alone, and no one else. It was precisely she who was that mysterious joy which I had awaited all the time. It seemed to me that I had already seen her face somewhere; I must have seen it in my dreams.

However, I did not lose my head. My love was no daydream—it was cautious, but passionate to the point of turbulence, to exhaustion. My pink delight was sitting, laughing in such a frivolous company, and her obvious permissiveness, her . . . *possibility* (I did not utter the word "accessibility" even to myself), increased my love all the more, it seemed. I *could* indeed embrace this frail body the following day . . . no, this day . . . no, in an hour, in half an hour . . . I could! I did not know what would have happened if I met her in the morning on the beach with her governess.

It seemed to me that no one would have been surprised to see her with a governess, for my pink one was so young. She was still a girl; she had barely made-up eyes and lips touched with scarlet; the make-up seemed to have been applied purposely, in jest.

Was she beautiful? I didn't know. To me she seemed beautiful. Dark, closely cropped, wavy hair. Dark eyes. A dimple on her chin . . . oh, it was all the same! Nothing was important. What was important was only that I was in love, that I was attracted to her to the point of trembling, of pain, of tears, in such a way that if suddenly she were, at the very moment, to vanish from the face of the earth, in all likelihood I would have fired a bullet through my head.

I did not even conceive that she might get up at that very moment, exit with the entire crowd, or go out alone with someone, with some sweetheart of hers. In an instant I would have won her away from a hundred sweethearts. That she also looked at me, transfixed and steadily, appeared natural to me. How could she help feeling *how* I looked at her?

I was waiting for just the right moment, and I practically did not even touch my dinner, did not notice it. As the minutes passed, however, it was becoming more and more difficult for me to wait. I decided to count to one hundred and then act, no matter what.

I had not even gotten to fifty when another group burst into the restaurant, obviously acquaintances of the first party, who jumped up from the table to meet them. All began speaking at once. Laughter and words resounded in snatches amid the music.

I did not listen to their words, but I also rose. It would not be hard now, after I had mixed in with the crowd, to head over to my pink one.

But this was not necessary—she herself anticipated me. Shining eyes, pink velvet (she again had her mask on), warm breathing by my ear, a whisper:

"Go out. Wait for me at the entrance."

I obeyed like a robot. On the sidewalk I stood motionless, not noticing anything around me. It did not appear to me that I had waited very long. But I shuddered when a thin little hand slipped into mine.

"Let's go away from here at once; it's too light outside."

We went somewhere, almost ran, then we turned into some side lane where it was darker. I had already embraced her—how delicate she felt beneath the soft, downy cloak! And how tall! I had to incline my head just a little in order to look into her shining eyes.

"The mask! The mask!" I pleaded softly (the pink velvet was in my way).

I did not know whether to use the familiar or polite "you." The tenderness of being in love does not wish to hear the rude, simple, familiar form. Yet this same form, if devoid of its rudeness . . . would seem premature for real tenderness. However— who considers time in such matters! And I whispered, using the more familiar form, my voice quivering:

"I love you . . . love you, love you . . ."

She laughed, then stopped, removed the mask, but at the same time gently released herself from my embrace.

"Oh, and I . . . love you, too. But wait, wait a moment. Listen to me."

"Let's go somewhere. Let's go quickly . . ."

"No, listen . . . All right, let's go. Do you live in Menton?"

"How do you know?"

She again laughed.

"Of course, I know. I have known you for a long time, for a long time . . . I have loved you. You are my *béguin.*"

"It is not true! Had I seen you only once . . . the minute I saw you—I fell in love immediately. Earlier . . . no, earlier I had only dreamed of you. I remember your face . . . only it was in a dream. Tell me, what is your name?"

"Marcelle. And are you an Italian? Gianino? You see, I know your name."

"Yes, you know it. Only I am not an Italian. Well, so let me be Gianino. Why are you moving away, if you love me? Marcelle, dear, I love you, love you . . ."

"It's impossible, impossible," she whispered, wrapping herself in her fluffy overcoat.

"Well, let's go. Wherever you wish . . . to your place."

I forgot, literally forgot about my Renault, which had been left behind at the restaurant. But it was for the better—we would hardly have reached Menton safely if I had been sitting at the steering wheel and if she, Marcelle, were next to me. A double exhaustion—love and passion, disunited and somehow engaged in a mutual struggle within me—deafened and blinded me. I saw only "her," heard only "her."

Very quickly, and perhaps not without Marcelle's assistance, we found a spacious limousine. Upon entering Marcelle turned toward me, looked entreatingly, and whispered:

"*Mais . . . vous serez sage pendant le trajet. N'est-ce pas? Vous me le promettez?*"

At this moment she looked just like a little girl, a shy adolescent. Oh, naturally I promised her everything; at that moment tenderness and love gained the upper hand over my passion. I merely embraced her, lulled her as I would a small child; I felt as though I were on a golden cloud of half-slumber . . . and the gentle ride in the limousine rocked and lulled both of us.

Even before we reached Menton this cloud began to grow hot, turn scarlet, and changed its shape. In the flashing lights her face also appeared to be changing.

"Marcelle, tell me, how old are you?"

"Sixteen . . ."

Her face, her parted lips, her chin with the small dimple— her face was so close . . . and the first kiss, when her lips met mine, seemed really to be my very first kiss. But the second, third, all the rest—I could no longer free myself from her lips— were exactly like the first; they penetrated the darkness before me with the same fiery zigzags.

"*Chéri . . . chéri . . . assez,*" Marcelle murmured, scarcely audible. "*Nous arrivons.* I implore you . . ."

We were already at my hotel; we had even passed through the gate of the park onto a circular road surrounding it.

What time was it? I had no idea. Perhaps it was late, perhaps early. The hotel was lit up.

"I'll put on my mask," said Marcelle. "It's better that way. Today all things are possible. Surely we won't stay downstairs?"

Downstairs! I really had no need for these hotel halls! And why the mask? But if she wished . . .

I had to regain my tranquillity—and I succeeded. I went out, settled accounts with the chauffeur, and we passed directly to the elevator through an enormous, brightly lit lobby.

From somewhere, it must have been from the halls of the restaurant, music could still be heard, mild and soothing. So it was not late . . .

In the hotel I was treated with respect, for I occupied one of the most expensive rooms and generally did not care at all about expenses. Marcelle's timidity surprised me a bit—even with the mask on she was still keeping her face buried, turning away from the attendant in the brightly lit elevator.

"You won't order anything else?" she asked when we entered my large, cool room. Through the door, which was opened onto the balcony for the night, there came a fragrance of mimosas.

"If you like, I will order something cold, some wine—they will bring it in a minute . . ."

"Oh, no, no! I beg you, it is not necessary! I need nothing, I do not want anything. Lock the door."

"My dear, my love, what are you afraid of? I am with you, we are alone . . ."

I locked the doors, the window, closed the curtains, put out the bright chandelier. Only a tiny lamp with a pink-colored shade was burning in the alcove.

Marcelle curled up on the divan, in a little corner, gathering her feet in light-colored shoes beneath her. The room was quickly growing dark. The dim light made it comfortable.

I knelt on the carpet in front of the divan and embraced my girl. She appeared again a timid little girl, but . . . I still remembered the automobile. Strong will and calm were no longer necessary, and my blood rushed ever more violently to my temples.

"My dear, my dear, I don't know what is happening to me. I have never yet loved anyone—as I love you. As I love you, you alone . . ."

I threw off her cloak. The frail arms embraced me. She smiled for the first time, almost playfully.

"Is it true? True? But I? Really, don't you feel, Gianino, that for a long time I . . . that you are my *béguin?* And how many times, while looking at you . . ."

"Have you also seen me in a dream?"

"No, wait . . . you will not understand this. There was even a vow here . . . And if it were not . . . But you will not understand . . ."

"I will not understand? If it were not . . . what? What?"

I kept on asking, but to tell the truth I was neither concerned with her answers, nor did I even desire them. Again these kisses, again these unusual "first" kisses, which melted my entire body. Indeed, this was "she," the only one who was pleasing to me in her entirety; that is, not just something about her, but all of her

—to all of me. I say "was pleasing," but this is a trite expression, for every fiber of my body was attracted to her, to her tall, slender body. There was something even cruel in this attraction.

Beneath the light dress I felt her frail nakedness. I heard the rapid beating of her heart.

"Gianino, oh my dear . . . so, it is true? No, no, wait a moment . . . Do you know? . . ."

She straightened herself up, threw back her head, then looked into my eyes:

"Do you know? Do you know?"

"I know nothing, Marcelle," I mumbled half-consciously, "and I want nothing but you. You—are you, I know nothing more. Don't leave, don't leave . . ."

She leaned over again toward my lips, lowering her eyelids in languor. And suddenly—I understood.

By this single second of my hesitation she understood that I understood. Her delicate body quivered in my arms, her eyes opened and immediately shut again.

These were the same eyes, the same lips, the same body to which every fiber of my own had been attracted. A second of hesitation—it was as though a cold wire had slipped through me. Slipped through . . . but changed nothing.

We felt this at one and the same instant, again together, while tightening our embrace.

"Marcelle, don't be afraid . . . Don't think. Isn't it really all the same? Isn't it really all the same, if you—are you?"

THE PEARL-HANDLED CANE

(Again Martynov)

I have been writing love memoirs, but I gave up because they contained only some incidental and brief anecdotes. Surely, there were more serious things to write about. Let me try again.

I shall not be tempted by brevity, nor shall I bore the reader with details. Rather, I will write sincerely and diligently. I shall not fear long approaches to the stories.

I
GRANDMOTHER

It happened during the years I was married to my "grandmother."

My grandmother does not have any direct connection with this story. I mention her in passing, for the sake of a very indirect relation—it will become clear later what relation. Concerning the marriage, I shall say only that it was a moment when I had to appear "married" or else put my head into the noose. The reason why is not interesting. Indeed, my dear deceased grandmother rescued me at that moment. (I am her grandnephew twice removed, but from childhood I loved and esteemed her and called her Grandmother.) It was at her place in Dolgoe, in the Tambov province, that we were married, early in the morning, and in the afternoon I departed almost immediately for Germany.

This is, properly speaking, all. Now there will be a new and long approach in the guise of an entire story—someone else's, not mine, but it is necessary to retell it since it pertains to my own story.

II
SOMEONE ELSE'S STORY. THE BEGINNING

Franz von Hallen.

He was my closest friend, perhaps my only friend among a crowd of acquaintances, all students of Heidelberg University.

He was older than I—well, it is true, I was then pretty much the youngest of all the students. I never thought I would meet that kind of man among (contemporary) Germans. I knew that such Germans had existed earlier, but I did not hope to meet one still living. He was very German (from a good, old German family, extremely rich, besides), and a most refined charm surrounded him, a dreamy silence combined with penetrating thought, always profound. He wrote verses, of course (they seemed excellent to me, no worse than Novalis's),[1] and he occupied himself seriously with philosophy.

Our attachment began with philosophy; it then developed further.

In my imagination, Franz, from his exterior, appeared to me as either a young Schelling [2] or even Novalis, one of those extinct Germans so dear to me—I adored them. He had nothing of the hefty *Bursche* about him. What eyes, flashing, pale blue sparks! A slender figure, perhaps too slender. The line of his lips was rather exciting—tenderly pink, it gave the impression of touching helplessness.

We became inseparable. I had no secrets from him. He, I thought, had no secrets either. Our relationship was an ideal friendship, like Tieck [3] and Wackenroder,[4] as I enthusiastically recalled.

There was not a single trace of condescending seniority in his friendship. Only at times, unexpectedly, there appeared in him something incomprehensible to me, some tenderly affectionate remoteness, as if he were cautious in his relationship with me.

I did not ponder over this, however.

Then we separated. Years passed. Did they divide us? Yes and

[1] Novalis, Friedrich von Hardenberg (1772–1801). German writer. His major works include *Hymnen an die Nacht* (1800) and a novel entitled *Heinrich von Ofterdingen* (1799).

[2] Schelling, Friedrich Wilhelm (1775–1854). German philosopher. His major works include *Vom "Ich" als Prinzip der Philosophie* (1795), *Ideen zu einer Philosophie der Natur* (1797), *Philosophie der Kunst* (1809), and *Philosophie der Offenbarung* (1854).

[3] Tieck, Ludwig (1773–1853). German writer, historian of German literature, playwright. His major works include a novel entitled *Geschichte des Herrn William Lovell* (1796), *Franz Sternbalds Wanderung* (1795), and with Wilhelm Wackenroder, *Herzensergiessungen eines kunstliebenden Klosterbruders* (1797).

[4] Wackenroder, Wilhelm (1773–98). German writer. Friend of Friedrich Schlegel and Ludwig Tieck. Together with the latter, Wackenroder wrote *Herzensergiessungen eines kunstliebenden Klosterbruders* (1797).

no. Over these years I saw him several times when I returned to Germany; however, not our meetings, but our infrequent yet constant correspondence drew us together . . . and in quite a new way. The youthful Heidelberg enthusiasm had gone—nothing to grieve about! I came to know Franz as he was, and I became humanly, loyally attached to him. I, by the way, am usually loyal.

Therefore, when this last letter arrived in which he asked me to visit him, even if only for a short time, I did not hesitate. Although I had not seen him for a long time, I knew what had happened to him two years before. Now Franz was calling me. His letter was calm, almost jovial, and I wondered why he needed me. I decided to go.

So I went.

III
THE DRAMA AND THE TRAGEDY OF FRANZ

Through the gauzy covering of the silky, pallid lilac wisteria we could see the Ionian Sea, poisonously green, at high tide. Only with moiré-like patches close to the rocks, nothing else. On the right and left of the veranda were the mountain terraces, wildly overgrown with shrubbery—this was the garden. The villa, a tiny house, was so concealed on all sides that it appeared to have vanished into the blossoming thicket.

"You're my friend," Franz said, "my closest friend. You know everything, you can grasp everything with your mind and heart. I need you sometimes more than anyone in the world. But I don't deceive myself—you cannot understand me."

His handsome, delicate profile was outlined against the lilac silk of the wisteria. His eyes were downcast.

"Franz, what do you mean by 'understand'?"

"As you would understand, if you were in my place . . . for one moment. But no, you would return to yourself, you would again forget. This aspect of human life and existence is the most elusive. It's also the most incomprehensible for people to accept in each other, if it's not common to them. By accident I can meet a man who is alien, stupid, repulsive, yet he'll be able to understand me. Together we shall form a 'we' . . ."

"And you and I—can never form it?" I interrupted. "You're probably right, if we have in mind such an understanding. Only you see . . . Are you listening to me, Franz? Some, like you, have understood themselves; for others, like me, everything remains mysterious, and I myself don't know exactly with whom I can form a 'we.' It seems not with you . . . definitely not with you. But—not with them either . . ."

"You cannot . . . anywhere?" Franz smiled as he arose. "That's untrue! This is what I know about you, and you yourself know. Let's leave it for the time being. Do you want to go for a walk? To the Wild Rock, below?"

Stepping soundlessly, one of Franz's servants entered.

"*Signor* . . ."

He said something to Franz which I did not understand, although I knew Italian rather well. I was not as yet accustomed to their Sicilian dialect.

"Sorry, I can't walk with you after all," Franz said, slightly shrugging his shoulders. "Giovanni informs me that something is wrong with the photographs which have been drying. I must examine them. Will you come in the evening? Before sunset?"

I promised. And, taking my hat, I went from the garden onto a dazzling rocky path.

I did not stay at Franz's house. He had arranged for me to live with the family of an acquaintance of his, a Hungarian artist married to a German woman, whose house was a beautiful villa on the other side of the town of Floriola.

Franz's house, so concealed that one could not see it from a distance, was called Rach. Franz told me he planned to remain in this tiny town of Bestra forever. And I believed him, although . . . for some reason I felt pain on his behalf, even a degree of indignation. For the rest of his life . . . yet was he even thirty-five years old?

Franz occupied himself with art photography. For his own

pleasure, of course. His photographs were really charming. He took almost all of them in his garden, and this wild, lush garden, with some of its trees strange and unknown to me, was somehow not like a garden, but more like Elysium—the paradise of happy days before the Fall.

Franz lived alone with several servants who were also his assistants. They likewise served as models when he took pictures in his Edenic garden.

At first I could not distinguish them, for all were dressed alike, all were of one Sicilian type—not quite Italian, but with some kind of admixture. Each one had a short, straight nose, and a special swarthiness with a golden tinge. Later I could distinguish Giovanni, Giuseppe, and Nino . . . and what was his name? The smallest one?

I also came to know Bestra a little; I knew why Franz had chosen it, when more than two years ago he had decided to seek solitude, having forever severed his relationship with his family and his native land.

He had written me about this drama. He had written in detail, openly, sparing neither himself nor the others. I well understood that a crude scandal, which had been enacted in crude Berlin society (or the so-called *beau monde* to which Franz belonged), could only have been a drama for Franz, and that he could not have concluded it other than the way he did.

I understood the drama entirely, to the very core. But beyond Franz's drama was there not a tragedy? He had precisely this tragedy in mind when he said that I could not understand it the way he understood it.

It seems I could not. Or could I?

IV
CONTINUATION

At my lodgings I found a bacchanalia of flowers.

Actually not in my suite, but in a huge, half-empty, beautiful room which served as a salon–dining room for my hosts. I was quickly passing through it when my hostess called to me from the loggia above.

The old Hungarian Marius, as always, was not around. He was probably in his workshop where I occasionally dropped in on him. It was pleasant there, only too hot! Yet April had just begun.

Flowers lay in heaps on the tables, on the chairs, even on the floor. All kinds, from lilies—and what strange, pale blue ones—to field and mountain asphodels, frezias, orange and pink daisies. Clara, my hostess, had artfully arranged these piles with the aid of three maids.

"Come and help!" she shouted, turning her lean, young face to me. There was a flash of her pince-nez, which she never took off. "My local friends have brought all this today because it's my birthday . . . Ah, *Donna Ciccia!*" She interrupted herself, rising to meet some wild Sicilian peasant woman carrying another sheaf of red flowers. She began to chat with her in Sicilian.

My hostess was very popular. I could not understand for a long time why she was popular and what kind of family this was in general. I had scarcely arrived when the villa Floriola struck me with its harmony of lines and its taste for severe, sparse interior furnishings. And with several pictures in oil, sepia, and gouache. There were women's faces of such charm that it was difficult to believe that they were only portraits. These pictures were painted by Marius, explained my hostess, Frau Zette (or Clara, as I called her in my thoughts). This Clara was, first of all, a terrible "German" from head to toe—she had rather flat feet and blonde hair with a slightly greenish tinge.

"Our mutual friend, Monsieur von Hallen, finds Floriola rather pleasant," she said in a melodious voice. "No one here will insult you."

I understood right away that this German woman was not simply a young German woman interested merely in being a good housekeeper. Besides her excellent housekeeping, she was a German interested in "reading" and making "inquiries." However, these "inquiries" are a purely Russian trait; to be a German, something different is needed—"dreams" . . . which do not hinder one's practical bent.

Why, for example, did she speak to me in French? In Marius's presence we would switch to German, but as soon as we were alone she would chatter away in French. She spoke fluently, with only a slight accent, but her intonation was thickly German.

And why was she married to Marius, this thickset, unrefined, savage-looking man with gray temples? Clara herself was rather plain, gaunt, even somewhat bony; yet her appearance was not unpleasant—she was like a bird in a pince-nez, and she was quite young. She had declared to me right away that she was twenty-five years old.

"Marius himself built Floriola according to his own plan, and he himself blended the paints for every room; we built it when we were married. Oh, it cost me a great deal!" Clara had indulged in confidences with me from the first day of our acquaintance. She did not think that I would remain here for good. She had arrived from Munich with her artist brother to stay in the area for a little while . . . Marius had already been living in the town for a long time.

I concluded from this that Marius was poor and that she was rich. Just why they married, I could not understand. It was all the same to me; nevertheless, such is my character—I like to observe people, to analyze them psychologically, to make guesses about them. Often one makes a false guess as he looks for certain meanings in human actions, but are those meanings always there?

Here I decided that Marius was not in love with Clara; he had somehow succeeded in seducing the rich, plain-looking young woman and in receiving along with her a villa and a marvelous workshop. But seeing with my own eyes the originals of Marius's pictures—pictures which charmed me so—I confess that at first I suspected Marius of having a harem.

This turned out to be one of my incorrect guesses: no, the three beauties—genuine beauties!—were beyond all question serving maids of the Zette couple. Very likely they had been selected as being fit for Marius's sketches; only in this way did they interest him. Clara taught them to work and treated them in the manner of a strict mother. They were three girls—quite young—the oldest, Maria, hardly past her sixteenth year. Prankazia, the darkest, with fiery eyes, was fourteen. And Giovannina was only twelve. My Lord, how pretty they were, each one different from the other! I will not describe them, let Gogol do it . . . Even Gogol gave up trying to depict his Anunciata[5]; besides, his conventional "Italian" Roman beauties never existed here. What was Anunciata's beauty compared to the face of Maria, which recalled the Madonna of some old Spanish artist, or compared to the angelic face of Giovannina! I could not help but think that Marius, nonetheless, had misrepresented them, had not captured their essence. And I could not decide who was better looking. Well, let's leave it at that.

"Today you will dine with us," said Clara, adroitly tying flowers together. Although three pairs of well-tanned hands were tying the flowers in beautiful bouquets, some long, some wide, the pile did not diminish. After *Donna Ciccia* there appeared still more of such *donnas,* and all with flowers.

"*Il signor dottore* will come also . . ." Clara named several people of "high society" in the district. Yes, Bestra had its "high society"—old Sicilian families. I even visited one such family with Frau Zette. Clara took me there, introducing me as her friend, a foreign baron interested in antiques. These Sicilians were presented to me, and I was amazed at the existence in the twentieth century of such people, with such customs, living in such homes. Stone staircases, eternal dampness, eternal gloom and cold, the windows are never opened. No one ever goes onto the patterned iron balconies. It is not their custom. We saw some old, stupid women—I could not make them out in the dark and could barely distinguish them. Young ladies did not show themselves. Furthermore, they do not even show themselves in the street. They take a stroll now and then, but only at twilight, with lace covering their heads. Strolling is not the custom. And what would happen if it entered the head of one of these

[5] Ref. to Gogol, "Rim" (1842).

signorinas to wear a hat! There is nothing less "in keeping with custom." Fortunately, such a thought does not occur to these signorinas.

"When I invite them for dinner, I do not entertain foreigners," Clara continued. "You are an exception, since you live in the house. We ourselves are foreigners, but we are considered local inhabitants as well. And ours, it seems, is the only house which they frequent. So, will you come?"

Usually I dined in my own suite, downstairs, if not at Franz's villa. On occasion I dined with my hosts.

"I . . . don't know," I stammered with a mumble. "I have . . . a headache. Please . . . pardon me."

The fact was—the flowers had overpowered me. They clouded my senses, stupefied me. They submerged me into a dream. I had the feeling that I had become satiated with flowers. However, I half-consciously continued to sort them out.

Clara did not notice anything.

"Do come! Or have you promised Monsieur von Hallen?"

I recalled that I had and rejoiced.

"Yes . . . I have promised him . . . Madame Zette. Excuse me, my head is swimming . . ."

"Oh, that is because of the *fiori di Portogallo!* You're not used to flowers in the room . . ."

"No, everything together seems to have affected me. How do you endure . . . this flood of flowers?"

She laughed. She clapped her hands and—*presto-presto!*—she ordered her girls to carry the pile off somewhere. The bouquets remained. My head continued to swim. No, I would go outside into the fresh air! I got up.

"*Je l'aime . . . Oh, que je l'aime . . .*" someone's quiet voice could be heard near me. It made no sense, for there was no one who could have said this, and therefore I became frightened— did it mean that I was becoming delirious?

"What a pity that you cannot!" said Clara. "You are beginning to betray us. And Monsieur von Hallen—since you have been here—has neglected Floriola entirely. It's your fault."

Laughing, she threatened me with her finger and kept on jabbering something, but I no longer heard her—I dashed onto the road. It would be good to breathe the fresh air—otherwise, even in the air here (I felt it distinctly), one could still smell the flowers, flowers, flowers everywhere . . .

V
CONTINUATION

I gave Franz an accurate account of my impression of Bestra. He listened very attentively, saying nothing, as if he wanted me to orient myself without his assistance. As if he were waiting for . . . what?

That evening, on the jagged Wild Rock, I informed him in a humorous tone how I had become "satiated" with flowers. Then I asked:

"What, really, do you make of the Zette couple? Have you known them long?"

To tell the truth, a different question had been on the tip of my tongue, more important than the Zettes. What were they, after all? I had known them for three days; I would depart and not remember them . . .

I was concerned about something more important. Why did Franz need me? Of course, since a long separation creates estrangement, one does not enter right away into a stream of open conversations. Time is needed so that even the intimacy expressed in letters, if it exists, can be transferred to conversational intimacy. Nevertheless, he was more tranquil than I had expected. His drama, well known to me, seemed to have receded into the past, but the tragedy . . . he said that I neither understood it nor would ever understand it. Why, then, did he need me?

He did not answer my question concerning the Zettes, seeming not to have heard it. He gazed at the sea below at high tide. From beyond the icy Etna, spreading in all directions, fell the last rays of the sunset; the sea looked like moiré.

"I am bored . . ." he said suddenly and turned his delicate

face toward me. I thought involuntarily—this often happened—that Franz was especially handsome in a spiritual sense. It was something in his features. Heaven knows what it was.

"You know that Otto is now married," he added.

Otto was the young Count X. Franz's serious drama had been enacted because of him. He had married? I did not know what to say, and so remained silent.

"Yes, he's married. And what's important, he's very happy. He's written me."

"So what . . ." I began and then quickly added, "or do you still love him?"

Franz knit his brows, his face became rigid. He shrugged his shoulders. And—it seemed to me—he looked at me with an expression of regret:

"But I expected . . . you wouldn't understand."

"Again?"

"Yes. But sometime perhaps you will understand. For your own sake, I hope you never will."

"Franz, you really annoy me. I very much want to understand. I'm convinced that I will understand. Don't put on this misunderstand act in front of me! For a long time I myself have wanted to ask you . . ."

"Later, later!" Franz interrupted. He was impatient and tormented.

We fell silent. Suddenly he said, unexpectedly:

"Didn't you ask me about the Zettes? It's . . . a remarkable family. Both he . . . and Clara."

I raised my eyes. I was surprised. On Franz's face so much kindness, of a melancholy sort, it is true, but almost tender. However, I also knew this trait of his—he was extremely kind to people, and not only to people, but to everything living. Somehow at times he radiated pity—not an offensive, piercing kindness.

"She's very unhappy," he said. "Clara, I mean."

I was amazed.

"Clara? Little Clara? What are you saying!"

"And innocently unhappy," Franz added, rising. "But you . . ."

"Again am I unable to grasp it? No, Franz, you're simply laughing at me . . ."

Franz really did burst out laughing, and so merrily that I looked at him and did the same.

We stood facing each other and laughed, as if we were two students again in far-off Heidelberg, as if the chalice of the southern sea were not looming green before us, as if the darkening hot air were not breathing on us with the shameless odor of "Portuguese flowers," and as if the wide Etna were not lying in a corner—rather, as if the gray, fresh, Heidelberg mountains were looking at us. A sweet, clean, brisk freshness, like youth itself!

VI
AN EVENING AT RACH

Franz did not live at all like a hermit, as I had first imagined. True, he did not associate with the old local families. It turned out that there were many foreigners in this remote, rocky little town, which consisted of a single street. For new arrivals there were two hotels—both very poor. The majority of foreigners, however, were not new arrivals—white villas were nestled here and there along the green slopes, and the owners were rich people who thought it worthwhile to settle down in Bestra—Englishmen, Americans, and Germans . . . somehow I do not remember any Frenchmen. All of them lived in seclusion, like Franz; not, however, as hermits—they did not shun one another. I had already met some of them at Franz's villa.

The city street was bounded on both sides—eastern and western—by ancient stone gates. All the villas snuggled on the steep slopes outside the city, beyond the city gates. They were not visibly evident; some seemed completely concealed in dense verdure, the flat roofs barely noticeable. From Franz's villa, Rach, one could not even see the roofs—the rocks obscured the view.

Our Floriola was, on the contrary, on a cliff. It had one low side facing the road, but on the other side it had three stories. My long, cast-iron balcony-gallery hung over a precipice, a deep, green slope. In the distance beyond it the sea at high tide looked misty. Rach was not so close—whenever I went to see Franz, I had to pass through the Eastern Gate, walk the length of the city street, and pass through the Western Gate facing Etna. I could, however, have gone around the city by the narrow mountain paths which curled round the town, but they confused me, especially at night.

I rarely saw Franz in Floriola, and when he was there he was not visiting me, but my hosts. Yesterday he came to invite me to a "party at Rach." This—he explained to me—would involve some music and several casual friends . . .

It was the custom of Bestra, probably. I was already used to the fact that there were many customs in Bestra; although they did not seem strange on the surface, they somehow remained peculiar. These customs were the same as everywhere, yet not entirely. Sometimes they were quite different.

The riddle of Bestra was simple, but it was so subtle that for a long time I could find neither the words nor an answer for it.

One thing was clear—I had entered a world which I had never entered before. The stormy south, Sicilian, resembled nothing else (although I had spent time even farther to the south)—grasping, sweet, heavily incensed—it embraced the body, penetrated within, and there, in the soul, it also seemed in its own way to change something. Indeed, the flowers made the head giddy to the point of nausea, yet I could not tear myself away from them. Without thinking, I was ready at times to spend hours fondling the silky petals, hiding my lips and face in them. And at night on the balcony, above the dark abyss, I surrendered with sweet passivity to the earthy fragrances which arose toward me like puffs of suffocating incense. And I even seemed to enjoy this passivity—of what? Of the soul or the body?

Bestra was a part of this special world—special in its outward appearance as well as within.

Here, although it is boring, I must say two words about myself —to make the rest clear.

There will not be complete clarity, of course. Franz was right in saying that the most incomprehensible side of man is his amorous side. Franz insisted that it is incomprehensible for another, whereas I add—it is incomprehensible for oneself as well.

Like any thinking person, I pondered over this a great deal. Both in general and over myself. I came to rather interesting deductions and conclusions. Little by little, I evolved my own theory, firmly constructed and not lacking in harmony.

I was quite content until I became aware that I was alive, that I felt, acted, and functioned as though I had no theory. I even live, love, and hate not in spite of, but quite apart from it. I forget it entirely when it is time for me to live and act.

When, in my free time, I recall the theory, it again seems to me harmonious, all-explaining, ideally beautiful; it is annoying and astonishing, however, that even in small things, in details, it turns out to be unnecessary and unsuited to life.

The theory (or my "philosophy of love," as I call it) is not at fault; of course, I myself am at fault for not yet being able to put it into practice. I myself have created it, with the better part of my "I," yet my physiology and even my psychology are primitive and behave in their own way, not wanting to take notice of anything—they are subjugated to their own primitive law.

Yes, it is very annoying. But I do not despair. Is there a discrepancy here? In the course of time will it not smooth itself out? Or am I wrong?

In any case, when I contemplated love, I never failed to express my theoretical views; I spoke about the great unity of love and the great freedom in love (although even objectively I somehow did not really understand or accept this freedom.)

Franz did not doubt that I upheld his sacred right to that love which befell him and which was sent to him. And I did not doubt it—how could I not have affirmed this sacred right!

I was a stern judge of human prejudices, the habitual and rigid kind. One form of love is called the "norm" because it is in the majority; people give the right to the majority, but they take everything away from the minority. They spoil life for themselves and for others; they envenom it with their suspicions, contempt, and persecutions . . . Did not the drama of Franz stem from all this?

And the fact that I occasionally, in the innermost recesses of my consciousness, also experienced both the norm—the norm of the ordinary—and something beyond it, which "we conceal and do not discuss"—this would plunge me into a deep terror. The power of the habitual, the prejudice of the Philistine? Even over me? No! No!

Here it is, dear Bestra, here is the clue to its joyful uniqueness —here "they speak and do not hide anything," here they do not drag their prejudices after them, here everything is simple, here everyone is free.

Once I solved the riddle of Bestra, I became overjoyed.

VII
IT

Franz's party had been postponed. Why? It seems as though some flowers had not yet bloomed. What nonsense! Maybe it was true? After all, Clara was not surprised—she received the news as if it were understandable.

However, something had affected Franz. I was about to believe that he was serenely happy and that he had summoned me so that I might see his serenity; but there had suddenly emerged from under it a new . . . or was it an old, an earlier torment? It was always present in him, it could be sensed in him. A tragedy which I did not understand?

Franz and I knew when to be silent and when to speak. Yet when something happened to me, or to him, neither he nor I would talk about it. Only if the other guessed, approximately, what the matter was, could we start a conversation.

Franz always guessed the things which concerned me. I was not as successful. There was much in him that was unpredictable. However, since I liked him so much, I often guessed what tormented him, although I did not understand the torment itself.

I suddenly felt that Franz was now becoming even more despondent. It had to do with Count Otto. But I could not explain to myself, why Count Otto? My question, "Do you still love him?" was rude, banal, and shallow. I knew that Franz did not love him.

I had not seen Franz at all for two days. Then, for an entire day, we walked together a long way, in the mountains, and kept silent. In the evening, at his place, we again were silent. When I arose to depart, he did not detain me. I descended the steps of the veranda. I stopped, gazing at the stars which were unbearably restless and immense above the sea. Slowly I returned and, I myself do not know why, said:

"Otto?"

Franz nodded his head, and I left.

During the night I woke up in terror—the darkness of the room seemed filled with an assembly of screeching witches. I did not yet know that this was the wind; I had no idea what the wind of Bestra was like. It was not real, and yet it was not a dream. I felt as if I were in a stifling heat, flying somewhere to a bottomless precipice together with this whole regiment of shrieking witches, of rattling and guffawing devils. It was like neither a tempest nor a thunderstorm; it was not like anything. There was not one thought in my head—only this shrill, piercing screech. It began to seem to me that I too, along with my body, was screeching and flying through the dark spaces.

Toward morning I regained control of myself, although the screeching continued. I attempted to rise—and I did. To my amazement I saw that beautiful Maria was bringing my breakfast. She was climbing the outside stairway to the doors of the balcony. Her golden hair was ruffled against her face; her dress, as if wet, clung to her legs.

I gathered up my courage, opened the door a little. I thought I would become deaf, but the sound, it seems, could not have become louder. Maria adroitly entered, placed the tray on the table, and said something, smiling; it was impossible to catch her words.

This entire day was a day of surprises.

Clara came to me. Since I could not hear her words, she took me by the hand and fearlessly led me upstairs—through all this roaring, swirling, gray terror. There, in a big and empty room, everything appeared to me even more unreal—some kind of metallic sound now accompanied the clanging of cymbals.

In the corner there was a table set for tea. A blue-black sea with white curls looked in at the window. Franz sat at the table.

He was smiling, Clara was smiling, the girls were laughing. I felt ashamed. I still could not distinguish Clara's voice, yet I began to make out Franz's shouting. It turned out that he liked this wind very much. He knew that I, being unaccustomed to it, would lose my head. But it was high time for me to recover it . . .

Clara smiled. Her face was pleasantly agitated, even flushed. Franz was polite, and our tea-drinking turned out to be very enjoyable; but I still could not understand entirely what was happening around me and what was being said—or even in what language. At times, it seems, it was in German; at times, in French. Or suddenly, in Italian. Not knowing who uttered them, I caught snatches of sentences, words, sometimes nonsensical, which evidently could not have belonged to any of us. For example, where did this suddenly come from: *"voglio bene . . . voglio tanto bene"* . . . ? The witches, of course, were screeching it in derision.

And—bang! Silence fell like a stone. I never thought that it could fall so heavily. I gazed open-mouthed at Clara, then at Franz. Everyone was silent. Franz was smiling.

"One also has to get used to this," he said softly (to me it seemed terribly loud). "Don't rejoice—the wind will return again. Let's take advantage, however, of the moment—walk me home."

He rose to go.

"But Monsieur will not be in time . . ." Clara looked at me with pity.

"No matter, it will be his first lesson. Let's go, *mon ami.* You don't need a hat, what's the matter with you!"

We went out.

Yes, an astonishing day! It began, continued, and ended with surprises. A tenfold howl and whirlwind came after the stony silence; Franz and I stood on a jagged path, holding each other tightly. And then our conversation in the whirlwind . . . why, however, was I now able to hear Franz clearly, and he me?

It seems I now understood Franz's tragedy. I also understood his latest, that is, his present anguish. To explain how I understood it, naturally, is impossible. Afterwards I shall relate it in words, but I know beforehand that it will not be right at all.

I also guessed that there was something else here involving Franz, something alien, some kind of chagrin, some kind of sadness for his tenderly sympathetic heart. I still did not know where it came from.

Later I learned.

VIII
RESPITE

The necessary flowers had apparently bloomed, because the party at Rach which had been postponed was arranged again.

Once, not long before, I had awakened with an unusual lightness in my soul, in my body, and in my memory. There occur such strange . . . well, not periods of life, for they are too short to be periods, but intervals when all important, disquieting matters seem to recede, to fall away from you. You know that the anxiety still exists; sometimes there is even a premonition of something important in the future, or something in the past . . . but on this day there is nothing except the sweet and simple present.

Bestra, I think, is a city where people more often experience this feeling. Such is its peculiarity . . .

My beautiful morning did not dawn so strangely beautiful for me alone: downstairs Clara was laughing with some old English ladies; Prankazia, running downstairs, was also laughing. When I went out to the Eastern Gate of the city and started chatting by the old wall with some boys I knew, I saw Franz looking so gay and with such a careless face that I felt really good. In his hands Franz was holding a bouquet of very unusual blue roses—they grew only in the garden of *il signore dottore;* this was his secret. Franz often dropped in on him in his garden, and this funny doctor of Bestra had proudly presented him with the roses.

We agreed that I would come in the evening; during the day Franz had to work. Indeed, he, like me, was not thinking about anything today.

And for the present I decided to climb Monte Venere. This mountain is not actually a mountain—it is a jagged gray rock (exactly like the one above the villa of Rach). On the top there is a dilapidated village and an old monastery.

This mountain—traditionally associated with Venus—is amusing. Everything is amusing and pleasant in warm, fragrant, blue-white Bestra! Since antiquity its citizens have been free, both the old and the young. This freedom is well known to everybody, as are the old habits and customs of Bestra's peaceful life. Youth, however, is turbulent, and therefore discipline is needed. The *carabinieri* (there are two of them) watch over it. Whenever a swarthy youth, either from the Eastern or from the Western Gates steps out of line, he is sent into exile with a fatherly admonition—not for a long time, and not far away, only onto Mt. Venus, to the old monastery. This monastery is not strict; nevertheless, the young people do not like it, so they usually behave themselves in an orderly way.

I liked being on Mt. Venus. Such tranquillity! The monks have gingerbread made with wine. I did not come across any exiles.

I spent the evening with Franz . . . we had not been in such high spirits for a long time. We chattered nonsense, guffawed, joked with Peppo and Nino; they also let themselves go as never before. Only Giovanni kept himself aloof. The most handsome of them! No, Nino was also very good-looking. From the garden of paradise there came such fragrances that my head whirled, and again there was quiet, torpid bliss . . . Finally we did not even want to speak—so delightful was our blissful languor.

The moon had disappeared long ago, the night was like India ink; just a short distance away I could not see Franz or his armchair, yet I could feel his presence. I felt him and myself as one, but what this "oneness" was I did not know; something not unlike an anguished happiness.

The city clocks struck far off.

"It's quite late," I said, but did not move.

"Wait. You can walk home in five minutes by using the lower path."

"No . . . It's too dark."

"Giovanni will walk you home. No, Nino will. Nino, bring a lantern."

A light shadow flashed across the veranda. A twinkling light flared up, instantly illuminating the armchair, the wisteria, the pale features of Franz . . .

"Ecco, signore."

Nino and I were on a steep, slippery path. On the left—a high rock; above it—the half-demolished walls of the city. On the right—a black nothingness; nevertheless, it felt like something huge and empty. Only dense odors filled it, but at this point I apparently no longer sensed them.

My hand was resting on Nino's narrow shoulder. I was much taller than he. (Franz and I were almost the same height.) I felt the slender shoulder through the thin fabric of his shirt. The swinging light from below lit up the tender, swarthy face, especially unfamiliar in these shady, uneven rays. My hand slipped, stretched out farther . . . It was already on Nino's other shoulder. He was closer to me, quite close . . . We were still walking, but more slowly. The circle of light was also wavering more slowly. My hand was slipping . . .

"Signor . . . Signor . . . " Nino whispered.

I also whispered some simple words. Bending over him, I sought his face, I sought his fresh lips with my lips.

"Oh, signore . . . Impos . . ."

I know, I know these whispers, this "no" which always means "yes, yes . . ."

But what had happened? It was as though someone's cold hand had gently pushed me away from Nino. I broke away from the embrace and leaned against the rock. Without moving or thinking, I gazed for a long, full moment on the now motionless light of the lantern on the ground, until the light again began to sway. I continued to hear Nino's whisper, but somehow I was neither listening, nor was I attentive. It seems Nino whispered that we were coming out onto the main road, that it was here, *"gia qua,"* and that *"i carabinieri sono adosso . . . sono adosso . . ."*

It definitely did not matter to me now.

At home I bolted the windows, the shutters, lit a candle, sat on the bed.

My heart throbbed with infrequent, heavy beats, as if it were terribly large.

What had happened? Why did I . . . ? No, Franz would not have understood me. After all, who would have understood, since I myself did not understand?

Franz would say, shrugging his shoulders, "Well, you're all alike . . . if Nino hadn't been a 'he' but a 'she' . . ."

But this is not true! Not true! In my memory there glimmered a remote story of my early youth, a carnival at Nice, the eyes of Marcel—whose eyes? Who was this, a "he" or a "she"? I did not know, I did not think about this; for me Marcel (he or she) was a "you" . . . The only "you" in the world . . .

However, Nino was in the first place, certainly not a "you." Therefore it did not matter whether he was a "he" or a "she." Because it this case he was—an "it."

I felt that I was becoming more and more confused, all the more hopelessly entangled in the threads of my thoughts. I was ripping away the threads, becoming irritated, but could not disengage myself.

I sat on the bed in such an absurd way half the night.

When I decided, at last, to undress and lie down, I only knew one thing for certain: that my respite, in any case, had come to an end.

IX
THE PEARL-HANDLED CANE

Clara had such an unhappy, careworn face lately that I could not refuse her anything. She asked me to go with her to visit a female English artist with whom she was acquainted.

I could endure neither these English lady-friends of Clara, nor the guests from the hotel, nor the local inhabitants. Because the local people, with their villas, were also numerous in Bestra. What they were doing here—who knows. A typical English-woman, usually aged and ugly, lives alone, but more often with another, a lady companion, and they occupy themselves with something "artistic"; it seems that they are always painting some-thing, writing, or collecting things . . .

Since I was very little interested in these acquaintances of Clara, I viewed them only from afar. The typical Englishwoman is well known on the contintent; I have not been to England, and for some reason I have never wanted to go there—neither the country, nor its people, nor even English literature, has attracted me. Such idiosyncrasies do exist.

I did not want to upset pallid, unhappy Clara and, although I did not feel like going anywhere at all that day, especially to see an Englishwoman, I went.

On the way I wondered what was wrong with Clara. Was she bored with Marius, with his gloomy appearance, and his thick gray-black mustache? And why did Franz so significantly say to her that she was innocently unhappy?

Clara tried to entertain me by talking about her artist friend—she would be glad to see me; Clara had spoken to her about me. She was interested in modern ideas in literature and philosophy, and in painting she was attracted by Cubism. Clara was not an admirer of Cubism . . . Yet she was curious about it.

I was not at all curious. When I saw the Cubist artist, I com-pletely lost interest. One thing, though, was comforting—this obese lady, with straight, obviously tinted, dark-red hair, turned out to be more German than English. Furthermore, it was pleasant to sit in the garden of her villa.

The garden descended down the mountain in semicircular terraces. On one of these, near a low, wide, stone embankment or parapet, a tea table had been set. Some kind of dense, dark tree, like a willow—it was not a willow, certainly—streamed long, soft branches downward, spreading them along the low, stony embankment. It seemed that the shade from this tree was especially fresh and quiet. The chattering of the English-German woman did not spoil the fresh tranquillity, for I was not listening. I do not even remember the language of the conversation—was it in German? In English? In French? Or all of them together?

There were footsteps on the gravel. A new guest. Clara and her hostess met her with cordial exclamations. I turned, rising from my straw armchair.

Our hostess asked the newcomer something in English. Clara turned to me and introduced us.

The guest was a little girl. So she seemed to me at first glance. Very little and thin—yes, but scarcely had she sat timidly on the stone parapet directly under the streaming branches, when I saw that she, perhaps, was not a young girl. Her plain, narrow, little face was even old-looking. All her features were sharp—a pointed chin, a long, sharp nose. Only her pale pink lips were those of a child.

Clara called her "Baroness" . . . I did not catch her family name. Our hostess asked something about the health of "*your mother.*" Clara, thinking probably about me and having been accustomed to speaking with me in French, interrupted:

"*Oh, parlons donc français!*"

"*Parlons français!*" agreed the little Baroness, yet I understood that this was not her language. Earlier she had said several words in German, then spoke in English, but even then I seemed to detect a barely perceptible accent. Who was she?

Our hostess now prattled exuberantly in French with the same force of garrulous eloquence. I did not listen. I did not look at her. I was looking at a short, gray dress and somehow pitifully crossed little legs in gray stockings and white shoes. She stooped a little, so that, sitting down, she appeared even smaller. She wore a wide jacket of English cut and an English straw hat.

"*Dites moi, Monsieur, qu'est-ce que c'est que le symbolisme? Dites moi . . .*"

I turned to my hostess, not seeing her.

"*Mais je ne sais pas, Madame. Je ne sais rien du tout. Je ne pense jamais à rien . . .*"

Fortunately, Clara interrupted. I continued my strange occupation—not thinking about anything actually, just gazing at the Baroness and the dangling branches.

The German-Englishwoman began to chatter about contemporary music. The little Baroness removed her hat and set it on the parapet next to her. I saw her brown hair with the golden highlights. Cropped in the French fashion, it rose luxuriantly above her forehead. Not in waves, but luxuriantly.

"What a beautiful walking stick you have," I said.

She silently offered her cane to me. The lower half was black wood, while all the upper half was covered completely with mother-of-pearl inlay. I almost did not see it—I saw only her eyes, very light hazel, with yellow rims around the pupils. And in them, as well as in the way she extended her cane to me, I saw . . . I do not know what, I cannot define it, the hour of fate, perhaps. I only know my feeling of certainty at that time—with this being I could do whatever I wanted, it was mine.

"Oh, Ella, this charming walking stick always delights my eyes!" jabbered the artist woman. "Madame Zette, have you seen Ella's cane? Is it not a thing of remarkable beauty? Where did Mrs. Middle procure this for you?"

Clara wanted to take the mother-of-pearl cane out of my hand, but I gave it back to little Ella.

She spoke shyly, not lowering her light eyes.

"It is ancient . . . *ma mère* found it in Egypt. I am never without it . . ."

Then everything was very simple. The three of us left the artist woman. Clara said that we would accompany Ella to her hotel, since it was on our way. Ella became cheerful, smiled twice in a childlike way, and, although Clara did most of the talking, I managed to learn something about Ella. She was a musician, a composer; she had graduated from the London conservatory, had always lived in England; however, Mrs. Middle liked to travel so much that they went far and wide over the whole world, it seems . . . They were now passing through Bestra, but they had spent some time here earlier. Ella's speciality was orchestral music. Mrs. Middle was very concerned about Ella's career; therefore, it was necessary to maintain connections in London.

Suddenly Clara fell silent. Franz came to meet us. He was frowning and his eyes were downcast; he raised them when he saw us. His face immediately changed its expression. It became kind and affable. To my surprise, he greeted Ella as if she were an acquaintance, although he had not known that she was staying in Bestra.

We spoke for a minute. The party at Rach was to be held the next day. Baroness Roon (what a strange name!) would also come, would she not?

We said good-bye to Franz, and since it was two steps from Bella Vista where Ella lived with her mother, we also took our leave of Ella.

Why, however, was her mother's name Mrs. Middle? And where was the Baron? Was this girl married?

Clara was strangely silent. On approaching the house, I nevertheless asked:

"Is she a good musician, this little lady?"

"Ella? Very good. And she's only twenty-four years old . . ."

"Has she separated from her husband?"

"What husband? She's not married! How did you come to such a conclusion?"

Clara laughed. She opened the wicket gate. From the balcony was heard the voice of Marius:

"Cla-ra!"

"*Ich komme!*" answered Clara, and hastened upstairs.

I went to my room.

X
FINALLY THE PARTY AT RACH

To tell the truth, I exaggerated when I declared that after my conversation with Franz in the wind I understood absolutely everything and that I only lacked the words to express it.

I understood, though not in the same way as Franz wanted me to understand. I understood more from the outside than the inside. Such understanding, although very profound, is based on faith. However, it is easier to talk about it.

First of all, I understood that in the soul of a man—more correctly, in the essence of a man—there can arise a whirlwind of great strength, great and insurmountable. That natural whirlwind which made me lose my senses was somewhat like it. By drawing nearer, I understood what was really important—insurmountability. It sweeps away everything the human being could use in order to master it. It is a useless struggle. This whirlwind will subside by itself. If it does not, let it carry you to its end. It is good that not every human being is sufficiently deep and magnanimous to enable such blinding whirlwinds to arise within him.

As for Franz . . . he experienced them. It was impossible to help him (it was insurmountable!); when he saw that I, standing near him, somehow comprehended it, felt it—he was comforted.

And then there was still another thing about Franz, which concerned Otto—something more personal, and which, frankly speaking, I did not quite grasp and took entirely on faith.

Franz could not and did not want to accept the idea that Otto was happy . . . with a woman. He said if this were so, it would mean that Otto, whom he, Franz, had loved, was not Otto at all, but someone different. And that the real Otto did not exist at all. However, the love of Franz did exist—was it for no one? This was what Franz could not endure. It was possible for him to go on living only by not believing in Otto's happiness. It seemed to me that he was hoping for some kind of help from me. But what kind of help?

Sometimes I sort of came to my senses—was not everything, en bloc, rolling along the brink of madness? And was not Franz himself a part of this madness, and even I myself, who analyzed his complexities and sympathized with some things that were absurd from a normal point of view? Franz did not love Otto. Where did this wild jealousy, this dry, loveless jealousy, come from? It was, moreover, absurd in its one-sidedness; there was nothing else—only his jealousy of Otto's wife! If Otto had betrayed him not with his wife, but as he had done before, just as Franz himself had betrayed him . . .

No, no, here at the very root there was some kind of unsolvable incomprehensibility, perhaps absurdity. Love had nothing to do with it. Are these whirlwinds which seize the being of a person—are they love? No, not love. Love is intertwined, entangled in all this, but how to release it, how to liberate it—I do not know. Perhaps we have not seen any love at all, and we do not have a real concept of it. God knows what we flounder in, and thus we die, not having seen love . . .

This is what I concluded. Memoirs about love, recollections of what never existed . . . lies, lies!

In such moments (of enlightenment) I want to cast everything aside. Especially since, speaking with the clearest conscience, I consider that "to cast aside love," or that which we attribute to love, does not at all mean casting aside "everything." This area of life is by no means everything and is of no particular importance, of no primary significance . . .

But I surrendered. I cast aside only rationalizations. They, truly, can lead to a madness which is completely fruitless.

Franz, whatever he was, was a living person. With his whirlwinds he lived a genuine life. And I did also, with my absurdities. Since I have begun to talk about people, about their loves— be it only their grimaces of love—I shall continue further.

Let God Himself understand us.

The Villa Rach, usually so familiar, today was different.

Wide doors, nearly the size of a wall, opened onto the veranda from a room with a red stone floor. There were colored lights from above, small patterned lanterns, but it was impossible to make out what color the light was—rose-lavender, perhaps. Anyway, it was bright and pleasant. A white tablecloth on a table glistened with silver, and a curtain of heavy material shone pink with wisteria. Farther off it was so pitch dark that it seemed as though the world were coming to an end. Nothing but darkness.

Some people were sitting at the table; others, at some distance, on low stools. There were six or seven people; I did not recognize them all immediately—the lighting confused me. There was a huge, young American with a childish, serious face. Also a German count, sinuous, thin, like the stem of an iris. And a taciturn, pleasant Dane. I had met almost all of the others earlier. Clara (she had arrived with Marius) sat near Franz who, in a gay mood, also appeared a bit absent-minded.

Servants flashed by in long, pleated, Sicilian garments. Giovanni, with a scarlet fillet on his dark black curls, was amazingly good-looking. What grace of movement he displayed when he, together with the other servants, lowered the tray in front of the guests! There were tall goblets on the trays, and something else which I could not make out.

Ella was alone at a distance, near the wisteria. I had at once glanced at the patch of her little white frock, yet I did not approach her; I searched for her mother with my eyes. Her mother was not there.

An animated but not very loud German conversation was in progress. The American only smiled, now and then exchanging a few words with Nino and Giuseppe in Italian; he did not understand German.

Franz arose and clapped his hands. And immediately from there, from the garden, from the black darkness where it seemed nothing could be, where the world was coming to an end, the first string sounded a high note.

Invisible musicians began to play a tarantella.

The Sicilian tarantella is of a special kind; I never again heard such music, even in Sicily.

It was a simple, fast, and strange tune—not exactly mournful, but heavy, as passion can be heavy.

Giuseppe and Nino began the dance. The secret of a tarantella (of this one, at least) is in the constant acceleration of tempo; the acceleration is slow, however. This slowness, with its gradual increase in speed, puts one imperceptibly into a whirlwind of movement—into such a whirlwind that, looking at it, it appears you are rushing along with it; rushing to—it does not matter where. What is important is to reach an end, faster, faster! Because it cannot last forever.

It ends abruptly. There is an instantaneous stop, a breaking off of movement. Giuseppe disappeared, and Nino stopped motionless in front of the thin count. This was his choice.

The music did not end, it did not return to the first slow tempo, it only became less loud and vibrant, as if it had moved into the distance. The count, then, coming out into the circle, immediately began to dance to a fast tempo.

He danced so well that, even in his contemporary clothing and next to handsome Nino, he did not appear ludicrous. In his own way he was very graceful, appearing somehow more frail, and in the whirlwind he looked more helpless.

Whether it was the strange wine in the strange glasses, or the flowers, or the invisible music from the black space, or the tarantella, I did not know—but I simply felt that the air, the atmosphere around us, was changing. I cannot say that it was intoxicating me, there was no haze, everything was clearly outlined; only an inner flame was flaring up in the air—and in me, of course, as in everyone else.

When Giovanni came out, it was difficult to take one's eyes from him. He was the handsomest of all, but this is not the point. I do not know what the point is. I recall jet-black curls under the scarlet fillet and the narrow line of his forehead, dark and smooth, with tiny beads of perspiration on it. I remember his fast, light, yet heavy movements to the heavy, monotonous, and soul-stirring melody. And most of all I recall the look of his black, seemingly lackluster eyes—thoughtless, intent. When Giovanni, suddenly stopping, stood before Franz, I became frightened of his gaze, for I recognized it. In the huge, completely **black eyes**, there was the same nameless, indefinable look that I had seen for a moment, not so long ago, in bright hazel eyes with topaz glints. The same look which had compelled me to feel with certainty—this being was mine.

Franz arose, smiling. He only did a few steps and stopped motionless in the middle of the veranda. Oh, yes, it was not necessary for him to dance. He had only to stand, occasionally turning his head toward Giovanni, who was dancing in front of him —for him and, hence, as though with him.

The clear-cut and ethereal profile of Franz was outlined against the cover of white wisteria . . . and suddenly, accidentally removing my eyes from him, I saw and again recognized the familiar gaze . . . what was it? Some kind of mental hallucination? Looking at Franz with this same self-abandoned, almost terrifying gaze, was Clara.

I could not endure it. I was not far from her, from the table, but I began to make my way still closer. Gray, bulging eyes, almost expressionless, were staring fixedly at Franz. It seemed to me that her lips whispered something. Inaudibly, of course. Was it that habitual sentence which I seemed to have heard so often, "*Je l'aime, je l'aime*"?

Yes, either I had imperceptibly become submerged in the psychopathy of imagination, or poor Clara was in love, body and soul, with Franz . . . What is more, he knew that she was in love. He turned, met her gaze—and nothing! He just looked at her with a very kind smile!

I did not succeed in reaching Clara—the music faded away; there was an interlude, everyone conversed, glasses clinked; Franz returned to his place at the table.

I took a glass of rosé wine from Nino's tray and drank it at one gulp. Shaken by my new discovery, I had completely forgotten about Ella. I saw her white dress also at the table—the young

American happily chattered away in whistling English, and the little girl in white would answer him animatedly.

I did not listen attentively, again forgot about her, and so it continued until the end of the evening when I was compelled to remember her.

The party was still lingering on—I don't know for how long; I only know that the ardor of the atmosphere was not weakening, perhaps it was even intensifying, and the monotony of changes, sounds, and the movements themselves were stimulating it. Toward the end I was not the same as I was when I had come in, and everyone, with the exception of Clara and Franz, also appeared to have changed.

I did not notice that many people had left—indeed, they had vanished, had slipped out, inaudibly and mysteriously, had disappeared into the vacant darkness.

Some people remained, but I could not see who. I stood on the very edge of the light, on the very boundary of darkness, facing it. Little Ella stood beside me.

I heard the voice of Franz behind me:

"Wait, now they'll play for you a farewell serenade. They don't play it often. It's an old Sicilian one."

He clapped his hands three times.

And for the last time music resounded from the darkness, again as though originating from there, from no one. It was not like the tarantella—or was it? I have my own idea about music, quite a unique attitude, but I shall speak more about this later. Now I was reading the music in the face of the girl who was standing next to me. She had the same sharp, delicate face as that of a small fox—short, brushed-up hair, chestnut-colored, luxuriant, above the forehead, yet her face had assumed an inexpressibly more serious look, entirely absorbed in listening. Even her eyes darkened, as if they were not looking, but listening.

The serenade lasted a long time. Finally it ceased; at last these eternally invisible musicians must have left, whereas we were still silent, as though waiting for something.

"*Oui. C'est bien,*" said Ella, in a barely audible voice.

She raised her eyes to mine. Again! Again! The third time today this delusion, this gaze. In these brown, topaz eyes it was different—it was turned toward me.

I even became angry. This was enough for me! I had indeed become mixed up in such subtleties! And as regards the little Baroness—was I in love with her? No, no. Not at all.

XI
WHAT A DAY!

The next day there was such a torrid brilliance, such a glitter, and such an idiotic confusion in my head, that I did not go out before evening. I longed for twilight and silence.

In the dusk of my shaded room I lay on the couch, doing nothing. Suddenly there was a light knock on the closed shutter. Clara slipped into the room from the balcony.

"Have you been resting? Have I disturbed you? Oh, excuse me! I came . . . perhaps, you will come up to visit with us about six, for tea? The little Baroness and *sa mère,* Mrs. Middle, are coming for a last visit. They're leaving tomorrow."

"Leaving?"

"Yes, to Rome, it seems. She's very charming, Ella, don't you think? And her *mère adoptive* is also nice."

"Is she a *mère adoptive?*"

"Of course. I thought you knew. Her foster mother. So we shall expect you? All right?"

I offered her an armchair, but she did not sit down. She spoke without expression, as though preoccupied with something else. Since my eyes were accustomed to the semidarkness, I saw Clara's face very distinctly, and it did not look as it had earlier. Perhaps I looked at things differently because of my recollection of yesterday. I felt embarrassed, both hurt and ashamed, and wished that she would leave soon. I hurriedly promised to be there at six and thought that the matter would end with that. However, that is exactly where it began.

Clara was on the point of going toward the door, when she stopped and turned.

"Are you planning to see Monsieur von Hallen later in the evening? Are you? Tell him that I love him . . . He knows it. He knows everything. But you, his best friend, please repeat it to him, *"Que je l'aime. Je l'aime tant . . ."*

I was struck dumb for an instant, but then I immediately regained control of myself. The best one could do in this situation was to remain calm.

"Why should I tell him, dear Madame Clara? Especially since he knows it. Why should I repeat it? It would be senseless, cruel . . . and indeed hopeless, wouldn't it? If you knew Franz . . ."

"I know, I know," Clara calmly interrupted, smiling. "I know that he doesn't love me, won't fall in love with me, and can't fall in love with me. It's hopeless. But why do you think I want his love?"

"What do you want, then?" I asked stupidly, losing all comprehension, if not my self-control.

"What I want, he will tell you himself. Yes, he will most likely tell you. And then, if he asks you about something, and if you answer him, remember, I implore you . . . remember my love. I love him so much!"

Although I made no sense of anything, I looked at her almost with respect—indeed, she really loved, no matter what her nature was. Love is one and the same with everyone. At this moment Clara indeed became prettier.

I decided to resolve with Franz that very day the whole muddle concerning Clara and myself. Indeed! I had arrived and behaved like a fool. Surely it was not for this purpose that Franz had summoned me, for me to make advances to his boys, observe a tarantella, and be the confidant of ladies who were in love with him? In a week I would depart. On my way I intended to stop at Rome and somewhere else in Italy.

Rome . . . Good Lord, and Ella? It was strange that I kept forgetting about her all the time, but while forgetting, I was all the time remembering. Very strange. Well, tomorrow she would be leaving; at least that would be finished.

I even said aloud, "At least that." However, I did not rejoice that it was "finished"—not in the least. I could not lie to myself.

The guests were sitting at a festive tea table when I came upstairs.

Clara (what a sweet, efficient hostess she was!), with her pleasant-sounding German intonation, was conducting a polite French conversation. She presented me . . . so there she was, the *mère adoptive!* Big, not at all old, white-skinned, obese, red-haired. Not bright, but light red hair. Englishwomen often have such hair; one seldom encounters the glorified ash-blond color which they claim to have. Mrs. Middle's yellowish-red hair was fluffed on her forehead in curls; chains, ringlets, and medallions dangled on her vast, lilac-silk bosom.

I noted at once that Mrs. Middle's French was very poor and that she understood almost nothing. But not being the least embarrassed, she attempted to speak all the while and even interrupted Clara several times. She was so large that behind her, and behind a lavish bouquet of white flowers, I could not at first see Ella. Only later did I notice her small figure, slightly stooping in the same gray English dress.

My English is poor; however, even if I did know it well, I would scarcely have been successful in converting the conversation into Mrs. Middle's native tongue. She liked to speak French very much, or perhaps she considered that precisely here, precisely at this moment, she felt comfortable and was convinced that it was fitting to speak French. Because of this certainty and because of her large size, she decidedly dominated the table.

I do not know what the conversation was about. I did not understand it and did not try very hard to understand. I only listened when Mrs. Middle would mention Ella's name (and she mentioned it often); however, even then I did not comprehend anything. There is nothing more obnoxious than an English accent—it can make any language entirely incomprehensible.

Fortunately, Clara would catch something and try to repeat

Mrs. Middle's phrases. Ella also began to do the same when the talking did not center around her. So I learned that they really were going to Rome now, that they did not know how long they would remain there, that Mrs. Middle had some business in England, and that they had been traveling for a long time . . . Then she related various *beautés* of their travels, then something else concerning Ella's musical career and her London success, then something about an ancient vase (*"la"* vase) which Mrs. Middle had bought in Bestra . . .

Ella was conscientious about helping *mother,* as she called Mrs. Middle. At our first meeting I considered Ella a very bashful girl. But at the party at Franz's I noticed that she was not timid; on the contrary, she was rather independent.

Very well, but why did I avoid looking at Ella? Why did my eyes glide past her face, without stopping to look at it? What did I fear?

Not the obese Englishwoman, in any case. What was this *mère,* moreover *adoptive,* and why?—I could not understand. However, what business was it of mine, when I hardly believed that she existed? Neither the vastness of her trembling flesh, nor the resolute sound of her guttural voice filling the room, was proof of her existence . . .

"I'm also leaving Bestra soon, and I'm also going to Rome."

I said this, without quite expecting it myself, and looked at Ella for the first time.

If I imagined that I would again see something "unusual" (who knows—I was perhaps even expecting it), I was mistaken. The eyes of the English girl (although she was not English, assuredly) were lowered, and her pointed face was calm.

My announcement, incomprehensible to myself, that I would also be going to Rome, was for naught. I was almost glad, since nothing annoys me more than my own incomprehensibilities and stupidities. But good Clara said, probably out of spontaneous courtesy:

"Oh, so you will meet in Rome, perhaps! Where are you stopping, *cher monsieur?*"

I wanted to say, "I don't know"; however, before "I don't know" had been uttered, I named the little hotel on Monte Pinchio where I always stay when I visit Rome.

All this slipped by quickly. Mrs. Middle did not understand a thing, and I had heard Clara ask Ella to play something (there was a piano in the corner).

"I am not a pianist, *chère madame,*" Ella half-protested. She smiled, as though excusing herself, but arose.

"Yes, yes, she is a composer! But sometimes we amuse ourselves together, and how well we do it! You recall, Ella, our '*Ça ira! Ça ira!*' Do you wish to play it?"

Mrs. Middle also arose—I was shocked by her immensity—then she sat down for some reason, probably waiting for the first chords.

Of course, Ella was not a pianist. What pianist had such hands, childlike and tiny, although sturdy and boyish, with slightly swelled fingers?

I saw only her sharp profile bowing and above it her brown, brushed-up hair (she had removed her hat).

I have already said that I have my own opinion of music, not resembling anyone's; I will not touch upon it. I shall only say that everyone (with the exception of Franz) strongly suspected that I did not like music and did not understand it. They were entirely correct, all of them—yes, I do not like music as they do, do not understand anything about it as many understand it, with subtlety and erudition. I am an ignoramus. I have never attended any concerts, I cannot bear them. And I especially dislike the piano.

As soon as the small stranger began to play, nothing unusual apparently happened to me. Only the room of Floriola vanished, along with Clara, the red-haired fat lady, the sunlight. I was at Franz's villa; I again stood beside the girl in the white dress, on the very edge of darkness. From there, from the black emptiness, came forth these strange sounds I heard.

When they ceased, I still remained for half a minute in a torpor. Clara too, it seemed, for she was silent.

I understood perfectly well, from the first note, that this was the serenade of yesterday. What was the source and the power of enchantment which compelled me not to recall, but to experience once more, with all my five senses, the past as the present? Was it the talent of the slender girl which had resurrected the past? What was this talent? Or was it in me, into me, into some dark depth, that these sounds, sent to me in exactly this way, had diffused? Was this magic taking place—in me?

Clara was also keeping silent. What if there were also some response in her—oh, but of quite a different nature!—to the same sounds?

Our silence lasted half a minute, no longer. Even less, most likely. The three of us were silent—Mrs. Middle did not even notice it. After half a minute, as Ella quietly rose from the piano, her *mother* exclaimed:

"Oh—yes, don't you want to play '*Ça ira?*' "

Ella shook her head. Following Mama's lead, we all rose.

"It's time for us to leave, *mother,* don't you think?" Ella said in English. "We must drop in on Miss Toll. You will get tired . . ."

Clara was engaging in some courtesies, having once more assumed her role as hostess of the house. I was also saying something. Or maybe I was not. I recall only my own tranquillity and shaking Ella's cold little hand. Was this magic? Yes, such things happen in the world. Many other unusual things can happen as well.

XII
CONTINUATION OF THE DAY

It was already dark, but what heat there was! Even here, very close to the sea, on the pebbles, there was no breeze.

We were both lying below the rocks. Something rustled near us. In the sky there was a sharp crescent moon, with its corners turned upward, as though it were smiling.

"Of course," Franz said. "You'll go and investigate. And

then you'll tell me the *whole* truth. I'll give you a year. I can't
live more than a year without the truth."

"It will be difficult, Franz."

"Of course, it will be difficult. But you can . . ."

"I can do it. That is, I can try."

"You can. You alone can. It doesn't matter that you don't
entirely understand why I need this truth."

"It seems, I do understand," I interrupted.

"Have I formulated it too abstractly? It doesn't matter. You're
the one who profits from it. You're able to find out the truth
and convey it to me. You're the only one whom I'll believe.
You have only one year. One cannot learn it hurriedly, at once.
Next spring we'll come together . . . it doesn't matter where,
and then you'll tell me."

We fell silent. There was a rushing among the pebbles. The
moon was smiling.

Nothing else seemed strange on this strange day. I accepted,
without argument, Franz's commission. When I saw that he really
was in need of something, I could not, I simply could not, go
away without offering my assistance. No one, except myself,
would give it to him, and the main thing was that he would not
ask for help from anyone but me. And, indeed, he did not ask
anyone else.

Franz wanted me to learn the truth concerning Otto within
one year. Not the external, but the inner truth of his existence.
(I, of course, understood at once what was meant by "truth.")
Otto was married, he was happy. Was he really happy? Could
he be happy? Had Franz's love for Otto, had this love been
—for "no one"? Or, at least, had it been for an unknown Otto, a
different Otto than Franz had seen? But then there would have
been no love.

Here I became entangled in my own reasoning, so I soon
abandoned my musing. I understood what Franz wanted—I was
well acquainted with Otto, I would find an opportunity to have
a good look at him from the proper angle. Besides, this Otto had
always seemed to be a rather uncomplicated man. I had not been

particularly interested in his inner world, and I supposed it would open itself to me without difficulty.

Well, enough! Franz knew, and it was unimportant that I did not entirely, not "from within," understand even my own explanation of Franz's desires (to learn *whom* he loved), and that I did not understand his dry, loveless jealousy, which was, moreover, absurdly one-sided.

And then he said . . .

"Listen, there's something else . . . something else, quite different."

Franz turned toward me, leaning on his arm. Having become accustomed to the moonlight, I now saw his pale face. It was astonishingly kind, with that expression of quiet tenderness which was so characteristic of my friend. For some reason, though, I became frightened. Something else? What something else?

"Don't be afraid. It doesn't concern the little musician. It's not about you."

About me? About her? What did he want to say? I looked at him, surprised, but did not answer.

"It concerns poor Clara."

Oh! I recalled everything. I recalled the previous evening and this morning.

"Wait, hear me out from the beginning," Franz continued. "Trust me—indeed, you always trust me—don't be surprised, don't laugh. Understand this, as you're able to understand many other things."

XIII
POOR CLARA

"She loves me," Franz began. "You know this, of course. You guessed it, or she told you—it makes no difference. Genuine love is a great gift to whomever it is given. It is both happiness and unhappiness. Clara's love for me is a tremendous, almost continuous unhappiness. She has known it from the very beginning. To whomever this love is sent, he is destined to bear it in the form it is sent. And through Clara, this small and entirely insignificant woman, the unhappiness of her love is also my unhappiness."

I could not endure it. I became angry, interrupted Franz, almost shouting:

"Franz, come to your senses! Your unhappiness? Pardon me, but I've ceased to indulge in such romanticism. I don't want 'high style' here. Is this the first time that an exalted, idle woman has fallen in love with you? I remember it happened before. And have you really suffered with all of them? Really, you remind me of those sensitive young men . . . who lived in the middle of the last century in Russia . . . They also spoke solemnly and made mountains out of molehills. Your unhappiness! A German woman you casually met obstinately fell in love with one she shouldn't have fallen in love with, and you're suffering because of this! And, of course, I'll stake my life on it that you're not the one who's guilty!"

"And she?" said Franz quietly.

"She? Whether she's guilty or not guilty—you don't know women, Franz! For them time is all-powerful; if you force them to submit to the cure of this doctor, everyone will recover. Do you want me to speak with Clara? She'll go to Germany for a rest, and you'll see that everything will turn out well."

"No, stop."

Franz was not angry, although I had spoken rudely and irritably.

"It's better that we finish our discussion later," he said, rising. "You're in a bad temper—I understand! You've forgotten my nature—if there's innocent suffering caused by me, I cannot be calm; in every way possible I consider and reconsider how to alleviate it. When I can."

"Deceive her . . . Get her divorced from Marius and marry the fool," I growled.

Franz laughed, but then he said seriously:

"You don't have to joke that way, Ivan. It's not me, but you who don't know women. Clearly, you've never thought about a woman. You fall in love with her, and then you have no time to consider anything. You ought to ask Clara whether she would rather have deception, or a marriage with me without deception?"

"What does she want, then, from you?" I shouted on the verge of despair. I nearly fell off the steep path, for it was dark, the air was stifling, and the moon had vanished a long time ago.

Franz, however, did not answer, and we parted.

XIV
FURTHER COMPLICATIONS

Nonsense and rubbish! Of course rubbish, if one thinks about it—this mission of mine to uncover the truth concerning the black-eyed, thin-legged little count, a fool, apparently (I did not know him, I was not interested in him), and this German woman who did not concern me at all, and Bestra with its winds, boys, serenades, little and big Englishwomen . . . After all, I had my own life, my own thoughts, my own cause—and what a cause! It was time . . .

Time for what? I was annoyed, irritated. I floundered in a nightmare, yet I saw above all that I felt sorry for Franz.

Why didn't I listen to him to the very end? Whatever he was, with his imagination and idiosyncrasies (you could not change him anyhow!), I loved him. Regarding Otto, I would go to investigate. Franz had to tell me something about Clara. I knew that he had something to say (it had also happened before that he had discussed his problems with me and had asked for my advice)—but I had suddenly and rudely interrupted him.

This concern for Franz had upset me deeply. (In my love for him there was so much piercing pity . . . no, such tender, thoughtful affection!) It was impossible to go to him to try to renew our conversation. It would again be rude. I had to wait, or work out something different.

I went away for the whole day to Catagna. I had planned to

return in the evening, but decided to spend the night there. A dirty city, dirty hotel, terrible heat.

I arrived in Floriola very ill. In the morning I could not get up. I did not know what was the matter with me. They say that this happens in Sicily, some enervating kind of indisposition, which is accompanied almost by delirium and which suddenly goes away in two days. The convalescence, although likewise very short, is of the type which follows a very serious illness.

In these two days I recall lisping and kind *il signor dottore,* then Franz, but, most important, I remember silent Clara, who was near me the whole time and who nursed me unceasingly with a truly maternal solicitude.

Although I really felt completely well, she still did not allow me to get up.

"Tomorrow, tomorrow," she smiled, sitting with some kind of needlework by the shaded lamp in my room. "Tomorrow you shall get up, though it will still be impossible for you to go out, and I will not allow anyone to see you, even Monsieur von Hallen. The day after tomorrow it will be over, and you will be free. It's nothing—just our sun; you were careless. Yes, perhaps you were upset . . ."

I looked at her, and in the quiet room she herself was so quiet that she seemed to me to be another person. As if she were not that stupid German woman over whom I had become so angry on Franz's behalf.

"Madame Clara . . ." I uttered.

She raised her nearsighted, light-colored eyes and looked at me. Then she asked simply:

"Did he tell you?"

I did not answer anything, although I understood the question.

"It is hard for him. He thinks that it's a great responsibility . . ." she continued, as if to herself, lowering her eyes to her work. "He understands everything, with the exception of this— what responsibility does he have? It is only my responsibility, and I want it to be only mine."

"Clara, but you know . . . You love him . . ."

"Yes. We know everything about each other, and it wasn't even necessary to say that word. He has always known that I don't anticipate and don't want his love . . . My own is sufficient for me," she added with a pretty smile, not at all sad.

No, I did not understand. What was the matter? Again some fantasy on Franz's part? Yet however sentimental, she remained the practical German. She obviously wanted something from Franz, which he . . . was not willing to give her.

Clara, unembarrassed by my silence, continued:

"He has guessed my heart, all of me, as no one could. As no one else could. I'm not a wife. I'm not a mistress. I'm capable of loving, as I am destined to do, but why must this love be reciprocated? No, my heart does not demand that . . ."

I sat up abruptly in the bed. There flashed, shot past, fragmentary phrases, words, some warnings of Franz, "Hear it out to the end . . . You don't know the woman . . . And don't laugh . . ." And now, "He has guessed . . . I am not a wife . . . I am not a mistress . . ."

"Clara. Do you want to have a child? His child?"

"Yes."

XV
THE DEMON

After this "yes"—as though by magic a complete picture arose before me, composed of the bits and pieces of what I had seen and heard earlier (though I had rarely paid attention to it), and so accurate that Franz later had to supplement it only with a few, though unexpected, details. Knowing Franz as I did, I could easily guess his feelings and his views concerning our dear Clara's little drama. For her it was not little. Therefore, with Franz's serious attitude toward human beings, Clara's little drama was not insignificant for him, either. He believed, of course (Clara and I also believed, and after all—who knows, maybe it was really so?), that this woman, indeed, was neither a wife, nor a mistress, but merely—though primarily—a mother.

Such women do exist. I did not notice them, to tell the truth. I simply did not give them a thought. Perhaps Franz was right in saying that I did not know women, that I had no time to think about them.

I understood perfectly, as if I had read it in a book, the whole complicated, emotional condition of Franz, the compelling power of his kindness and, in addition, his eternal feeling of responsibility . . . and what else? Yes, yes, my love for Franz understood everything, it seems. But . . . here I, regretfully, again must say something about myself. More accurately—about my demon.

In truth, it is an accursed demon—it always attacks me unexpectedly, and always at the most inappropriate time; it strikes at exactly that which I would most want to protect.

It is unmerciful, this demon—forcing me to laugh at the most inappropriate moments—this demon of the most crude, mocking laughter. Naturally, I myself am its favorite target, although it does not spare anybody or anything.

I still remember—several years ago I was in love with two women—two at once. I swear, seriously in love, deeply. I loved both with the same intensity, but differently, and they were both quite different. A mother and her daughter. The daughter was my fiancée. And the mother, quite unforeseen for both of us, became my mistress. The most terrible thing was that I really loved both of them, I needed both in the same way. And they loved me; I had only one way out—having deceived both, to separate from them.

I recall the tragic night when I was suffering so deeply, severing a relationship which was incomprehensible to me, fully aware of what this severance would mean to me, to both of them, and to each of them individually. (Besides, could I tell the truth to those whom I had deceived? Could they understand it when I could not understand it myself?) Well, during this night, suddenly, on top of everything else, the infernal demon of laughter took possession of me. I not only laughed at myself, but mockingly guffawed and crudely teased myself, as though I were Khlestakov, "Anna Andreevna! Marya Antonovna!" Was it possible to retire with both of them "to the refuge of the streams . . ." ? What did it matter if one of them was "to a certain degree married" ?

No, it is not worth talking about now. I know that I almost blew my brains out because of this intolerable laughter—how much worse it is than "laughter through tears"! [6]

I remember this because all my thoughts—Clara's significant "yes," my understanding of her, Franz, and the entire picture, my increased love for my serious and affectionate Franz, my pity for Clara—all these kept me from closing my eyes until morning. And then there was that foul demon of laughter that so oppressed and exhausted me. Instead of Franz, the demon was showing me such a stupid, comical figure that my sides split with laughter. And Clara appeared to me in a many-faced hysterical mask—such women flit from one celebrity to another, begging, "Please make a child for me! And right away!"

These are the tricks of the devil—to bring together external facts in order to confuse them, to destroy their living, inner content where it exists. To convert a drama not even into a comedy, but into a dirty vaudeville.

I spent the whole night indulging in these pictures, jeering at Franz. (He had gotten into a scrape and still dared to sigh.) At Clara. (And why didn't she desire Marius?) And at myself. (Adviser! Next they would ask advice about what obstetrician to call on! But from the beginning—was this my role, *tenir les chandelles?* Oh, I will agree, I have such an appeasing nature!)

Only toward morning did I doze off. I awoke in a cold terror—what would happen if the demon seized me in Franz's presence? Or in front of Clara? What if I should not get myself under control and laugh in their faces?

[6] With the words "the laughter through tears invisible to the world," Gogol used to describe his own works and their basic tenor, which combined social criticism with the mysticism and political conservatism that alienated him from many of his contemporaries.

No, this was decidedly a figment of my very real madness . . .
I listened—the accursed demon was silent.

Maria brought in coffee, then inquired about my health. The
signora said that if the signor felt better . . .

"I am certainly completely well, *mia figlia!* Tell the signora
that I am strong and that I'm getting up now!"

XVI
A TELEGRAM

I spent my last week in Bestra in the most intimate association
with Franz, in long conversations with him. We took walks far
into the mountains. Whenever we came across a tiny hamlet, we
would spend the night there.

At Floriola I frequently ran into Clara, in the evening, on my
terrace. Little by little we established a frank relationship. I
hardly ever saw Franz and Clara together, and they, it seems,
did not spend time together. Now and then Franz would come
for five o'clock tea.

They really and truly did not need to hold long conversations
with each other—everything was understood and said immediately in a few words.

I had correctly guessed Franz's attitude toward Clara—I simply
accepted it.

I also accepted Clara in the same way, with her love, her persistent will, and . . . her practicality.

I liked her determination. She "most certainly" would separate
from Marius and would leave Bestra forever. She would give
Floriola to Marius. She still had means and a small villa on the
Italian seacoast (she did not say where); her old aunt was living
there now.

"We shall arrange something with Monsieur von Hallen,"
she added, "before my departure. He can come for several days
. . . best of all to San Remo. If, of course . . ."

She did not complete her sentence, she never completed it. For the first time, upon hearing these words, I became terribly frightened—what if the demon were suddenly to seize me? But she said this so simply, with such unaffected *naïveté*, that I did not burst out laughing. I did not even smile.

Well, and what about Franz? He knew of Clara's decision to leave Bestra; he, apparently, knew everything; he also accepted everything, apparently . . . Yes, but he was not Clara, and my conversations with him were different. It seemed impossible for us to become closer, and I clearly pictured to myself what was taking place in his serious and complex soul. I began to think that kindness—his radiant kindness—would conquer, that it must conquer. Now I no longer laughed—our conversations always took this special course.

I did not even laugh when I suddenly noticed that some new complication was tormenting Franz. I only became helplessly angry and immediately decided not to think about it, since I saw at once that I did not understand it and would not understand it. I became angry with Franz—was it possible to let oneself lapse into such entanglements? To become entangled to the point where everything became meaningless? How did he, in his understanding, connect Clara's story (and this unfortunate San Remo) with my promised investigation concerning the little count? No, it would be better for me simply to close my ears, to turn my back, to forget—to look at that Sicilian peasant woman walking with a jug on her head, at the little girl playing with a cat by the door, at a rooster crowing somewhere . . . what a sweet, coarse, understandable life! Why do people twist and turn it so!

Franz guessed, it seemed, that I was angry and why—he did not explain, did not insist on anything, but with a smile passed on to something else.

No, enough! Bestra wearied me very much with its enigmatic events and its unexpected complications. Something had become disentangled—I understood now why Franz needed me. Now I could breathe with relief. Of course, the absurdity of these events remained—both Clara, and Franz's commission . . . It was not worth thinking about, though. This was Franz's nature and, therefore, I would go in due time to try to get some information about Otto. Concerning Clara—he knew how I felt.

And with joy, even with emotion, I eagerly looked forward to becoming free in two days, to traveling . . . where would I be going? It made no difference—to Syracuse, to Palermo . . . from there, through Naples—to Rome. I know Rome. Sienna, Orvieto . . . what if I went there? On the return trip it would be necessary to stop in Berlin, if only to begin with that stupid Otto . . . Well, it was still a long way off! Now I anticipated my journeys, as though expecting a "secret joy in the future."

Whistling, I was packing my suitcase (though I still had two whole days!) when Maria, with my morning coffee, brought me a telegram.

I opened it but did not understand a thing. What language was it? French? Italian? Oh, English! It asked when I planned to be in Rome. . . *"Could travel with you . . . Mother goes England. Ella."* I stood with the open telegram in my hands, staring at the strips of words which were pasted on it. I turned it over—yes, it was for me. Evidently it was necessary to answer it. But where? It was from Rome—my hotel, where I always stayed.

I was slow in grasping the situation. *"Mother goes England"* . . . Should I show it to Clara?

Immediately I decided that I would not show her. I would go to the city myself and answer. When would I be in Rome? In a week? Earlier? And Syracuse, Palermo? Well, maybe I could skip Syracuse. I would stay a day in Palermo. It takes a night to reach Naples . . . I could be in Rome in five days.

JULIEN, OR
NOT JULIEN?

Why is it that no one thinks of Julien when one is in love? After I had read Stendhal's *Le Rouge et le Noir*[1] I understood right away—that's a real hero for you.

I have to admit, however, that this is where my second love got mixed up in it. Yes, it was my second one, and this was saddening in itself. It also worried me.

I knew about first love—angels rejoice over it, and it is noted among them up there. Even if nothing results from it here on this earth, it is not lost—and later on, "up there," its effects will be seen. About second love I had no information, and it seemed that it was good for nothing.

But one suffers no less because of it, although, I must admit, there is no less joy in it, either. Because of this knowledge I felt sorry for myself in advance—how would I feel when I stopped loving her?

This second love of mine was the priest's

From *Russia Illustrated*, no. 47, November 14, 1931.

[1] Stendhal, pseudonym of Henry Beyle (1783–1842), novelist and critic. Author of many works, among them *Le Rouge et le Noir* (1830), *Mémoires d'un touriste* (1838), *La Chartreuse de Parme* (1839), *L'Abbesse de Castro* (1839), etc.

daughter, Marya Ivanovna. That made her the daughter of our high school divinity teacher (all this took place in Moscow). He was also our parish priest at the Church of the Resurrection on Ostozhenka Street, the Archpriest Father Ioann.

I saw Marya Ivanovna frequently—occasionally in the teachers' room (she would come for her father) and in church, but these meetings didn't mean much. The most important fact was that she often visited my cousins' home where I was a regular guest. My cousins lived two steps from the church along Ostozhenka Street, and I was not far from there. So on my way to high school I went past all these cherished houses; Marya Ivanovna lived in the one belonging to the church.

She wears a black dress with a wide, black velvet band around her neck. Her face is very round and full, her gray eyes are somewhat bulging in addition to looking askance, so that it's impossible to tell whether or not she is looking at you. Everything about her seems somewhat pleasantly round and plump. The expression on her face is always nonchalant (or haughty). Behind her shoulders she wears two long, even braids tied together at the top with a small ribbon.

I know nothing about her. My cousins never mention her, and she says practically nothing when she is at their house. As for myself, I remain silent, too, just looking at her . . . I think about her, I make guesses about her. Whom could she resemble? Could it be that she is Melita from Spielhagen's *Problematische Naturen?* [2] If this is the case, that would make me Oswald; but I am not Oswald at all, nor do I want to be Oswald. Instead, I am Julien from *Le Rouge et le Noir.* In any case I long passionately to be a Julien, and this is sufficient, for most likely I have the makings of one.

However, the realization that I was Julien entered my mind later. (Having conceived this second love, I began to devour every novel which came into my hands, searching frantically

[2] Spielhagen, Friedrich (1829–1911). German writer. His major works include *Problematische Naturen* (1860), novels *In Reich und Glied* (1866), *Sturmflut* (1876), etc.

in them for information about love—its psychological side, of course, for I knew about the physiological part from my friends. But for some strange reason I was not interested in those things then, despite my fifteen years, thank God!)

Thus I started out not so much by being Julien, but by studying my lessons to the minutest detail for our divinity teacher. It wasn't that I would engage in lengthy discussions, but I took to memorizing and spouting off whole pages in Old Church Slavic, things which weren't even demanded of me.

I wasn't scheming to please her father. What good would a scheme like that have been? I had, however, a vague feeling of being somehow tied to her through my knowledge of God's law. Her father is a priest, and that means she probably also takes part in it. Perhaps she, too, knows all of this by heart. I tried to clarify this confused connection for myself, to define it, but nothing came of it.

One time at my cousins', when she was there and someone was asking me about high school, I took the risk. I declared with disdain that I had received a low mark in Greek but that I couldn't care less about it, since I was interested exclusively in God's law. Right there in one breath I recited in Old Church Slavic an entire chapter from the Sermon on the Mount.

My cousins' grandmother listened to me, deeply moved, and sighed. The oldest cousin, Yulya, shook her head: "Have you, perhaps, decided to become a deacon?" Yet she, Marya Ivanovna, didn't say a word. I became exasperated (maybe at myself; it only appeared to be for another reason).

I did not stop memorizing my lessons (some kind of subterranean connection with Marya Ivanovna still remained), but at the same time I began to search for new approaches to this love of mine.

Isn't it strange that one always wants to do something with one's love? Why is that? Wouldn't it be sweet bliss just to sit at my cousins' in the gloomy dining room, to steal a look at the black velvet band, the gray eyes, or perhaps not to look, but only to know, only to feel with the whole of your being, to the very

depths, that she is here? And wouldn't it be sweet bliss for one at
home in bed, in the darkness, to cry out from the sweet pain of
one's own solitude and from the incomprehensibility, the in-
expressiveness of love?

Of course, it would be sweet bliss! But the special quality of
love, as it appears, is that it is not satisfied with sweet bliss. Love
does not remain in one place. Since I didn't know what to do
with it and really didn't want anything from Marya Ivanovna, I
unwillingly turned my attention toward myself. And it was exactly then that I came across Stendhal's Julien Sorel.

What if this love (which perhaps was not my second love by
accident!) had suddenly been given to me for the reworking of
my character? It had been given in order to test me, and certainly
not for me to be thrilled and timidly enflamed by it while indulging in boyish delight. I must act, I must gain a victory over myself in all things, even in defiance of myself. If I can't say a word
to Marya Ivanovna—still I must. If I can't dream of kissing her
hand (and I don't want to at all)—I'll make myself do it. Finally,
there is one last thing, something, of course, which I had only
considered with a shudder of despair, a thing which was the
most impossible—maybe I'll even tell her that I love her . . .

This was not going very far, but it was enough to plunge me
into total horror. The task which I laid before myself simply
weighed me down. It even suddenly seemed that I had stopped
loving Marya Ivanovna a little. Oh no, my dear boy, you are trying to deceive yourself, you are using a very cunning device so
that you can get out of it! Julien would have been ashamed . . .
Just what I have decided to do—I will do. I may die, but I will
do it . . . even if I don't reach the final stage, that is, the dec-
laration of love, I will do it anyway.

They dismissed us for two weeks for Easter vacation. The
spring was terrible, cold, and gray; the brown snow was like
watery porridge, and something thin and sharp fell from above.
I wandered along the streets, bewildered by my thoughts; I
slipped into puddles. I would go walking—where I didn't know
—and then I would return.

Near the china shop by the church I felt as though something pushed me—it was she! I had never really met her in the street before. This was a clear sign.

She wore a small, black lambskin hat with her braids over her fur coat, and her cheeks were red.

"Marya Ivanovna!" I said firmly and in a loud voice. "My respects to you. I wish you all the best. That is, I mean, how are you?"

I removed my school cap while making a bow.

In surprise Marya Ivanovna looked to one side; she did not answer my smile, but held out her hand.

"Where are you heading?" I continued. "Aren't you going to my cousins'? "

"No, I'm going home," she said. The surprised look didn't leave her face. After a while she added:

"Are you coming from there? "

"Yulichka isn't well," I lied unexpectedly, myself not knowing why.

Marya Ivanovna looked at me askance.

"Really? Well, good-bye."

We parted. It turned out well for the first time, and I was very pleased with myself. In the evening I went to see my cousins, vaguely thinking to find her there and at the same time secretly hoping not to find her.

I did find her. However, instead of my former bliss, I felt bewilderment. Yulichka did, in fact, turn out to be sick—again this was a clear sign.

I began chattering in a most unusual way, mumbling some sort of nonsense, for I was thinking of something else. I was thinking that Julien himself was not left alone after such a short time, yet he even took her hand in front of her friend, in the darkness, that's right, in the garden . . . Should I volunteer to walk her back? Never, it's not proper. Her servant usually accompanies her from my cousins' house in the evening. But what has the mud got to do with it? The street is not a garden, anyway . . .

I arose to go earlier. As usual, I kissed my cousins good-bye, and I squeezed Marya Ivanovna's hand especially tightly and held it in my own for an instant. I made myself do it.

I really did—my word of honor!—even if she didn't notice. What if I were to kiss her in church, after matins?

This insolent thought, however, put me in such a state that I didn't go to matins at all. At home I said that I was sick and didn't go. I felt that I couldn't go, that there would be a catastrophe. By the same villainous weakness I didn't visit my cousins either on the first day of the holiday. It was only on the third day that I made up my mind—"Even if you run into someone on the third day, you don't have to give an Easter kiss. And it is hardly likely that she would be there . . ."

She wasn't there but arrived soon after. I didn't have to give her an Easter kiss; still, having seen a "sign," I felt in myself a surge of strength and an iron steadfastness. Not a trace of bliss was there. I hardly noticed the velvet ribbon and that "she" was not wearing black but a light gray dress.

I gave her my best wishes for the holidays and sat down next to her. I declared that I was sick.

"I even missed matins. And how have you been?"

"I am feeling fine," Marya Ivanovna said, surprised. "We were at home. The weather was terrible, so we couldn't go to the Kremlin."

"Do you like the sky at night all lit up like this? You like this spring air, don't you?"

I moved my chair closer to her.

"What sky are you talking about, when it's raining?" exclaimed Yulya (my other cousin was not home). "And why do you keep pestering her? Manichka, do you want some fresh paskha? The fresh one is ready, I was just going to bring it in. Come on, let's try it."

Yulya rose and went out. I was left alone with Marya Ivanovna.

Alone with her for the first time!

That was the end of my reflections. The end of my hesitation.

The only thing necessary was will power, an action. Was I, or was I not, Julien?

Marya Ivanovna's hand, somewhat plump and not very white, with small dimples on it, was resting on the table. I leaned over and kissed it with a smacking sound.

"What's this all about?" Marya Ivanovna said in amazement, turning her face toward me.

I said firmly and loudly:

"My dear Marya Ivanovna. Are you listening? I love you."

Since she said nothing in reply, I continued:

"I love you, I adore you, I am in love with you . . . Are you listening? I am in love with you . . ."

It seemed that everything had been done, everything had been said . . . but I sensed with horror that this wasn't everything. Something had to be added. Phrases from books floated about in my head, those things which usually come next—"Be my wife," or just "Be mine," or "When and where will we see each other," or even, "I ask for nothing, nor do I hope for anything." But I couldn't say any of these phrases to her! And I began chattering away, like a woodpecker, "I love you, I adore you, Marya Ivanovna," although I felt neither love nor adoration, but only wondered how I could get out of all this now, wallowing as I was in inexpressible shame.

Yulya's footsteps were now heard along the corridor. The inspiration came to me.

"I ask one thing of you, just one!" I whispered. "Not a word to anyone! Not a hint! Be merciful! Least of all to Yulya! I beg you on my knees to be silent! Silent! Forever!"

I glanced at Marya Ivanovna (I had not looked at her before). She was just the same as ever. She shrugged her shoulders and said:

"Of course. Why talk about it? Really, these are such silly things . . ."

That was the end of my second love. That was my liberation from Marya Ivanovna. I had lost my bliss, but I felt no regret.

In fact, it was just the opposite—some sort of new feeling of ease.

I was only tortured by uncertainty, for it really hadn't been decided whether or not I was Julien. I behaved as he did, or close to it, but for some reason it was apparent that I wasn't Julien anyway.

REST, HEART

I met her, this beautiful old woman, during the war, in 1915. At the time no one had become accustomed to the war even on the line of battle, not to mention on the home front. People were terribly distressed about the mothers who were tormented continually by hope and fear. They recalled Nekrasov's "Heed the terrors of war" and "The tears of the poor mothers . . ."

It was at this time that I met Marya Markovna. The meeting so affected me that I wrote a description of it right after I was injured, and before returning to the front, and printed it in one of the St. Petersburg newspapers. A great volume of letters flooded the editorial office after that. Most of them were written by mothers. Some were in praise of Marya Markovna, others envied her, still others were outraged, condemned her, or even heaped insults on her (and on me too, by the way). This was despite the fact that I only put down what I had heard from her without making any judgment. I did not know how to judge her then; I do not know how even at this time. Possibly the question of a mother's suffering does not sound very timely now—there is no war, and the mothers of today are different in some way . . . Indeed, so much have we endured—we in partic-

From *Russia Illustrated,* no. 46, November, 1932.

ular—that what we have undergone is worse than any war. But I believe that basically the question of spiritual, lingering suffering still remains. The person for whom it remains will find my Marya Markovna interesting. I regret that the notes which I took at that time have not been preserved, and in the course of so many years I have forgotten a good deal of it. I will write down briefly what I remember; I still recall the essentials.

I was discharged that summer from a St. Petersburg hospital; although no longer an invalid, I was not yet at my full strength. It was impossible to return to the front sooner than the fall. My aunt and uncle, the only relatives I had, advised me not to remain in the city since I was still a sick man, but to take a trip to their small estate and spend some time there. They themselves had not been there for a long while, preferring to travel abroad, and were now going to the Crimea. The house was an old one in a virtual wilderness, but the place was marvelous, or so my aunt had said. I was happy that it was a wilderness and hastily packed my things.

It was indeed very pleasant there. There was a narrow stream with a steep bank, the village lay beyond it with a green-domed church, there were forests in the distance . . . My little house was a ramshackle one, the watchman there was deaf, and the watchman's wife could fix nothing but omelettes and cabbage soup . . . All this pleased me very much.

Across the stream there was a footbridge to the high bank opposite me, and behind it a steep path ascended straight to the church. From my bank the church was distinctly outlined in the sky; next to it, just as distinctly a dark canopy of age-old trees was visible, and on the most precipitous part of the bank, nearly overshadowed by trees, there stood a white house with columns. I was attracted to the house—it was so lovely in a conventional way, in the style of an antique picture. It was a real manor house, one of those which were sometimes even called "palaces." Evidently it was quite ancient, and the most surprising thing of all was that it was not vacant—the windows were not boarded up

and, although they did not exactly sparkle, they showed clear signs of life.

From down below, from the footbridge, I would often stare at this house, lost in reverie. At that time, incidentally, I used to look at everything, people, the sky, in some kind of strange reverie which I did not wish to abandon. It seems that this began after I had experienced the long lapse of memory which followed my injury.

It was August, and the charming canopy of trees between the church and the white house was dappled in red and gold. The old birches by the church were also turning gold. I loved to sit in its graveyard. It was pleasant and clean there, with benches between the monuments and tombstone gratings. There was never anyone in this spacious graveyard except, perhaps, the lector whom you might occasionally run into—he lived somewhere in the vicinity.

I do not remember when I first saw a slender woman in a dark gray dress on a far-off bench in the graveyard. A veil of the same steel color was thrown over her carefully arranged, silver-white curls. I noticed this and everything about her, although somehow unconsciously. Only the second time did I remember that I had seen her already, and that I had seen her precisely on my bench near a graceful and apparently newly erected marble monument. The pedestal was concealed by bushes on which some smallish, late roses were blooming.

I stared at the woman's face—it was thin and, while not stern, somehow amazingly tranquil. It was so tranquil that in looking at it I felt as though I were infected by this tranquillity. I did not take my eyes from her, I did not think about anything. I just sat as she did, watching. I came to my senses a little only when she rose and, with a light step, disappeared beyond the trees.

I waited and then strolled along the pathway up to the monument where her bench was located. The monument was simply a pillar of gray marble, finely sculptured. Its modest gold lettering read, "Valentin Borovikov: 1894–1914." A boy twenty years

old; no doubt it was her son. Perhaps he died in the war? Hardly
. . . Borovikov . . . some sort of half-felt remembrance, not
reaching total consciousness, flashed in my mind and vanished.
I sat down on the bench again in my aimless reverie, but I
jumped when I heard near me the voice of the lector, who had
appeared from somewhere:

"What delightful air we have! It's heavenly! Have you been
taking a walk?" He took a seat next to me on the bench.

"Very pleasant places we've got here," he continued in a talkative manner.

"We have a fine parish here, too. And all due to the efforts of
the Borovikova lady . . ."

"Is that who was just sitting over there?"

"Of course. Her home is behind the park, and the entire
estate is called Borovikovo. They were once wealthy people. As
for now, she has been here two years without ever leaving it. She
lives like a hermit. The only other people are the cook, the
watchman, and some maidservants. She has a coachman who
exercises the horses, but she never goes anywhere."

"What about this grave here," I pointed to the monument,
"was this her son?"

The lector pursed his lips in a somewhat strange way, looked
at me askance, and said:

"Her son. Yes. Her son."

He fell silent. Then he suddenly leaned toward me and whispered mysteriously:

"But his remains are not here."

At first I was astonished, but then I realized that during the
war such an event was not rare.

"Then did he die in the war? This happens when it's impossible to recover the body. They only issue a verifying certificate."

The lector smirked and shook his head.

"Certificate! Not only did Marya Markovna want nothing to
do with a certificate, but she gave orders that no one was to bring
her anything from the post office. And no one has. And no one
has come to see her. In the spring there was some gentleman

who tried to see her, but she didn't receive him, didn't even allow them to take his calling card. When her money does arrive, the steward has the power of attorney. Yet you talk about a certificate!"

I shrugged my shoulders. It was strange. Was she insane, or what? But the lector again shook his head:

"Not at all. That's her character. Once she has decided something for herself—it has to be that way. She is a kindhearted person, she does perform many good deeds around here! But she has quite a character."

"In what way? What has she decided?"

The lector, however, either didn't want to or was unable to explain anything to me intelligibly. He shrouded himself in mystery and shifted the conversation to God knows what, saying that they would hold no requiem but that, in spite of this, the monument was built on consecrated ground because she had "authority." Having passed on all this gossip to me, the lector departed—his wife was calling him. If he wanted to arouse my interest, he had succeeded in doing so, I must admit. That day I thought of the woman from the white house more than once. Furthermore, the next day I purposely went to the graveyard toward evening, hoping to meet her.

It must be said that war—life at the front, in the trenches—produced a change in many of us in the sense that it simplified our relations with people, especially our social etiquette. Take myself, for example—I was, as they would say, a "dashing" young man, accustomed to the *beau monde*. I was, moreover, starting out on a diplomatic career; I suppose I was socially polished. Yet all this was gone from me after a year in the trenches. It was not that I had become hardened, but I had become more direct, less sophisticated. The conventions drifted away somewhere—nowadays something more important was continually stirring within my soul and thoughts.

Before this, could I ever have conceived of going up to a strange, respectable lady and having a chat with her just because the radiant tranquillity of her face had attracted me? Now I was doing just that, without even thinking about it. I went up, bowed low, and asked, would she permit me to sit down beside her and have a few words with her?

She was not surprised and said in an even voice, also contrary to etiquette:

"You're an officer, aren't you? There is nothing for you to discuss with me. I do not want to hear about the war."

"I myself had no intention of discussing the war. I wanted to ask you . . . indeed, I don't know exactly what, at this moment. However, it was not about the war. I haven't thought about it for two months."

"That's good," she said, not looking at me. "You may sit down."

She spoke neither coldly, nor dryly, nor with indifference, but calmly.

We fell silent. Suddenly, gazing somewhere in the distance, she asked me:

"Is your mother still alive?"

"No, I don't even remember her. I have no one—no close friends, no close relatives. I'm all alone."

"That's good," she said again.

At that minute it seemed good to me, too. I didn't notice how I again became lost in thought, gazing at the evening sky, so clear that it appeared to be almost a vacuum. Below, far away, was a motionless dark line—a forest, presumably.

"When you look for a long time at a motionless object," I said, "it seems that time doesn't pass."

My companion smiled silently.

"That's true. Or that it all has already passed . . . Did you see my house?" she added unexpectedly.

"From far away. I like it very much."

"Come, if you'd like to, any time in the evening. When it gets dark. We will drink some tea. I have books. Good books. Old ones."

"But you don't receive anyone . . ."

"Oh, they have been talking to you. I will receive you."

Of course, I went to see her. And it soon happened that I began spending time at the Borovikov house almost every evening.

I would enter into some kind of new world, as it were, once I entered these rooms. I won't describe them. Far better than any description would be an etching depicting our country life in, let's say, the 1830's. I have seen such pictures. In an etching, however, you can't recognize the smell, you don't feel the air, yet I felt it, completely special, and I didn't doubt that this was exactly the same as it had been a hundred years ago. Do books from the beginning of the past century retain that smell? Marya Markovna had many such century-old books. We would read them together, in the "greenhouse," where we usually spent the evenings. Here, even familiar books became unfamiliar—they sparked a new fire in me—because they were bound by this fine leather cover and because their delicate rag paper caressed my fingers. It was not the past, it was not its aesthetic aspect which was so alluring—I myself do not know what it was.

Marya Markovna did not worship the past. She did not regret it, did not sing its praises, did not prefer it to the present, as do all old people. This is very difficult to explain, and for a long time I could not fathom it. She would take equally from every period of her life those things which pleased her. She would pass over them calmly in her mind, or they would remain somewhere outside her, if they had not already left her mind completely.

In the astonishing tranquillity which flowed from this woman there was something akin to my reverie at the time. I was able to sit for hours, motionless, almost without thoughts, in some kind of profound, boundless repose. There, by the monument, Marya Markovna had struck me as not entirely comprehensible; she had interested me with her "strangeness," but now I no longer thought about her strangeness. I had forgotten it, and it came up of its own accord that we began discussing her son.

We would read Zhukovsky[1] . . . it was as though this de-

[1] Zhukovsky, Vasily Andreevich (1788–1852). Russian leading pre-Romantic poet and translator of Gray, James Thomson, Southey, Scott, Moore, Byron, Uhland, Bürger, Schiller, and Goethe.

lightful book in the soft brown leather were alive before me!
At first I would read, then Marya Markovna would take up the
book:

> "The roses are beginning to bloom,
> Rest, my heart . . ."

How wonderfully she read! And what magical verses these
were!

> "The heart will be serene,
> The heart will bloom forth
> Like a beautiful rose . . ."

"Do you like roses?" I suddenly interrupted. "There, in the
churchyard, on your son's grave, the roses are still in bloom. Did
he die during the war?"

I asked without curiosity, very simply. She likewise answered
simply:

"I don't know. He died when he first entered the war."

"When he first entered the war?" I questioned her a second
time with awakening surprise. "Where, then? In what way?"

"In this way. Here. You saw his grave. I haven't abandoned
it since that time."

I was dumbfounded by these answers. I wanted to ask further,
but I could not immediately find the words for the necessary
question. Seeing my distress at not understanding, she smiled and
calmly began to explain:

"You don't remember your mother—it's better that way. Perhaps you will understand me more easily. It is a simple thing, yet
people are accustomed to see mothers differently. Valentin was
my soul, he became my very life. From his youth, even from his
childhood, I knew what it meant to be tortured by love and hope,
by the fear of loss. So that by the end my heart no longer had
the strength to continue suffering. Not my heart alone, but my
whole soul grew weary . . . and I could not bear a new torment.
Valentin knew this—we understood each other so well that
sometimes we conversed with our eyes alone. And if on the first
day he said that he was going to war, it meant he wasn't able not

to go. I pleaded with him anyway, 'Think it over until tomorrow. Tomorrow once and for all. I will decide then.' We both tormented ourselves in vain until the next day. It was impossible to change anything."

She paused, staring at the pitch-black window, as dark as though there were nothing at all behind the glass, as though the world had come to an end. In the greenhouse it was warm and comfortable, the ancient oil lamp was burning, hissing gently— a carousel, I think, it is called. Marya Markovna's face was tranquil. For the first time this tranquillity did not soothe me—it was disturbing.

"Well, and later," she summed up, "later I gave him up. Gave him up completely. One night, right then and there, I lived through his death from beginning to end. It was the same as if on that night he had actually died in my arms. I bade him farewell, as if he were already dead—I kissed his lips in a final kiss. He understood, he accepted it that way. And now . . ."

"What if he is alive now?" I whispered in inexplicable, stupefied horror.

"I don't know. But it's all the same. People don't experience one death twice. Whatever takes place today, whatever will happen tomorrow—it doesn't matter. Everything has already happened, as far as I am concerned."

"What if he has even escaped alive, totally unharmed! And what if he returns alive? Then what?"

I was upset, my voice faltering. Half-smiling, trying to pacify me, Marya Markovna rested her pale hand on mine.

"Then . . . he will be born to me a second time. But I don't think of that. I keep him in my heart. This heart of mine has made a final effort to accept his death, and it has accepted it . . . so that it may rest later on."

"You believe in God," I muttered. "If you do believe, then this is a sin. You are renouncing hope. This is not love."

"Not love? Then what is it? Besides, I am not renouncing hope at all. If I say with Zhukovsky, 'Rest, my heart . . . ,' certainly you have heard the rest:

'The roses are beginning to bloom,
My heart, be hopeful—
There is, as they have promised us,
A better place somewhere.
Eternally young,
Spring dwells in that place.
There, in the vale of Paradise,
We have another life,
Which will bloom forth
Like a rose . . .'

"You see," she added, lowering her book, "I have a better hope, and not a sinful, but a singularly pious one. Love here, in this world . . . worldly hope . . . is all this worth the torture which may come? Listen to the words of the saints: 'Everything of this earth is meaningless, unnecessary . . . There is another, better Paradise.' And to that place, as Zhukovsky also said, 'To that place the road lies through the grave; only in the grave can man find rest.'"

She became silent. In her silence, as in her words, there was no sorrow. All the while there was that radiant, even restful tranquillity. What could destroy it? It was invulnerable. Her hope was a shield against fear. A dear grave, roses in bloom, my heart—be hopeful . . .

After leaving Marya Markovna, I went home. The night was calm, dark, and black. I will not hide it: at that precise moment —though it was only the turning point of my active life—the coldness of the grave touched my soul. It was as though I were looking at a quiet, dark, caressing precipice. Where is she now, this woman? Who is she? Was there something more to the gray, death-inspiring pillar at the monument, standing above the grave in the graveyard? He, whose grave this is, is perhaps alive . . . and what about her—is she alive? . . .

My heart was overcome by a strange fear. By now life itself had inflicted a wound upon it. And for that reason, after my blind fear which had somehow become subdued, I also felt . . . envy. Certainly everyone is destined to know the meaning of the torment of hope, the fear of loss, and the torment of love. But mothers are destined to know it to its fullest degree. Is she not indeed blessed who has the strength to drink willingly her cup to the very bottom at once, so that she can say to her heart, "Be reposed," in a hopefulness which does not resemble the deceptive hopes of this earth?

I tried not to make a judgment, knowing that I would not be able to reason it out to the end. I departed soon after that. Many years went by, and I heard no more of Marya Markovna. As regards her son, I remembered what I had heard earlier before—that some Borovikov had been wounded on the northern front. Perhaps it wasn't the same one.

Several times during these long, difficult years the tranquil face of Marya Markovna would rise up before me. The fence around the church, the native maples, the roses above the grave . . . I thought of Marya Markovna also when I learned of the mother of my friend Volodya. A thousand days, a thousand nights she had spent tortured by hope and fear, and when the Reds killed Volodya in the south, her heart did not succeed in finding rest. After a month she herself died from grief. She had not been able to believe that

> "There, in the vale of Paradise,
> We have another life,
> Which will bloom forth
> Like a rose."

WITH THE STAR

When the procurator's sister-in-law passed away in 1913, her funeral service was held in the town monastery and she was buried there, in the churchyard. From that time on a close relationship arose between the monastery and the procurator's family. The wife of the procurator, after each mass, would drop in on the Father Superior, Archimandrite John; the monks would also come to visit the procurator's home. But the guest of honor was the deacon of the monastery, Father Nathaniel.

The procurator occupied a large house on the outskirts of the little town, and his home was like an estate. Beyond it lay a shaded, verdant garden where a creek flowed, with a swimming area sectioned off, a grove nestled behind the garden, and farther in the distance were fields and clusters of trees. The so-called "grandmother's chamber" was located in the corner of their spacious home—this was the room of the procurator's mother-in-law, a simple-minded old woman who wore a bonnet, sat with an eternal stocking in her hand, used a flat, birchwood snuffbox, and had a predilection for the "divine."

Father Nathaniel would begin his visits with

From *Russia Illustrated*, no. 52, December 24, 1933.

this chamber; there he would usually be treated to tea with preserves and bagels. Then, little by little, he started coming at any time at all, and in the evenings he would go straight to the parlor, remarking that "Of course, Grandmother is already in bed."

Father Nathaniel addressed everyone not by name, but just as he heard—he would call the mother-in-law "Grandmother," the procurator's wife, "Mama," the procurator himself, "Papa," and their twelve-year-old daughter, simply "Zinka." When the son, a St. Petersburg student, arrived, the deacon began calling him "Vasya." No one was offended, for everyone saw that Father Nathaniel did this because of his unaffected nature. At first the student was surprised, but he soon found the man to be a curious "child of nature."

The student was pale, delicate, and his shoulders were somewhat lopsided. Nathaniel—practically the same age as Vasya— was the flower of health: stately, handsome, with dark eyebrows; and yet there was something very babyish about his face. His crowning glory was his hair—he had an unusually thick chestnut braid reaching almost to his knees. Zinka envied him. He presented her with a photograph of himself in a sitting position, with his hair let down from beneath his cowl. It was so wavy that it enveloped him like a mantle, and in the picture one could not even see how far down it extended.

"Father Archimandrite doesn't approve of my holding service with my hair like that. I can only let it down a little, just to my shoulders, but the ends have to be under my cassock, and that has to be securely fastened at my neck. It's probably better that way, for the ladies would touch my hair and be very surprised."

He went on, laughing heartily and good-naturedly, so that on his cheeks, framed by his curly beard, the dimples of a child appeared:

"Now Zinka, don't look so sad. When you get to be my age, you'll have the same kind of braid as mine."

"But I don't want to go to a monastery," Zinka would retort

not to the point, and Father Nathaniel would laugh out loud even more lightheartedly:

"Well, what a little oaf you are! If you were to go to a monastery, you would lose every last bit of your braid! For our salvation we are ordered not to touch our hair, but as for your friends, the nuns, their little heads get completely shorn under their veils."

The spring there—unlike the northern ones—came all of a sudden. The mud along the streets, so watery that it was impossible to cross, first dried up into small mounds, and later it turned into a thick, downy floor of dust. The cherry orchards became green, and the procurator's garden was converted into such a paradise that no matter how hot it was there was shade and sweetness with a moist coolness drifting in from across the river.

Whenever Father Nathaniel came, he immediately would be drawn to the garden and, always in cheerful spirits, would lie down on the bank next to Vasya, the student. Father Nathaniel would place his small black cowl by his side so that one could not see it in the dense grass. Vasya treated the monk with curiosity and, of course, with a certain patronizing sympathy—this poor "child of nature"! How had he ever wound up under that cowl! He was born a Cossack, and a Cossack he remained.

"That's the way it is," Father Nathaniel explained. "I do come from a Cossack village, but it was impossible for me to stay there. While she was dying, my mother revealed to me that I was a son promised to God. After her death I went to the region town. I roamed for a long time on foot. At the time I was just about to turn fourteen. When I arrived, I began to look around —where could that monastery be? I finally reached my goal. They accepted me as a lay brother first, and later on they said to me, 'You are a bright lad, you have great zeal,' and they arranged for me to enter the seminary. I caught up with the other students. Yes, I got along all right. Then, as soon as I felt the desire, I took the monastic vows. But I was ordained here. The local Father Superior likes me. And my voice as well."

"So, in other words, you have studied, Father Nathaniel?" Vasya asked in astonishment.

"Well, what kind of studying do they have in the seminary? It's better for me to rely on my own mind. What do you say, Vasya, why don't we go for a swim? The water looks awfully good."

"Very well. But are you . . . allowed?" Vasya asked hesitatingly. He had never before come in contact with monks, but had only heard something vague about them.

"Not allowed to swim?" the deacon laughed aloud. "What did you say, you little oaf! Just watch me swim! I don't like to go into that swimming hole; why should I swim in such a box? I would rather be out in the open."

He was already getting undressed. Vasya was also—rather reluctantly, by the way. The river bed was covered with silt and was, therefore, mushy. For some reason he felt ashamed to go in right in front of the deacon.

"Wait, wait, I have to tie up my braid with a scarf so it won't get soaked! Oh, Vasya, your body, it's as scrawny as a little chicken's. Well, God be praised." He sprang from the footbridge, splashing the student with a whole spray of multicolored drops. Then he began to swim with a powerful crawl stroke.

The student, after paddling about a bit by the shore, climbed out and was almost dressed when the other, having swum his fill, undid his braid.

"Lord, Father, Heavenly King! How splendidly Thou hast arranged everything!"

But for some reason Vasya was in a bad mood.

"Yes, how splendidly everything is arranged! Yet in the long run—please don't be offended—it's still not known. Maybe there isn't any God."

"You little oaf," Father Nathaniel uttered without taking the least offense. "You don't know, but someone else knows. If He didn't exist, then the people to whom He revealed Himself wouldn't exist."

"Maybe those people only made it up," the student muttered.

"Well, look at them, they wouldn't even have the intelligence to make it up. Who's telling this slander to you? The people of God wouldn't be giving you such ideas. It must have been those others, the no-goods, they're the ones, by their own father's command . . . Keep away from them, think for yourself."

"I don't understand," Vasya said, raising himself up from the grass. "What no-goods are telling me slander? What father are you talking about?"

"What father indeed? The sons of the enemy, that's who I'm talking about. God sowed the seed, created real people in His own likeness. But the devil immediately scattered among them his own sons, completely soulless creatures, shells, for no purpose other than temptation. To look at them, they're the same, but they aren't real people, for from the very beginning they were different. You little oaf, perhaps you have forgotten the story, so just listen."

He recounted in detail the Gospel parable about the good seed and the thorns and then added:

"And so that the people would not begin to misinterpret it, the Lord explained at once how it was to be understood—'The sower,' He said, 'was God. The good grain is His creation, His people. The weeds are the sons of the enemy, sent among the people for greater temptations.' For his evil deeds the devil can prepare as many of them as he wants, all looking the same. The enemy cared only about tempting, and then he would disappear like a mist. This is explained so firmly in the Holy Scriptures that it couldn't be firmer."

"W-well . . . I don't know," the student mumbled. "You have gone too far, Father Nathaniel. You have been indulging in some sort of mysticism . . . But, supposing I accept your point of view, whenever you run into such a weed, should you destroy it as it deserves?"

"No, no, no!" The deacon shook his head; he even frowned. "You aren't permitted to touch them! You have no right to decide who is a weed and who is not a weed. It is your job to recog-

nize the temptation, to keep yourself away from the temptation
which he might bring your way. Naturally, if a real man has been
tempted, he himself can also lead you into temptation. For temptation—oh, how widespread it may become! Like a stone which,
when thrown into the water, creates ripples far away . . ."

"If one is forbidden to recognize these weeds of yours," Vasya
burst out laughing, "then let's forget about them. Explain to me
just this, holy father, again from your own point of view—
why has this God of yours, this kind and blessed One, given
His people over to . . . temptation, as you say? Is it to make
them worse, in your opinion? Isn't it true that He didn't even
let the angels get rid of these weeds? Would you say that this
was a good arrangement?"

Father Nathaniel regarded the student with a sympathetic
sigh.

"You are an oaf, a little oaf, you are completely ridiculous!
You have no capacity for reasoning. Did the Lord make His
people His pawns, or what? Do you think He set them down on
the railroad tracks, the straight path, saying to them, 'Roll to
the place I have shown you'? He surely has no need for such
people! He created men in His own image; He left them to
their own free will. What He needs is for everyone himself, without compulsion, to choose his own path to follow. The sons of
the enemy are made by machine, they haven't been given free
will; they must do as they are told, and that's all there is to it!
Therefore, like scarecrows made of straw, they will be burnt up
in a pile and won't feel a thing. Well, I've chatted long enough
with you, you little oaf. It's getting dark already. The dusk
gathers fast in July. Look up there, above the grove, the little
star has begun to shine. There, it's twinkling! Take a look!"

But the student stretched himself, yawned somewhat affectedly,
and uttered:

"Indeed you like these old wives' tales, Father Deacon. It's
interesting how all this is stored up in your head, this business
about free will and all kinds of temptations and roads, as though

they were written for you somewhere, for you to unravel . . ."

"So what?" the deacon began, and suddenly cheerfully interrupted himself:

"Is this Zinka running along the path toward us? Yes, it's her! And she has the little puppy with her, the one which I brought yesterday. They must have served the tea already, and she is running to call us."

"You said yesterday, Father Deacon, that you were also prompted by temptation when you brought the puppy here in your cassock sleeve. Does this mean that here, too, there was some sort of 'temptation'?"

But the deacon was not listening or did not hear the student's casually mocking words. He was walking, smiling his trustful, happy smile, toward the little girl with her tiny yellow bundle, barely visible in the twilight, on the darkening, sandy path.

These were not Father Nathaniel's last "old wives' tales" and good-natured precepts to the "little oaf" Vasya. Perhaps they were not precepts, but rather a sort of consolation, something like saying, "Take heart, you little oaf, just keep on asking questions, and an understanding of these temptations will be granted unto you."

The summer passed. Another one like it never came again. In January the procurator and his family moved to St. Petersburg. The manor house, together with the entire estate, as well as the garden with the river, was deserted. And then came the disaster—the war. The years lingered on, one bleaker than the other, one more frightening than the next . . . How many of them passed? Four? Five?

He regained consciousness—everything was still the same. It was dark, cold, painful, terrifying. It seemed to be colder, still more terrifying because of the silence. He thought, "I'm wounded. They've left me here, the scoundrels." He wanted to move, but moaned aloud from the pain and remained lying there motionless on his back. He was lying very low, with his head completely buried in the snow. From the corner of his eye the ruffled snow seemed to hang in icy heaps, and Vasya, the former student, now a wounded Red soldier, could see nothing from the the side but the nearby blue snow. But it was difficult to look sideways without turning his head. It was more comfortable to look straight ahead.

Straight ahead and high up there was something still darker and bluer than the snow. In the midst of this blue expanse there was a small golden spot; it flitted along the edges, quietly trembling. Vasya gazed at it a very long time and then thought, "It's a star," the thought accompanied by a strange indifference. By now he stopped feeling the cold, which was becoming more intense all the time; even his fear was growing stiff within him, as though it were becoming frozen. If only he could lie in this very same way, unmoving, forever! His thoughts were silently extinguishing . . .

All at once something large, black, bent down and shielded the star from his view, and immediately such an inexpressible, gripping pain seized him that he could barely cry out. Then, all of a sudden, everything disappeared somewhere, both his pain and he himself.

But then, once more . . . he opened his eyes. It was dark, cold, painful; he was lying on his back, as he had been lying, yet something had changed—he felt the cold, but the snow was no longer turning blue and there was no star.

Only very slowly was consciousness coming back to him. He had been wounded, and they had left him in the snow . . . However, now he was not in the snow but on some sort of bedding covered with his military coat, as though in a shack or tent. Over there, in a corner, a light was shining. Again he attempted to stir but, groaning from the pain, he shut his eyes. When he opened them, he caught sight of a stranger's bearded face above him. His fear suddenly returned—"I'm a prisoner of the Whites!"

"Now, now, don't move, your shoulder is bandaged," the stranger said in a somewhat harsh manner. "You'll only make it worse. How did I ever drag you away from there, with all that blood underneath you! But now everything will be all right, God be praised. Amen."

"Have you . . . am I a prisoner of the Whites?"

"What's the difference, whites, grays . . . If I report to the Cossack chief,[1] you'll find out. Just sleep now, or wait, you little oaf, first have something hot to drink, I'll bring it right away . . ."

Everything seemed once more to have disappeared. Yet from somewhere, as though from a mist, something old, ancient, almost otherworldly, began slowly to emerge. And when the bearded man in his army jacket brought in the steaming mug, the former student Vasya, half-asleep, uttered the words, "Father Nathaniel."

The bearded face broke out into a smile.

"So, you have recognized me, you little oaf! And I recognized you—as soon as I brought you in here. After the battle I always go to see whether or not anyone is alive from those left behind. They don't even pick up their own men. They wouldn't understand anything like that, since they haven't been given the understanding. Just consider what a night it is tonight! Tonight the stars are twinkling, there is peace on earth, good will among men. But instead of this, at the moment that star came out, they began running around, bang-bang, shooting everyone in sight, attacking anyone who came their way, defiling the face of the earth. There's your humanity for you! And these people have even forsaken their own men. They don't understand, these children of the enemy."

"The weeds?" asked Vasya, smiling faintly, again as though in a dream, as though it were not he who was saying it.

"What weeds!" the bearded man replied, not surprised in the least. "They are people, men who have fallen into temptation, that's what they are! How about you, did you know what you were doing?

1 Presumably Makhno, Nestor Ivanovich (1889–1935). Ukrainian anarchist leader. For more information see D. Footman, "Nestor Makhno," *St. Anthony's Papers*, no. 6, *Soviet Affairs*, no. 2, 1959.

"Lord, Heavenly Father, temptation has now spread itself far and wide, including even the paths which lead to God. I, too, have had my share. Is it like me to take up my rifle against these confused people? But I have no choice, for this is not an offense against me, but against the King of Heaven. When this outrage against Him began to take place, there was much destruction, they even killed the abbot—so I threw off my cassock and came to help the Cossack chief. I thought I would do my share and maybe even accept my death. Now I have done my share. The Cossack chief has given us orders for tomorrow—everyone is to try to get to the border, while my instructions are to go to Mount Athos. And there—it will be as God wills."

He went on after a brief silence:

"I have a feeling that your Papa and Mama have died. I feel sorry for Zinka because she might go astray. But what about you? Was it by your own free will that you joined them?"

"I don't know . . ." Vasya groaned.

He really felt as if he no longer knew anything, but only half-heard, half-understood the words of Nathaniel. He just huddled up, like a cold, sickly, deserted child.

"You . . . you won't leave me, Father Nathaniel," he whispered. "Take me with you, anywhere you go . . . even to Mount Athos."

Nathaniel smiled and nodded his curly head.

"Don't talk nonsense, you can't walk! Look at this little oaf —he wants to go to Mount Athos! Well then, I'll have to get a horse and some sleds ready for tomorrow, for it will take a long time before you get well. The path is long. It's bitter cold this time of year, and God might grant us as difficult a journey as the ancient Hebrews had while crossing the desert in Palestine. But have no fear. The Lord is faithful to those who are faithful to Him. We'll reach Mount Athos . . . wait a moment, this shabby coat is wet, I'd better give you my own, it's drier."

He brought it in, wrapped Vasya with it and, pitying him, said:

"There, there, little oaf. Go to sleep, don't be afraid. We'll get where we have to go. Our future is in God's hands. Whatever He wants us to do."

Vasya's pain subsided. In his drowsiness certain images were floating and rocking about—something very near and immemorial at the same time. A green star flickered and trembled before his closed eyes—perhaps it was the one which he saw while lying on his back in the trampled, bloodstained snow? Or was it the one he saw on a July evening very long ago, rising from beyond the grove above the river? Or maybe it appeared that way to him simply because from the tiny corner of the shack, where the light was shining and Father Nathaniel was busying himself, there came the scarcely audible, murmured singing and the words:

"With the Star the free-willed souls do go . . ."

METAMORPHOSIS

. . . What a curiosity, that encounter I had yesterday! Maybe it wasn't a curiosity, I don't know; it was some kind of sudden pitfall, incomprehensible to me. Judge for yourself, but I must admit that I ceased to understand many things a long time ago. I ceased to fathom them. For example, what is happening in Russia is like looking into murky water—I am even afraid of all kinds of discussions. Since the time I acquired my little farm and planted potatoes—it is the third year already—I have not even been able to keep up with the events taking place among the émigrés. I have become alienated from them. I visit Paris quite often—after all, it is only a forty-minute drive! And my little room is always ready for me at Blagovo's—yet I still do not pay attention to what is going on. I do not even pay attention to the newspapers. You open them up, and there is so much in there that you do not understand. It is true that I have no time to follow what is going on, but I love Parisian life, I love Paris itself. Wherever I happen to have free time, I go there. I see a few people and go roaming around.

Yesterday morning I arrived there to spend two full days . . . but wait a moment—if I am

From *Russia Illustrated*, no. 46, November 7, 1936.

to give an account of it, I must start from the very beginning. For our meeting yesterday actually was the second one, the second chapter, as it were; nothing but rubbish would result unless I accounted for the first meeting; without such an account, there would be nothing remarkable. The first meeting took place a year ago . . . no, more than that. I had never spoken of it. I had simply forgotten it, I confess; it had completely slipped my mind. It happened this way: in early spring I was walking along Montparnasse Boulevard. At that time, like now, I also came to relax, to have a change of pace. The day was really pleasant, a little chilly, but not humid; it was still light, although dusk was approaching. I was strolling along, looking at the people, deciding in which café I should stop. Suddenly I saw an old man before me. He was stooped over, taking short steps, and beside him was a broad-shouldered, somewhat awkward young boy. In Paris you meet so many figures of every shape and kind that nothing surprises you, yet for some reason I fixed my attention upon this old man. He was walking so oddly and, although he was not dressed shabbily—as a matter of fact, he was wearing a rather new overcoat—he was strange-looking, as though he did not feel at home in that overcoat. In the young lad I also perceived something strange. Were they Russians? For nowadays not everyone could distinguish Russians among Parisian crowds, and even a gray beard would not be a sure mark . . . However, I quickened my pace and, overtaking them, unceremoniously gazed at them straight in the face. Unceremoniously, simply as an ordinary passerby would. To my surprise, the old man recoiled—I even became alarmed—and stopped.

"Monsieur . . . Monsieur . . ." he prattled, his eyes fluttering.

I was going to say "pardon" and pass by, but suddenly he leaned toward me and whispered, "Are you, perhaps, Sinel'nikov? Valeryan . . . Am I correct?"

I began to scrutinize him. No, I did not know who this old man was.

"You don't recognize me, well I can understand that; nevertheless, I'm glad. Although I shouldn't be glad, I am glad, glad for at least a second. I am Baykov, yes, Leslie, maybe you remember Leslie . . ."

That hazy, distant past suddenly began to flare up before me, and in the remote past I recalled Leslie. But what does this old man have to do with it? Indeed, recollections flash by as quickly as lightning, and everything comes to you immediately, in a single picture. All at once Baykov-Leslie appeared in front of me, just as when I was young I had seen him in St. Petersburg—five or six times in all. At that time he was heavyset, with a thunderous voice, a handsome representative of the intelligentsia. They said that he had been preparing himself for a diplomatic career, but had turned to journalism and wrote occasionally, though very smartly, in the left-wing newspaper. Although I myself had dreamed about becoming a journalist, I did not like Leslie. Instead, I liked his wife (he had just gotten married then)—she was a young, vivacious, dark-haired student from the Women's University. How was it that I suddenly remembered all this? My Leslie had nothing in common with this old man.

He had nothing in common with him, yet it was he just the same. It takes long to tell a story and, since it is quicker to act, I managed with the greatest effort (do not ask me why) to drag the old man into a nearby café where I sat down across from him, scrutinizing him while listening to his mumbling, yet still understanding nothing:

"I will tell you everything right away, right away," he muttered. "Why not . . . It's good we're in a corner. There are lights, of course, and it's a public place. But after all, we were once acquaintances . . . As for you, Markusha . . . maybe we will find out something about these playing fields."

The old man's lad also followed us into the café. He looked at the old man and myself rather disapprovingly, every once in a while jerking his shoulders. He had an ordinary face. Incidentally, it would have been pleasant-looking, were it not for his eyes—unusually dull, like those of a fish.

The old man kept on muttering and half-whispering, as rapidly as though he had been given five minutes to say a million words.

"We've been here a week, a whole week already . . . Oh, what luck this is! I used to go to Paris, I know what it was like, but not what it's like today . . . after what I've gone through, you have no idea, no one does, no one can imagine, only I can . . . And only she, Anna Fedotovna. (We've been divorced for a long time, it couldn't be helped.) She tried as much as possible not to forget me. She helped me a great deal, but then she said to me, 'No, you had better go, Ivan Stepanovich. You are a burden to me here with your clumsiness, you hinder me, you have no tact at all. Go, but watch out! If you aren't as quiet as a mouse—first, I will put a stop to everything, and second, you know that if I want to I will get you back. So in the future, don't complain!' Oh, now she can do anything she wants! And, indeed, I'm ready to see whom I am supposed to see, although I don't understand for what purpose. All I cared about was not staying there . . . I couldn't! I couldn't stay there! I've had enough!"

"Cut it out, Gavrila!" the young lad rudely interrupted. The old man shriveled up and grinned guiltily.

"What of it? There isn't anything special. This was exactly what she herself had decided. That I should go. Yes," he turned again toward me, "as she had decided, that's how we did it. But Markushka wanted to tag along, asked her if he could go, said to her, 'I want to go look at these filthy bourgeois . . .' She agreed—she was always spoiling him—on the condition that he would be sent right back."

"I couldn't care less about the bed," Mark's bass voice again was heard. "What's more important to me right now is to find out what kind of playing fields they got here, and what these people have rigged up here . . ."

"He doesn't know French," Leslie said in a apologetic tone. "I knew French, but I am still mixed up after my ordeal! In the beginning we picked up a few words here and there . . . But what I'm going to do with him and his playing fields, I still haven't figured out. 'He's a clever boy,' Anna Fedotovna told me, 'he is bound to have a big job one of these days.' She knows best, she took pains with him, put her whole heart into it, so naturally . . .''

"Can he be the son of Anna Fedotovna?" I managed to put in.

"Come now, come now, certainly he is our own son. He was born during the second year of the massacre . . . that is, the war. Anna Fedotovna took care of him, he stayed with her. As for me—where could I go, after what I'd been through? So that was the reason for our divorce. But her heart isn't just any heart. She herself saw that I couldn't stay there. And so, getting back to those playing fields . . .''

"Wait a moment, Ivan Stepanovich, I don't understand. Do you mean to say that you aren't planning to return? Will you become an émigré? Will you be writing in the newspapers here?"

"In the newspapers?" the old man was thrown into confusion. "No, no, no! I am just here to take a look around. As far as going back—no, no! Anna Fedotovna herself has agreed, and she is going to help me. I am as quiet as I can be. I'll take a look around, we'll see about the playing fields. After I send him right back, I'll spend the rest of my life here very modestly, just as she's ordered me to. I'm all right, you know, but I couldn't stay there and hinder her. She understood that. The Komsomol is waiting for this one. He has an active part in his group, so he can't stay here."

For me this muttering, mumbling, and nonsense, in which I could not discern any particulars, was becoming rather boring. About the young boy it was perfectly obvious—he was "one hundred percent" of the kind you see there. I know the type, although it is true they are usually a little older. He'll make out well if he stays with his mother. The mother must be a real big wheel there. And what about the old man himself? He is obviously not lying about his "ordeal," for he's certainly nothing but skin and bones! He seems to be satisfied that he got away. Evidently he must have become too boring for his former spouse, for her to have given him a pension just for behaving himself and keeping quiet. All the same, it's nonsense! However, we grew out of the habit of being surprised a long time ago—even if we don't understand something, we still accept it, it's over and done with.

I began wondering how to get away, but at the moment Baykov himself, when he heard that I knew nothing whatever about the playing fields, started to tear himself away from me. He jumped up, shoved some francs into my hand to pay for the beer (I didn't accept them), muttered something completely absurd, and said good-bye. I asked him where he lived. He didn't say, but replied, "So . . . we . . . have taken shelter here for a little while . . . So long . . ." He did not ask me anything at all. It was strange that he had recognized me, even more so that he had remembered my name. By the way, while looking at him, I noticed that he wasn't that old after all—it was his skeletal thinness, his beard, and the fact that he was practically toothless which made him an old man. Of course, he was half-insane, but all people who come from there seem that way to us as soon as they arrive. He will soon snap out of it.

He grabbed his young boy, who did not even nod his head to me, and shuffled out, looking about helplessly. They disappeared at once.

That very evening both of them evaporated from my mind and, as I have already told you, I did not think of them again.

The year has been a difficult one for me—I have had other things to worry about. Only now, with summer just ahead, has life become easier. It was precisely here that the second chapter unfolded. Taken together, both of them really form a remarkable story.

After nine o'clock last night I was sitting in a café, again on Montparnasse, but in one of the more luxurious cafés where there are always many people; at this time, however, in early June, every café there was noisy and filled to capacity. I found this refreshing, since I had just come straight from the country.

I sat watching, thinking about nothing, when suddenly—it was as if I had been struck by something—there was Leslie! He was not at all the old man from last year, but a man as I had known him before, that is, large, well-built—he even had quite a paunch on him—clean-shaven, handsomely attired. Upon my word, it was that very same St. Petersburg journalist with the thunderous voice—he had lived, died, and come to life again. Of course, I looked him over—his full cheeks sagged, his hair was sharply turning gray, yet look how he was laughing with someone, see how his teeth sparkled!

He stood by the door, then moved in my direction. The whole time I did not take my eyes from him. I was indeed astounded! He caught sight of me and headed straight in my direction, extending his hand with a flourish, just like in the old days:

"Well, hello, my good man! How many years has it been! May I join you? I am expecting someone here."

Imagine, even his way of speaking was completely different, in the style of St. Petersburg; that is, he spoke distinctly, with assurance, not mumbling. It was as though at our first meeting in Paris it was not Baykov at all, and now it was he in person. When he saw my surprise, he started laughing:

"A metamorphosis? Yes, my good man! Let's drink something a little more exciting. Are you alone? *Garçon!*"

I asked him, "Did you send your son home a long time ago?"

All of a sudden he frowned, his face became wrinkled, and he seemed to grow older. He came closer to me and said less loudly:

"He's the only cloud upon my horizon. I can tell you that you caught us at that time in a lamentable condition. I had just come in from Wonderland. Since then much water has flowed under the bridge. Oh, yes! He didn't leave! He hasn't been living with me for some time. At first I thought I'd be punished. For I was afraid of Anna Fedotovna! But an intelligent man must never despair. As for Anna Fedotovna, isn't she a smart one? She threatened me first, but then she came to my rescue. What do I care? If I can stay here, I can handle everything. Let her catch Markushka herself, if he gives himself up."

"I don't understand anything," I said angrily. "If your son has disappeared, you can find him with the help of the police."

"There, there, my good man, you don't understand! If you had been through the same thing, you'd understand. If only he had disappeared! But it's worse—he's gotten caught up in such a line of thinking . . . And it has been terrifying for me. He demands money from me. I tremble with fear (Anna Fedotovna doesn't know about this), yet I give it to him. The boy is a black-mailer. If the money is his mother's or mine—well, he shouldn't take it if he doesn't like it. Let him side with whomever he wants. He doesn't let me set foot on his doorstep—he only agrees to meet me at the café. That's how it is."

Again he seemed like a madman to me. I remained silent.

"But look, there he is! He wants to have his own ideas, yet he always comes back to me for his money. How on earth can you know such people—this is the new breed!"

I raised my eyes, and at that moment I was so surprised that for want of habit it was even pleasant. A stately young man was approaching us, smartly dressed, in a suit with a sporty flair. He wore no hat, in the style of the younger men of Paris, and his dark hair was smooth and sleek. I recognized his face . . . yet not entirely. I recalled his fishlike eyes, but now they were not really fishlike. God only knows how to define them, only they weren't dull. Brazen, perhaps, or else simply young, impudent eyes.

Not offering his hand to his father but nodding to me, he sat down at our little table. He shouted something to the passing waiter—and what a free and easy manner he displayed! Yes, indeed, this was a clever lad!

"Well?" he said to his father with his former rudeness (the rudeness was still there). "Do you have it?"

Baykov slightly moved his shoulders and smiled half-heartedly.

"Now don't you worry about it. You'll sit with us a while, won't you?"

Mark glanced at his watch.

"Ten minutes. That's all the time I have for you."

"Yes, yes, yes, that's how it is," Baykov started to become like the old man of a year ago. "Look at them, our children," he winked at me. "They neither resemble their mothers, nor their

fathers . . . That's what they call post-revolutionary consciousness, you see . . . The devil knows how many types of this consciousness there are."

"Shut your trap," Mark interrupted. "Besides, an agreement's
an agreement . . . It wouldn't take me long to ruin you."

"And yourself at the same time," Baykov remarked spitefully.

"If I didn't have your money? If I really wanted to, I could
get along without it!"

He straightened his shoulders, and it was apparent that he
really could get along without it.

Baykov conceded, "Yes, well, all right, all right . . . wait a
moment." He noticed someone in the distance and jumped up.
"I'll be right back . . . in two minutes . . . there's just this one
little fellow . . ."

He dashed off. Mark regarded this with indifference. He muttered through his teeth, "He won't get away . . ." and busied
himself with some kind of concoction which had been brought
to him. We were silent.

"Are you an émigré? White?" Baykov's offspring suddenly
began to question me.

"If I'm an émigré, that means I cannot be a Red."

"No . . . it still doesn't mean that. That one over there is also
an émigré . . ." he nodded toward his father. And he added,
"Don't become too chummy with him . . ."

"How's that?"

"Just what I said. Those old fogeys have no control over their
minds. Self-interest's got the better of them, without exception.
He shakes all over from fear, trying to please everybody. If only
he could 'drink tea,' [1] like Dostoevsky's heroes. Ideologically, I
spit in the face of my mother and everyone else over there. And
as for him, he had some ideas of his own! He succeeded in plead-
ing with her. He accepted an assignment among the émigrés. But
he'll fall flat on his face."

"What assignment? And you, what are you? A Communist?"

[1] Ref. to Dostoevsky's heroes who discuss religious, political, and historical
issues at great length.

"Me?" the young man snorted, "with these old fogeys? Communism has outlived its novelty! It's time to bury it. Besides, there aren't even any Communists. Like my old man, for instance, who cares only about how to fill my belly. Now it's time for something new. We kids won't give these scoundrels an inch. I'll take his money, even if its stolen, while I'm going to school —all of us know this and think it's okay—I don't want him to kick the bucket too soon. But if he does, it wouldn't upset me at all. We'll get by."

"But where do you fit in?" I asked in amazement, understanding less and less.

He casually mentioned the name of some émigré youth circle, of which I had heard in passing and had only a vague idea. It was either a group of neo-idealists, or neo-monarchists, or even neo-democrats; in any case, something rather chaotic. Abandoning this thought, I asked the neo-youth:

"And how are your sports coming along?"

He grew animated and something childlike flashed across his face.

"Things have been going just great for us. There are all kinds of things going on. We have one idea, that is, our ultimate goal, and that's to make work out of sports and sports out of work. Sure, we still have a long way to go, but the idea itself, as you can see, is quite an idea! We're the generation of tomorrow. In the meantime, we're getting ready. But this one . . ." At that instant the former rudeness again returned to him—his father, maneuvering among the small tables, was approaching us—"Let him have his fun for now. After all, he's carrying out his little assignments . . . what's it to us? Our job is to pass it on . . ."

Smiling, Baykov sat down at the table, but I got up.

"Where are you going, my good man? Wait a moment! We haven't even had our little chat as we should have! How many years has it been! Where are you living? I haven't seen you once in our émigré circles, among the writers or in any other group . . . I'll admit that it's not interesting in all of them . . . But sometimes things do happen."

This thunderous outburst of his was the last straw. I hardly remember how I got out of the café, how I said good-bye; maybe I didn't even say good-bye. I wandered for an hour along the streets, not thinking of anything. My head was in a whirl.

I am not thinking today, either. I have told you what I saw and heard—on first sight, transformations are rather curious affairs. But what they signify, who has been transformed, and into what—one can't understand. Once you try to grasp it, you might, God forbid, come to the conclusion that all of us live in some kind of bedlam. That's why I am going out to my vegetable garden today, to my potato patch—things are simple there.